NO QUESTIONS ASKED

NO QUESTIONS ASKED

THE SECRET LIFE OF WOMEN IN THE MOB

By

CLARE LONGRIGG

miramax books

HYPERION

NEW YORK

Introduction

PORTRAITS of Mafia wives in popular culture tend to be exaggerated, often to comic extremes. They are easily recognizable from their thickly applied makeup, permanent tans, teased-out clouds of bleach-blonde hair, and fingernails too long and ornate to have done a day's work. Part of the easy comedy of Mafia women is that they move in brightly colored packs: they flock together at social occasions, while their husbands retreat to discuss business. At nightclubs, they are herded into booths and guarded by mob heavies as though they were so many designer handbags. Unembarrassed about making a spectacle of their wealth, they offer a highly visible, almost laughable counterpoint to the violent underworld on which their husbands' status is based.

In other ways, Mafia women are nearly invisible. Traditionally debarred from the men-only inner sanctum of organized crime, they are excluded from acts of violence, and none has ever been made a member of Cosa Nostra. Mafia women have also been noticeably absent from criminal investigations. If a mob wife answers the door when a police detective comes knocking, it's because she knows the drill—she doesn't know where her husband is or when he's coming home. Officially, she knows nothing about her husband's criminal activity. She never asks any questions—if she did, she might get a slap, but not an answer. Privately, she may know a good deal, but she's not saying *anything*. Secure behind her veil of ignorance, she is assumed to be, at most, a passive witness to her husband's affairs.

When, in the early 1990s, I began researching a book about

women in the Italian Mafia, I discovered a reality far from this cultural stereotype. These were turbulent years in Sicily, marked by tragedy: in 1992 two anti-Mafia judges, Giovanni Falcone and Paolo Borsellino, were assassinated by the Mafia. Shortly thereafter, a seventeen-year-old woman named Rita Atria killed herself. Rita's father had been in the Mafia and was executed by his own clan after a conflict over a drug deal. Her brother had been killed because he had sworn to avenge his father's death. I soon learned that Rita had been cooperating with Judge Borsellino, feeding him information about Mafia activity in her hometown. Rita's would be the first of many stories that revealed a more substantial role for Mafia women than anyone had given them credit for.

Following the murder of the two Italian judges, magistrates began a major crackdown on organized crime, sending many mafiosi away for long prison terms. While the men were out of action, an extraordinary transformation occurred: the women started to take over the daily operations of their husbands' criminal organizations. During my research, I found a woman who had been directing a drug ring in Naples, one who was running guns and commanding interfamily guerrilla warfare in mountainous Calabria, and even one woman who had organized a bombing raid in Sicily. The Italian Mafia, clearly more concerned with practical matters than with maintaining traditional roles, had decided to take advantage of the perception that women are never involved in organized crime and set them to work.

Until the 1990s, most Italian judges believed that Mafia wives had been forced to obey their husbands, without any recourse. As such, women were not considered responsible for their actions and were excused from moral judgments or legal action. A succession of female cooperating witnesses eventually convinced the world that Mafia wives had more of an influence over their husbands than had been previously understood. "A woman can make her husband do anything she wants," said Rita Atria's sister-in-law, who also cooperated. "The wives of mafiosi know everything." As increasing numbers of female magistrates filled the higher offices in the courts, the belief that women had no moral responsibility ebbed away.

Despite an eagerness on the part of the Italian judiciary to retain them as cooperating witnesses, and efforts by women's groups to en-

courage them to rebel against the Mafia's patriarchal and violent system, the women, even more than the men, expressed deep-rooted
adherence to Cosa Nostra's values. I met women who spoke nostalgi-
cally of the glory days of the Mafia, when men of honor were worthy
of the name. In 1994, an Italian news agency was surprised to receive
a phone call from a Sicilian woman, Giusy Spadaro. She and her
sister-in-law wanted to make a public statement in condemnation
of their husbands, Mafia soldiers Emanuele di Filippo and his brother
Pasquale, who had recently been arrested and had begun to cooperate. "They'd be better dead, it would be better if our husbands had
been killed," Spadaro declared. "This way I am dishonored. It would
have been better if he was dead."

When I began researching the stories of women in the American
Mafia, I was told that, unlike their Italian sisters, they played no part
in organized crime. Italian-American families, I was informed, tend
to be conservative and retain the traditions of the old country—even
customs that have long been abandoned by their European counterparts. I'd been led to believe the same thing, of course, in southern
Italy, where the classic image of a Mafia wife is a woman dressed in
black who spends her days stirring pasta sauce and watching the street
from behind a beaded curtain. Having discovered the truth about Italian women, I suspected the situation in the United States might also
hold some surprises and complications.

There were a few things in particular I was eager to discover about
American women connected to organized crime. I was interested to
learn whether Mafia women are really as passive as their representa-
tions in the popular culture suggest; whether they are as ignorant of
illegal activities as they claim to be—and, if so, at what emotional cost
they maintain their ignorance. I also wondered whether the legal immunity historically granted to Mafia women would continue to prevail in the United States, where senior positions in the judiciary are
increasingly held by women. Such questions led me first, inevitably,
to the beginnings of the American Mafia and the experiences that distinguished them from their Italian counterparts.

The Italians—like the Irish and the Jews—who came to America by
the thousands in the early part of the twentieth century were for the

most part tough, aspiring men. Immigrants were not well served by the laws of the state and consequently felt excluded from the new order. Thus Cosa Nostra, as it was first called in America—literally, *this thing of ours*—was born, an affiliation that established its own system of justice. In the opening scene of *The Godfather*, Don Corleone lays down the law, dispensing advice and favors to grateful Italians. The new social system wrought from Cosa Nostra was presided over by men capable of extreme violence, and was held together by loyalty, savage brutality, and fear.

As one tracks the odyssey of Italian Americans who settled in New York, from Lower East Side tenements to small townhouses in Brooklyn, and then onward and upward to mansions and sprawling estates in Staten Island and New Jersey, the road gets easier, the living more comfortable, and the young men more accustomed to luxury. Accordingly, the mob began to view their operations less as a matter of survival and more as a means of exerting power for material gain. Most mafiosi have abandoned paying lip service to old-world notions of honor; today, it's all about making money. The mob still wields influence through the threat of violence, but no longer under the pretence of administering justice.

In America, a mob boss enjoys his fortune in style. As soon as a capo has the financial means, he will build himself a minimansion in the suburbs, where his children can lounge in a swimming pool and his wife can drive to her hairdressing appointment in a Cadillac SUV. Paul Castellano built himself just such a mansion on Staten Island for $3.5 million; nicknamed the White House, it was a sumptuous place with marble floors, gilded mirrors, and Renaissance statues that doubled as lamps.

As a Mafia don's wealth grows, as his power takes root, he tends to adopt a personal style reflective of his new status. The suntanned mobster wearing Armani sunglasses, a designer suit, and a heavy gold watch, with a cigar in one hand and bleach-blonde girlfriend on the other, has become a familiar character in the American imagination. And yet, despite being able to walk the walk, second- and third-generation Italian-American wiseguys are, in many ways, poor replicas of the old-style Mafia boss celebrated by Hollywood and on television. As crime reporter George Anastasia writes in his book *The*

Goodfella Tapes: "They value form over substance. They have little sense of history. They assume instant gratification as a birthright. And, time and again, they have shown, they cannot deal with adversity."

The long, slow decline of organized crime in America is by now well documented, and the figure of the stressed-out, beleaguered Mafia boss has itself become a cultural cliché. Beneath such familiar icons, however, lurks a psychological drama that is less easy to stereotype—and much of this drama is centered on the changing role of Mafia women.

Although traditionally relegated to the sidelines of mob activity, women have always had to accommodate themselves to the mob's violent ethos. This is often handled with a slippery morality, one that employs justifications along the lines of "They only shoot at each other," or "Anyone who got whacked probably got what he deserved." Such defenses often betray a deeper unease. Do Mafia women feel good about spending their husbands' money, knowing it was secured through violent means? How does the loving daughter of a murderer come to terms with his past? What does a mother tell her children when so much of the family history is unspeakable?

As if these questions weren't provocative enough, the domestic affairs of mobsters are now, more than ever, wide open to public scrutiny. If *The Godfather* made the Mafia glamorous, *The Sopranos* brought it next door. Owing to modern surveillance techniques (and, more pertinently, to the vanity of mobsters themselves), the American Mafia is no longer a secret society. Mobsters' daughters have become media figures. Turncoat mafiosi have written tell-all memoirs, and no detail is too intimate to be left out of such accounts.

Since the days of *The Godfather*, when Michael Corleone closed the door in the face of his wife, Kay, as he attended to business, the role of Mafia women, too, has undergone a transformation. Many people agree that the most complex and interesting character in *The Sopranos* is Carmela, the boss's wife. Sympathetic though she may be, her character is beset with moral uncertainties: How can a religious woman, devoted to her family, excuse her husband's lifestyle, or his line of work? How much of an accomplice is she? And how many of her own values has she been forced to sacrifice on the altar of her husband's wealth and power?

The lives of many Mafia women are predicated on such uncertainties and sacrifices. Rosalie Bonanno, the wife of Bill, writes in her memoir of her mother-in-law's uncomplaining attitude as she hid out in a cellar for months to avoid a subpoena and protect her husband, Joe Bonanno. Although Fay Bonanno was an unquestioning servant to the cause, Rosalie herself adopts a slightly more rebellious stance: she expresses anger at her husband's infidelities, his financial lapses, his long absences and unreasonable demands. One New Year's Eve, when Rosalie heard that her husband had been arrested after spending many months on the run, she admits the news gave her a certain grim satisfaction. "Not only did I know where my husband was, but for once in my life I knew what he was up to on New Year's."

Whatever the state of a Mafia marriage, however many girlfriends the husband keeps on the side, a wife is traditionally expected to come into line when her man is in prison. One woman, whose husband has been in jail for most of the past thirty years, has campaigned tirelessly for his release, even though she no longer loves him. She claims, with good foundation, that he was wrongfully imprisoned, and, with a sense of responsibility that goes deeper than her feelings for him, sees it as her duty to have his sentence overturned.

"I don't really give a shit what happens to him," she admits. "But he's been framed, he's the father of my children, and that's how it is. It's not fair."

One theme that dominates the lives of several Mafia women profiled in this book is control—or their lack of it. Mob families always face upheaval, whether from the criminal underworld or from a police raid. At a moment's notice, they may need to pack up house and go on the lam. If a mobster decides to negotiate a deal with the government, his wife will have no choice but to follow him into witness protection—that is, if she ever wants to see her husband again.

As trapped by circumstance as Mafia women often feel, many have been able to wrest some control over their situations. As I conducted the research and interviews for this book, I found women had to fight hard to achieve anything resembling equal status within the male-dominated world of the mob. The wives and daughters portrayed here have never, however, submitted wordlessly to the demands made by their husbands and fathers. To the contrary, most of these women have struggled admirably through the vicissitudes of mob existence. Many have made an uneasy accommodation with the darker aspects of organized crime—or else, realizing there's no escape, have exploited their insider status for personal gain. Only one of the women in this book rejected the Mafia life outright and betrayed the mob boss she once loved, at great cost to herself. These are not stories of sacrifice (the new generation of mafiosi are not, in any event, well versed in the meaning of that word). They are stories of rebellion and self-assertion, as striking and various as the women who lived them.

The Mafia daughters I interviewed have, with few exceptions, defined themselves in relation to their fathers' oppressive influence, often trying gamely to win their approval while never being admitted into their world. Unlike most Mafia sons, a daughter is not compelled to join the organization; neither is she free to make her own choices. If she suffers the misfortune of being endowed with her father's overbearing character, she is nevertheless not allowed to express her ambitions through a life of crime. She must find another way to assert herself, to control those parts of her nature that are like her father while preventing his legacy from destroying her life. In telling the daughters' stories, I offer their perspective, rather than their fathers' or husbands'—who were, in most cases, either deceased, or incarcerated.

Many daughters of well-known criminals have turned their fathers' notoriety to their advantage, making a career of being mobsters' daughters. Often this is done in a way that honors the father's role as the pillar of the family, a hardworking man who always provided for his wife and children. After the mobster dies, his daughter may spend the rest of her life trying to create the rarefied atmosphere of her early childhood, a time when she basked in his strength and generosity. In some cases, however, the father is not treated so warmly. One woman, far from being her father's public defender, challenged his authority all her life. She repeatedly called him a psychopath. She constantly provoked him, even threatened him, demanding to be recognized as a person in her own right. She was probably the only person who ever dared to confront him in this way.

Mafia wives, in general, aren't as ready to mix it up with their husbands, or to capitalize on their criminal fame. The late John Gotti was flamboyant and ostentatious in a way rarely seen among mobsters. While he attracted attention to himself, his wife stayed out of the spotlight and stuck to the traditional script. (Mrs. Gotti once memorably told investigators, "I don't know what he does. All I know is, he provides.") Gotti's daughter, Victoria, on the other hand, surpassed her father's courtship of the press and launched herself as a media personality, solely on the strength of her family name.

When I spoke to the widow of one New York mafioso, and then to his daughter, I was struck by how differently their experiences had affected them. The widow, who had coped with financial disasters and her husband's repeated imprisonment, was resigned to her fate. Through the various periods of her husband's incarceration, she had done her duty and taken the children to visit him as much as she was permitted. Even when she no longer loved him, and hated the life he led, whenever he was moved from one prison to another without notification, she says: "I was there."

His daughter, however, was fiercely loyal to her father's memory, and very angry. Her rage at the system had finally boiled over during her last visit to her sick father in prison, when she screamed at the guards and caused a near riot among the prisoners' families (her mother describes her own demeanor during prison visits as "goody two-shoes, nicey nice"). The daughter took issue with the way the family had been treated by the authorities. She was still furious about a police raid on their house some years ago, during which her bedroom had been turned over and her possessions strewn about, including the contents of her underwear drawer.

Not all Mafia women are born into the mob—some come to it late in life, usually after an uneventful childhood. Most such women are drawn to the underworld for the excitement of lawlessness and the apparently irresistible attraction of dangerous men. Criminals have always held a great fascination for women longing to break out of repressive small-town life, who see a life of crime as a cure for boredom. In an early scene in *Bonnie and Clyde*, Clyde tries to convince Bonnie to return home to safety rather than risk her life on the road with him. "You'll have no peace," he warns her.

"You promise?" she replies.

The lure of the Mafia lifestyle is intensified by our modern obsession with celebrity, which can transform a wiseguy with a little style into an outlaw hero. Caught up in the thrill of her husband's stardom, a Mafia wife or girlfriend can happily subsist for years on his notoriety, power, and money, and never question her own role in the relationship.

In time, however, she may grow weary of her sidelined status and seize any opportunity the mob offers to make her own way, realizing her ambitions in defiance of the male-dominated culture she's chosen. These women might start as passengers in their husbands' mob careers, but they end up as accomplices. Perhaps they've become hardened—most of them have at least one close friend or relation who has met a violent end—or they may have an eye for making money. In Italy, a successful career in the Mafia depends not as much on family connections as on individual ability and character. In America, such valuations apply, to a degree, to women. A wife with ambition equal to her husband's will find a way to get involved in Mafia business.

Most of the women in this book have sought to assert themselves within the Mafia, either by participating in their husbands' endeavors or otherwise exercising influence over the family business. Only one decided to wage an all-out war. After fifteen years of marriage, she could no longer accept her husband's crimes or his abusive behavior, and was determined to prevent their son from following in his footsteps. The only way she could be sure of getting away from her husband alive, with her son, was to destroy him. In the process, she transferred her loyalties, and her affections, to the FBI. Her story is one of tremendous courage, an ordeal in which she lost everything but gained control of her young son's life.

Mafia marriages that haven't been broken by the stress of criminal life—the violence, the conspiracies, the constant threat of danger—are nevertheless often spectacularly ill-equipped to handle the quiet ordinariness of small-town life, if and when they are placed in the witness protection program. A couple that goes into hiding together is left to survive entirely on their own resources. In cases where the Mafia marriage is based on an equal partnership, in which the woman accepts responsibility for her husband's life of crime, the couple is often able to stick it out. But if the wife is at all uneasy about her husband's activities or the choices she's made to abide them, the result is usually a disintegration of the marriage.

The profiles in this book herald a generation of women who are more assertive and less governed by fear or resentment. Having long been heavily involved in the mob's financial management (a wife's bank accounts and real estate holdings provide a perfect haven for her husband's illegal income), today women are playing a more active, significant role within Cosa Nostra. Not all of these stories end happily, and none of the women's choices is entirely free of compromise. But as their role continues to evolve, and as we gain familiarity with these women's lives, the cultural stereotypes of mob wives inevitably give way to a more intimate picture. As we watch them struggle to take charge of the emotional dramas raging around them, they are no longer caricatures. They are recognizably human.

1

"I'M grateful to my father for making me a tough son of a bitch," says Lana Zancocchio. "It helps me deal with situations."

Lana's father, Anthony Graziano, is one of the triumvirate at the head of the Bonanno family who, prosecutors claim, has long been a powerful figure on the landscape of organized crime in New York, feared and disliked in equal measure. Most people know him as TG, or the Little Guy.

To his daughter Lana, he is a "real man."

As consigliere of the Bonannos, Graziano had a small army of criminal manpower at his disposal; with illegal gambling operations in New York and Florida, and tens of thousands of dollars on the street in loans, he made millions out of other people's weaknesses. Anyone who fell behind with payments could expect a new and not particularly friendly business partner. Graziano's crew members were afraid of him; an aggressive taskmaster, he had an uncanny knack for knowing when people were not telling the truth. His telephone conversations were a barrage of screaming and curses; in the background, his terrified interlocutors often heard the sound of objects smashing against walls.

The eldest of Anthony Graziano's three daughters, Lana, born in 1961, was always treated like a son. Though she was never given an active role in the criminal enterprise, she was brought up strictly, taught the rules, frequently yelled at and beaten if she disobeyed. The scion of a powerful mafioso, she was spared none of his abusive behavior, and learned firsthand what it takes to be boss. Like her father, Lana assumes a controlling role in all her business dealings. "She's a nice lady," says her attorney, with a nervous laugh. "She can be pretty tough, too. You don't want to cross her."

Some call Lana a princess, others a bully. If Adolf Hitler had had a daughter, a law enforcement source once said, she would have been something like Lana. Such remarks may reveal more about the father's nature than the daughter's—an abusive, power-crazed man does not beget meek, sweet-natured children—but investigations by the Brooklyn U.S. attorney's office have confirmed that Lana has indeed inherited her father's character: "Almost without exception," reads an internal memorandum from May 2002, "witnesses described Lana Zancocchio as a verbally abusive, abrasive, unpleasant woman who used her father to get her way, both with her husband and with outsiders."

Growing up with such a frightening father—not just occasionally bad tempered, but the sort of man who makes grown men afraid, whose professional standing depends on his ability to terrorize—was bound to have an impact. Mobsters operate through the fear of violence as much as by violence itself. They are aided by an overdeveloped capacity for outrage; any imagined slight is an attack on their self-importance, and their eagerness to avenge an insult determines their status. A successful mobster is frightening all the time, and to everyone: his crew, his hangers-on, his debtors, his lawyers, his wife, his children.

Most of the detectives and agents who spend their careers hunting "bad guys" are drawn to their quarry's humanizing traits: they pride themselves on finding something good, or at least interesting, about the most notorious criminals they come across—a love of fishing or homing pigeons; a talent for cooking. Anthony Graziano is capable of a dry, gallows humor, cracking jokes even from the dock, but he also possesses a deliberate, ostentatious rage. He bullies lawyers, his own and other people's, and screams at everyone in his way until they are dinned into submission.

Lana's response to her father was to become like him. She absorbed his lessons in intimidation and took on the world. She learned how to turn his abusive nature to her advantage, exploiting his reputation to get her own way, threatening to bring down her father's wrath. Because she has grown to be like her father, inevitably Lana has clashed with him. The two have been engaged in a lifelong power struggle, she trying to resist her father's control while he unleashed his fury whenever she stepped out of line. She hates his behavior but knows she behaves just like him.

"My father was very strict. He told me not to trust anyone, not to talk on the phone, all that. Everything was like an image kind of thing. I was overweight, and he'd want me to be thin. He was domineering, yeah, he was a bully. And then he'd be great, very funny. It's so hard: you want to hate him, but . . ."

The "image kind of thing" went deeper than a typical father's concerns about his teenage daughter's appearance. A mobster's family is an extension of his status. If a child misbehaves, it is a symptom of his lack of control. By criticizing her appearance Graziano had the power to hurt his daughter's feelings, yet her public behavior had the potential to do him real harm. By dating the wrong kind of man or disobeying her father, Graziano's daughters could damage his reputation. Acting out became the one way they could exert some power of their own under a severe Sicilian father's regime.

While she was engaged in these power skirmishes, Lana enjoyed all the positive aspects of Mafia inheritance: people around her were always anxious to please. When she was as young as twelve or thirteen she would get the best seat in a club, without having to wait in line or even buy a ticket. She once went to see her idol, Welsh crooner Tom Jones, and was shown to the best table in the house, at the edge of the stage, where the star joined them after the show. She knew this was not how normal kids lived. Graziano made sure his little girl had everything she wanted.

"My father gave me everything under the sun. While I was at school, every six months I had a new car, I mean a Jaguar, Mercedes . . . and I had twenty or thirty dollars in my pocket every day, which is like two hundred to three hundred dollars now," Lana says. She is quick to add that she paid for these luxuries in other ways. "He kept me strict, not like my sisters. He wanted to control everything I did.

"He still tries to control me. He's always on the phone"—she impersonates his rasping voice, shouting—*"Don't do this, don't talk to them, don't do that."*

When she was growing up, Lana's father told her flat-out whom she could mix with and how she should behave—and yet she defied him, again and again. In her late teens she hung around with a biker gang in Brooklyn, and even dated one of the bikers. When she introduced this boyfriend to her father, he held the edge of the table with both hands to contain his rage. She dated another man covered in tattoos. "Anything to get my father's attention," she says.

If Lana was desperate to provoke her father, the boyfriends were probably less eager to do so. "He used to get hold of them and say, 'This is my daughter. If you get excited, you go in the bathroom.' I was horrified. Most of them did not come back."

Although Lana generally knew how to get a rise out of her father without getting killed, sometimes it was a close call. Graziano used to spend a lot of time in Florida, leaving his wife, Veronica, in sole charge of the ungovernable girls. There was a phase when Lana stayed out late with a group of friends. Her mother repeatedly told her to come home; receiving no reaction, she threatened to tell Lana's father. Tired of being ignored, Veronica eventually did tell Lana's father. His reaction must have gratified her at some level. He hired a jet to fly him back from Florida that night, and, armed with a baseball bat, arrived at the house where his daughter and her teenage friends were hanging out, and swiftly broke up the party.

"He wanted to dictate everything. At one point I suggested to my boyfriend that we should get married, split the money and go our separate ways. Anything to get out of the house. When I called my parents' house and told my father, 'I'm marrying Bradley,' he put his foot through the TV. I could hear my mother screaming."

After all the abuse and the criticism and the beating, she wanted to hate him. And yet, she admires him. Certainly, she is proud of what he has achieved.

"My father had a terrible childhood. He had to care for his sisters. They were very poor, the bathroom was outside," says Lana, thinking, perhaps, of the spacious luxury of her New Jersey mansion, with her marble-tiled bathroom suite and her cosseted children. "He was fending for himself at fourteen."

Anthony Graziano grew up in a tenement building on the Lower East Side, the grandson of Sicilian immigrants, a large, struggling family in cramped quarters. By the age of twenty, Graziano was married to Veronica Gebbia, whose family originally came from Reggio Calabria; they owned a pasta store and Italian restaurant in Hell's Kitchen—a welcoming, unpretentious place with checkered tablecloths and red sauce on everything—where Anthony worked shifts. The walls were covered with portraits of severe-looking Sicilian family members, stony-faced brides, square-jawed uncles. Veronica was only fifteen when she had their first child. Her family was wary of their daughter's husband: he was a young tough always trying to make a dollar, and it was their impression that he didn't much mind whose pocket it came from.

From court papers and interviews with prosecutors, IRS and FBI sources, a picture emerges of Anthony Graziano's career as he progressed from burglaries and minor scams to more serious crime. In the 1970s, he ran a successful bookmaking business; according to prosecutors he was initiated as a made member of Cosa Nostra in 1977. When, in 1987, Bonanno capo Joey Massino was sentenced to ten years for racketeering, Graziano stepped up another rung of the ladder.

People feared Graziano: he was intimidating and abrasive. Although he had only a sixth grade education, he was street smart and savvy, a good judge of character, expert in assessing people's strengths and weaknesses. He was hands-on in all aspects of his business dealings, personally directing operations and missing nothing.

Following a trend of New York–Italian migration in the early eighties, he moved his family from Brooklyn to the relative calm and prosperity of Staten Island. An FBI source says the move was a significant step up for the young captain. Staten Island in those days was not under the exclusive control of any one of the five New York Mafia families, and there was money to be made by a fearless operator; Graziano became the Bonanno family's representative in the borough.

The timing was good: the Bonanno family was out of the limelight after having been thrown off the Commission of Cosa Nostra due to the internecine warmongering of its top members; thanks to the injudicious behavior of John Gotti, the Gambinos were in the

public eye and under intense investigation. In these favorable circumstances, Graziano was earning serious money, and increasing his
status. He exacted a tribute from every criminal organization operating on the island, and invested in a number of legitimate businesses that laundered money and served as meeting places for his
associates. In 1984, Graziano was arrested for criminal usury. After
pleading guilty, however, he was granted a conditional discharge.
The rising star of the Bonanno family had still not seen the inside of
a prison cell.

This period of rising fortunes should have been a good time for
the Graziano family, but Anthony's behavior at home was often abusive. Veronica endured her husband's continual tirades; and while
the three girls were still living with their parents, life proceeded at a
pretty high level of stress. The girls got angry, and stayed that way.

Government surveillance picked up evidence that their father's
business was no secret at the house: Anthony Graziano brought his
work home with him. He talked loudly and indiscreetly on the
phone, especially when he lost his temper. If one of his partners had
the temerity to put him on hold, he would yell: "Who's the boss
here, anyway?" (Detectives listening to a wiretap on his bookmaker
had been wondering who this furious, rasping voice belonged to.
Now they knew.) A former investigator with the Staten Island DA's
office said: "He did not have good phone discipline. When he got
mad he would call everyone under the sun." Graziano's associates
would often visit him at home, bringing tributes. The women might
not have been in the room during the meetings, but they knew all
the people who came to call.

As a Mafia boss's wife, Ronnie was strictly old school: she enjoyed good social standing but didn't flash it around—she dressed
with taste and restraint. Detectives noted that she got the best treatment at the beauty salon, was shown to the best table in restaurants;
one of her husband's men drove her wherever she wanted to go, and
people were always pleased to see her. Many of her husband's assets
were in her name, but apart from passing on messages, she did not
get involved in his business.

In 1986 Graziano started building a massive house in Staten Island,
with an adjoining apartment for Veronica's mother, subsequently

occupied by Lana, and later by the middle daughter, Rene, and her husband, Hector, one of Graziano's crew members. Graziano registered the house in his wife's maiden name, but later divorced his wife and registered the house, then said to be worth half a million dollars, to his three daughters.

After his morning telephone rounds, Graziano would go out to see about his collections, or else stop by the sports club, the restaurant, or the topless bar he used as his social club. For most mafiosi, Cosa Nostra provides an easy camaraderie, an alternative family. They may be discussing scores, but they are mainly hanging out. For a Mafia wife, her husband's prolonged absences are to be expected, and she soon learns not to question them.

Veronica Graziano not only had her husband's absences to cope with, she was also faced with the customary *goombada*. At least, that was what law enforcement thought. In the late 1980s, Detective Joseph Rauchet of the NYPD, who had been conducting surveillance on Anthony Graziano for five years or so, received a phone call from naval intelligence in Ohio. They had a list of names and wanted to know if he recognized any of them.

"One of them was Graziano," Rauchet, who is now with the New York State Organized Crime Task Force, recalls. "I said yes, I knew him. They said, He is visiting one of our recruits every weekend. He takes a hotel room, and his men take a room on either side, and he stays there and parties for the weekend. They said he's here with his wife, Susan Ransom.

"I said, No way, that's not his wife. But they said yes, they'd seen a certificate. I said, You'd better check that. Turns out, he's legally married to Susan. I thought I had him on bigamy, but it turned out that he and Veronica were divorced."

Susan Ransom was much younger than Graziano, who was in his mid-forties at the time. She was pretty, she had a good figure, and she'd been seeing Graziano for a couple of years. Originally from Staten Island, she had been living in Pennsylvania when they met. Graziano had apparently supported her decision to join the navy, convinced it would be a good career move, that she'd receive proper training and so on. Of course, it would also keep her at a reliable distance from his family. Detective Rauchet advised naval security to test Ransom for cocaine, as Graziano was rumored to use the drug recreationally, although he has always denied this. Susan tested positive and was discharged from the navy.

As far as the agents conducting surveillance on Anthony Graziano were concerned, Susan was his regular date. He was almost never seen out with Veronica. And, in time, his relationship to Susan became known to the rest of the Graziano family. Although mafiosi are more or less expected to have mistresses, they are supposed to be subtle about it and avoid doing anything to humiliate their families. You don't want vengeful women in a secret society: it's messy and noisy and can lead to unwarranted acts of public revenge.

If publicity would have been bad for Anthony Graziano, it was potentially far more dangerous for his mistress. Before they got married, Susan was seen on his home turf on Staten Island on more than one occasion, boasting to friends about how Anthony was going to marry her and showing off a big rock he had given her. (To the amusement of investigators, this later turned out to be cubic zirconium.) Police detectives monitoring Anthony Graziano's telephone conversations heard him saying to an associate: "That problem I have in Pennsylvania. Can you make that go away?"

The silent listeners on the line froze. If law enforcement working undercover or conducting electronic surveillance hear a murder being planned, it is their duty to prevent it. A couple of detectives called on Ms. Ransom in Pennsylvania and warned her of the danger she was in. She thanked them, but dismissed their concerns and their suggestion that she disappear for a while.

"I understand," she said, "but he would never do that."

Clearly this was another woman who thought highly of Anthony Graziano, in spite of everything. Graziano did not, in fact, harm Susan, who has put her relationship with the mob boss behind her and is now happily married with a child.

Lana never spoke to me about Susan Ransom. She told me she would not discuss anything that would embarrass her mother or her father. Even though I could sense that part of her was eager to tell her story, she shrank from the wrath of her father. If she occasionally entertained thoughts of revenge, she could never, ultimately, do him harm.

Although she rebelled against her father, Lana did what was expected of her when, in 1984, she became engaged to a mobster, a member of her father's crew known to Staten Island investigators as a bookmaker. Her father couldn't have chosen a better match for her if he had arranged the marriage himself. But if Lana had bent to her father's will during her formative years, she had also internalized his manner. The man who was about to become her husband had no idea just how like the boss his future wife could be.

2

LANA'S marriage to John "Porky" Zancocchio, a well-liked rising star of the Bonanno family, was a full-blown, traditional Mafia occasion. Porky (who got his nickname because of a slight stammer not unlike Porky Pig's) was already a favorite with the boss. His bookmaking business was a good earner for Graziano's crew, and by marrying the boss's eldest daughter, he stood to improve his position.

The wedding was held at the La Mare ballroom on Eastern Parkway in Brooklyn in September 1984. In attendance were the bosses of all the major New York families. John Gotti was there, at that time a little-known figure in the Gambino family who was yet to achieve the notoriety he later enjoyed. The usual complement of celebrities from the legitimate world was in attendance; actor Tony Danza was there, as well as baseball player Joe Pepitone. (James Caan failed to show up due to personal problems, an omission Lana still remembers.) The bridegroom took home envelopes stuffed with more than $70,000 in cash.

The Staten Island District Attorney's squad had been watching Porky for six months and was also on the premises, photographing guests and license plates. "The FBI took the best pictures," Lana observes dryly. (Like her father, she has a mordant sense of humor and often makes dark, ironic references to her situation. She will also send up members of her own family—her impression of her father yelling down the phone is particularly funny.)

After the wedding, a detective asked Porky to identify the men who had been photographed standing on the steps outside the hall greeting the bridegroom. Porky agreed to do it, on one condition—he wanted a copy of the photo to keep. The same detective later saw the black-and-white surveillance photo framed on the couple's dresser at home. This photograph sat next to a picture of Lana and Porky's first child, named Anthony Graziano Zancocchio in honor of her father, dressed as a gangster and holding a toy machine gun. Lana and Porky are clearly amused by references to the gangster image: on their dresser in the New Jersey mansion is a mocked-up Wanted poster featuring Porky flanked by their two youngest children, all in cowboy hats and brandishing fake rifles.

The happy couple spent part of their honeymoon in Los Angeles, where they made another date with James Caan. Lana remembers trying on every one of the many outfits she had brought with her before she could decide what to wear to meet the famous Hollywood actor.

"John must have really been in love with me when we got married," Lana reflects. "Because I was a real head case at that time."

Lana and Porky's first meeting, according to her own account, was inauspicious: she was drinking with a friend at around 5 A.M. after she had been bouncing around clubs and bars all night. Porky sent over a drink, and Lana, somewhat the worse for wear, started pelting him with little plastic shot glasses. They exchanged a few words, and he asked her out for dinner. "He was a very happy-go-lucky guy, very well liked, not at all like my father," she recalls.

He might have seen some sign of what was to come in that flirtatious volley of plastic cups. Home life for Lana and Porky was not peaceful. Although Lana knew what was traditionally expected of a mob wife, she certainly wasn't going to follow her mother's example and act like a doormat. She admits she was manipulative and sometimes violent. Detectives monitoring phone calls from their house heard streams of verbal abuse, most of it directed at Porky. They began to feel a little sorry for this young, up-and-coming mobster who had married the boss's daughter. If she didn't get her way, she would invariably threaten to tell her father.

Porky's own parents were very different. His mother is a silver-haired grandma well liked in the neighborhood. His father, who died when John was young, was a legitimate businessman, and John made pizzas at his uncle's restaurant throughout high school. From pizzas he graduated to petty crime, says an FBI source, and then to bookmaking. By the end of the 1980s, according to government records, his bookmaking ring was bringing in at least $5,000 a day. Like other members of organized crime, he had to guard against ostentatious spending: it was important to conceal his earnings from the IRS. Try to find any trace of John Zancocchio and you'd think he didn't exist: no credit cards, no car, no home, no bank account— all his assets were in his mother's and wife's names.

Zancocchio's crew was hijacking trucks and selling whatever merchandise they could get their hands on. Of course there was always room for error. In one hijacking incident on Staten Island, Joe Rauchet remembers, Porky and his crew stole two shipping containers of frozen shrimp and lobster—a great favorite with hijackers, as there's always a market for it in New York, especially just before the holidays—and unloaded them in a field. Unfortunately, the two massive containers were dropped off with the doors facing each other, so—to the amusement of detectives—the men couldn't open them. They had to wait till morning, when they could buy drills, hammers, and bolt cutters to get through the steel walls. Unhappily, they soon found out this particular load of frozen seafood belonged to another made guy, so they had to give it back.

Apart from the occasional setback, Porky was doing well for himself and he began to take himself more seriously. He was frequently at the side of his father-in-law and after a while became indispensable to him. In 1987, court papers show, he got his "button." He had a union job with the teamsters, which brought a lot of benefits and influence. His stammer, which always got worse when he was stressed, was by now pretty well under control. He let it be known he no longer wanted to be called Porky. Lana signed the papers on mortgages, on bills, on almost everything they owned. She made their monthly payments in cash. She and Porky played the money-go-round like everyone else.

An FBI agent who investigated Porky's business affairs describes him as "very savvy, very charming, very personable, very engaging. He grew into the role of being the capo's son-in-law." Unlike Lana and her father, Porky saw the value of being civil, even to the enemy in the NYPD uniform.

Joe Rauchet recalls: "The first time I arrested John I had a four-wheel-drive vehicle, and I had John handcuffed to the roll bar, with his hands up over his head. We were going over to arrest another guy and we end up in a car chase, another squad car got into a chase and we joined it. I had John sliding around in the back, every time I went around a corner he slid right over to the other side of the car. . . .

"We got to the station and John called Lana and was telling her about the chase, how exciting it was. He asked her to bring six pizzas, from the family pizzeria, Mama Rosa (named after John's mother, Rose). When Lana got there he was joking about how this guy wouldn't take money so he's going to try to bribe me with pizza. . . ."

Over the years, if everyone behaves respectfully, a sort of camaraderie tends to grow between the mafiosi and the police detectives who make careers of tracking them. Even so, Lana never found it in her to be civil to the opposition.

On one occasion, Rauchet recalls, he went to arrest Zancocchio and found him at home. To spare everyone's feelings, he waited until they were at the front door before snapping on the cuffs. He radioed for backup to take Zancocchio to the station for processing, and as the two men waited for the squad car to arrive, Lana threw open an upstairs window with a crash and yelled out at the top of her voice: "John! John! While you're standing there put out the fucking garbage!"

Her husband looked up and motioned helplessly to his bound wrists. Rauchet turned to his captive and said: "You sure you don't want to go into witness protection?"

John just shrugged.

When Detective Rauchet later went to the Graziano house on Staten Island to deliver a notice of intercept to Mrs. Graziano, informing her, as the law obliged him to do, that their phones had been tapped, he would receive a swift rebuke from her husband. His son-in-law would deliver the message. At the Richmond County Supreme Court, Detective Rauchet was walking through the corridors, observed by a small group of wiseguys. As he passed Zancocchio, with whom he had developed a cordial, if adversarial, relationship over the years, he nodded a greeting. To Rauchet's great surprise, Zancocchio said: "Anthony says, stay away from his house, stay away from his wife or he will cut your balls off." (Cross-examining Detective Rauchet in court about this incident at a later date, Graziano's lawyer inquired: "I take it that to this day you remain fully intact?" Rauchet confirmed that he did.)

Porky, like his father-in-law, received his mob associates at home and conducted meetings in the house. Lana would become livid—not because she didn't want Mafia business in her house, but because her husband never seemed to have time for her. When Porky had his friends over, their conversation was always private; she had to stay out of their way and either sit in her room or go out. It made her furious. On one occasion she grabbed the vacuum cleaner and started cleaning noisily around them during their meeting.

Sociable and convivial, a keen cook and golfer, Porky was nevertheless no match for Lana. She soon beat him down. Again and again he came up short in comparison to her father. "My father is a real man," she says. "John would say, 'If you need to smack me, Lana, smack me.' I'm not saying I didn't abuse him verbally. My father was just very tough."

Lana had done the right thing by her family and her own ambitions when she married a successful mobster—even better, she married a man her father respected and held very dear. But John's successes were never enough: he constantly disappointed her. He didn't hold the same ineluctable power over her as her father did. She wanted to control him, but at the same time she despised him for being weak. Detective Rauchet, who over years of surveillance had plenty of opportunity to observe the couple, puts it simply: "She is her father's daughter."

In 1990, the family would suffer a major setback: John Zancocchio and Anthony Graziano were both arrested for tax fraud, and Lana was indicted separately for bank fraud. Graziano and Zancocchio made a bargain with the prosecution: they would plead guilty if the government would dismiss the charges against Lana and drop their intention to indict John's mother for tax fraud. Graziano was sentenced to two years in jail, Zancocchio to one. When John went to prison, his second son and namesake was just a few days old. Lana struggled to cope, aided by her mother.

John got out in 1991 after serving less than a year, and Lana decided they should move away from Staten Island to the Jersey countryside. She wanted him to start over. She tried to make him change his ways and go legitimate, she says, to make a new start for the sake of the children.

Come on, Lana, you were brought up in the life, your husband is part of that. You're not going to change that by moving to Jersey, are you?

She pauses for a moment. "At the time, I believed it. I did."

Lana had first felt the desire to move out of New York a few years earlier, after a particularly nasty episode that rocked the world of organized crime. In 1988 Gus Farace, a wild young Mafia wannabe, got out of jail after doing seven years for manslaughter, hopped up on steroids and eager to get into drug dealing through his prison contacts. He contacted a dealer to negotiate the sale of a quantity of cocaine, but before the deal was done, Farace received a warning that the man who had introduced him to the dealer was an informer. There was a chance the dealer was setting him up. Farace decided to meet him one more time, to check him out.

The dealer was in fact an undercover agent for the DEA named Everett Hatcher. He was told to meet Farace late at night on a deserted intersection in Staten Island. The place was exposed, and Hatcher's backup team had to wait some distance away. Farace arrived along with his cousin, Dominick Farace, and they ordered Hatcher to follow him. Hatcher followed, with the backup car trying to keep pace, but at some point they lost radio contact. The cars stopped at a diner and the men talked. The Faraces left the place apparently reassured that the dealer was legitimate, but somewhere along the route Gus changed his mind. When they got back to the deserted intersection, he drew level with Hatcher's car and shot him dead.

Unlike its Sicilian counterpart, the American Mafia has a rule about never killing cops or lawyers. Like most Mafia rules, it is a matter less of honor than of pragmatism: dead cops attract too much heat. The murder of Everett Hatcher was a disaster for the Mafia. Every law enforcement agency was brought into the hunt for his killer, and before long Staten Island was crawling with detectives in lock-on surveillance. They knew Gus Farace was the killer, and within hours they were knocking on the doors of all his friends, family, Mafia associates, and criminal pals.

Dominick Farace later became an informer and gave his account of what occurred that night. After the murder, Dominick told detectives, he had called Anthony Graziano for advice. Dominick was seeing Rene at the time, and it was she who answered the phone. She wanted to chat, but Dominick was panicking and yelled at her to get her father. When Graziano picked up, Dominick started to tell him the story, but Graziano just slammed down the phone.

Graziano didn't want to get involved—but everyone was involved. The police applied pressure on the Mafia to force them to give up Farace. They flooded Staten Island with detectives, who followed the mafiosi step for step. It became impossible to do business.

After the shooting, Gus Farace ran for cover. He went to see Margaret Chilli, known as Babe, a rather needy, lonely woman. Babe's father and brother were connected to the Bonanno family. Gus persuaded her to hide him, and when the police knocked on her door looking for him, he was in an upstairs room, rifle in hand. She told the police he wasn't there, and they went away. Soon after, she arranged for him to stay in a friend's apartment.

Babe and Gus were both friends of Lana's, and they were all part of a rising generation of Staten Island's Mafia dynasties, now in their mid-twenties. Lana and John were newly married and looking for an apartment. As they went house hunting, they were followed everywhere by a detective in case they should give away the murderer's whereabouts.

After several months, more shootings, and hundreds of arrests, Gus Farace was shot dead in a Mafia hit. Babe went to prison for hiding a fugitive. To Lana, it seemed as if all her friends were dying or going to jail. On one occasion, on her way to her parents' house to visit her mother, she passed areas cordoned off by combat troops in full armor, machine guns at the ready. They had closed off the area around the Grazianos' house. "There was a whole SWAT team, with guns drawn. Growing up, you're kinda used to certain things, but this was extreme."

Things were getting too hot in New York, and Lana wanted a more peaceful place to bring up her family. But no matter where they moved, Lana would not find any peace—she was angry and dissatisfied, and continued to attack and berate her husband. Once she had found an idyllic rural setting for the family home, she more or less drove her husband away.

3

I N 1992, Lana and John moved to Old Bridge, New Jersey, but
trouble soon followed them there. Through the teamsters union,
John Zancocchio had a no-show job at the Jacob Javits Center in
New York, where he dropped in a couple of times a month to collect his paycheck. After a major operation to eradicate the influence
of organized crime in the unions, Zancocchio lost his cushy job with
the teamsters, and with it, as far as Lana was concerned, his only apparently legitimate income. Family life did not improve.

Lana and Porky decided the neighborhood in Old Bridge was
going downhill, so in 1995 they left to find a nicer area. They
wanted a more rural setting, where the boys could ride their quad
bikes and go to the shore in summer, where the air would be cleaner
and they might find a better class of neighbors. They bought a big
house near the Jersey Shore, which they decided to expand and fix
up. As contractors came and went, their fighting intensified.

The countryside where the Zancocchio house stands is picture
perfect: behind big wooden fences, thoroughbred horses canter
about; the houses are big and ostentatious, with huge decorative
columns and fancy neoclassical porticos. Many have elaborate
wrought-iron gates, and a few of the wealthier residents, who include sports stars and hip-hop millionaires, adorn the gates with
their initials in gold. Most of the houses have infrared electronic
security systems, as well as the more traditional barking and biting
kind. There is a small airport nearby for convenient commuting to
Manhattan.

Lana and Porky made a down payment of $100,000 in cash for the eight-thousand-square-foot house on thirteen acres of land, and mortgaged the remaining $300,000. They rebuilt the house, and between 1996 and 1997 spent $50,000 turning it into the mansion of their dreams. The house was gutted and extended, and they converted the top of the barn into an apartment. The endless procession of workmen attracted the attention of the IRS, and when investigators spoke to the contractors, they were most interested to learn that so many skilled laborers were working for Mr. Zancocchio for free.

The house was always filled with visitors, mostly members of Lana's family. Lana's parents and sisters would arrive on weekends; John's mother would visit. Local police detectives cruising by observed Lana's father holding talks with Porky and other associates on the porch on Sunday mornings.

The Zancocchio family did not blend in particularly well. Local old-money types disapproved of the Zancocchios' flashy cars and noisy dirt bikes. Porky and his friends made some effort to join the local crowd: they made up a foursome to play a round of golf for a charity match at the golf club across the road. Halfway around the course they were disconcerted to come across Detective Ron Jennings and three of his colleagues from the police department. The encounter did not improve their game.

Lana, too, began to have ideas about her position in her new neighborhood. At Christmas she called the local police department and offered them her children's old toys for charity. A police van took away armfuls of stuff her kids no longer needed. She also saw herself as a mentor for deprived children. She offered to take in poor kids from inner-city areas and give them a rural holiday over the summer but was shocked to learn that she would be considered unacceptable mentoring material. She also applied for permission to convert her barn into a refuge for battered women but was advised against it.

When I paid a visit to Lana at her Jersey house, I was immediately struck by its size and grandeur. The house is set back from the road but its grand entrance is in full view of anyone driving past. Two huge English mastiffs bark at intruders; at night the place is lit up like a beacon. The family owns more than ten acres in back of the house where the kids ride their quad bikes. From the garage, we entered the house by stepping over piles of discarded household items populated with mewing kittens. The kitchen is the heart of the house, with a huge modern range and a fridge the size of a walk-in wardrobe. "I love to cook," Lana told me, picking over some deli packages on the shelves. A marble-topped dining table, big enough to seat ten, extended into a deep bay window. From here you could see the swimming pool. The pool guy had stopped by, apparently, to dump a load of chemicals in it, but the water still appeared murky from neglect.

Upstairs were the boys' bedrooms, full of artwork, toys, and clothes strewn on the floor. Across the corridor was the room of Lana's ten-year-old daughter, Sonni, designed for a little princess: pink walls and custom-made wooden furniture; a walk-through closet; her own prettily appointed bathroom in pink and white. It was better than Barbie. Lana's own room was palatial: a huge bed on an acre of thick carpet, swathes of heavy curtains draped artfully to the floor, gold lacquered walls. Her walk-through wardrobe led to a huge bathroom lined in lustrous marble. She pointed out the bidet, a new acquisition not yet installed. She was impatient to have it connected and learn how to use it.

Downstairs, a room big enough for a bowling alley contained a new sofa and a wall-sized television, but the floor and the walls were unfinished. Lana had run out of ideas at this point, run out of people to fill it, and, critically, she'd run out of cash. The mansion, conceived for a busy extended family, was echoing around her.

Both Lana's house phone and her mobile rang constantly, often simultaneously, all day: there was a crisis at her restaurant. This was their busiest time of year, with the shore people opening up their beachfront homes and partying on the weekend, and after a series of disagreements, the chef had quit. Lana shouted, cajoled, begged and bullied her staff into keeping the restaurant open. Wearing a short black toweling housedress and big fluffy slippers, she would grab a yellow mop and pad back and forth across the kitchen floor, phone clutched to her ear, bossing around her kitchen staff. This is apparently her habitual mode of conducting stressful phone conversations: mop in one hand, phone in the other, pacing.

The restaurant was a pet project of her husband's. When Lana and Porky moved to the Jersey Shore, they had an idea about how to make their mark on the new neighborhood. Unwilling, perhaps, to give up their New York habits, they wanted their own fancy restaurant, a place that would draw people from miles around, that would far outshine the local restaurants and the seafood places on the shore.

They found a place being renovated by the owner, an eccentric millionaire—a huge, ambitious project just a five-minute drive from their house. Before long, Porky and his associates had muscled in on the project. Whether the owner was aware of what was happening is hard to tell. The Mafia has a way of getting into bed with legitimate businessmen and before they know it, the legitimate guy has been shoved out and is sleeping on the floor. Work began in 1997, and it shaped up well: the restaurant had two floors, space for live music, an elegant vaulted roof, a stylish zinc bar, a cigar room where patrons could keep their own humidified boxes of Havanas, and a sushi bar. They gave it an exotic, Franco-Italian name.

The local authorities soon realized they were dealing with a substantial figure in organized crime; they also saw he was not a leg breaker: on one occasion Detective Jennings walked in unnoticed and looked on silently as the Mafia guy and his cronies discussed the best way to arrange a flower vase and a pink linen napkin. Porky Zancocchio was always well dressed in suits and sunglasses. He was never rude or abusive to the police when they dropped by, but he never hung around to chat either: if he caught sight of a detective walking in, he would vanish out the back.

When the work was finished, they threw a launch party and invited hundreds of local guests, as well as associates and friends from Staten Island. The police, who were conducting a routine background investigation before a liquor license could be issued, were impressed. By this stage the legal proprietor had been sidelined. When people asked who the owner was, they were shown to a laughing group of snappily dressed wiseguys. The real owner was left leaning on the bar.

Rumors that the place was owned by mobsters drew curious crowds, politicians who wanted a free meal, and others who just wanted to rub shoulders with gangsters. But as the liquor license failed to materialize, the local press began to run stories that there was something not quite right about the place. The smarter set began to stay away.

Without a liquor license, they hired the place out for private parties. It was a perfect setting for a gregarious fellow like Porky to play host. He invited his gentlemen friends to a "cigar and lingerie" party, with models posing in underwear. The place was packed. Lana threw a fortieth birthday party for her husband. The guests arrived in stretch limos, and her father held court.

Perhaps eager to score points with her new neighbors, Lana tried to hold a fund-raiser for the church school her children attended. Police informed the parents' group that they couldn't legally hold their fund-raiser at the restaurant, incurring the righteous fury of the local worthies, who had no idea that the legal status of the restaurant was in question. Although the event went ahead after much wrangling about bending the rules for a good cause, the whole incident did not reflect well on Lana.

In the end, the liquor license application was rejected. The owner was found to have links to organized crime through his associates and was forced to sell. In the months that followed, workmen and tradespeople repeatedly complained to the police about money they were owed for materials and labor.

Porky, whose name had never appeared on any of the restaurant's legal documents, looked elsewhere. He found a place in an unpromising strip mall just inland from the shore, and in 1999 he opened a little restaurant with modern Italian cuisine on one side and a pizza oven on the other. Porky had worked for many years in his uncle's pizzeria on Staten Island, a place popular as much for its pizza as for its ambience, and he knew what he was doing. In the early days, the Jersey restaurant was always full, drawing summer trade from the shore, attracting both tourists and locals.

Despite its initial success, Lana and Porky began fighting over the restaurant, which was owned in name by his mother, Rose. Lana saw herself as manager of the modern Italian side of the restaurant and would complain that his pizza oven was killing "her business." He was heard to say on surveillance tapes that she was driving his customers away, that she had no aptitude for the restaurant trade, but just showed up on the weekends to act the part.

The fighting escalated. On one occasion, patrons of the golf course across the road were bemused to witness the full rage of Lana Zancocchio. Porky and a friend had come into the clubhouse and were sitting in the bar having a drink when in flew Lana. She was just about to let fly at her husband when his friend muttered something that sounded like, "Here comes trouble. . . ." Hearing this, Lana swung around and smacked him. She bellowed at the two men and stormed out as fast as she had come.

John began to stay away from home. He took an apartment on Staten Island, where most of his work was centered, and hung out at the restaurants and bars that doubled as business premises and social clubs for the crew. One of these was Hipps, a topless bar. It was generally known that Porky was seeing the barmaid at this place. It also became known to Lana.

Not wishing to humiliate herself by confronting the woman face-to-face, Lana let her sister Rene pay the woman a visit. If Lana is formidable, Rene is no shrinking violet herself. Lana's father also had a strong word with Porky about keeping up appearances. Lana tried to make Porky promise never to set foot in Staten Island, but he couldn't give it up. He loved the camaraderie of organized crime, she says: playing cards, playing golf, hanging out and trips to Atlantic City, where, investigators claimed, the Bonanno family did most of its business until Joey Massino, identified by prosecutors as the boss, was banned from all casinos.

As her world began to fall apart, Lana started seeing a therapist. The children were also getting help to deal with the emotional fallout from their parents' breakup. John was told to attend family sessions, but, according to her lawyer, he didn't take it seriously and stopped coming. This may have been a little shortsighted: since the success of The Sopranos, therapy has become rather fashionable among mobsters, who tend to cite their psychological problems as mitigating circumstances at sentencing. Hector Pagan, now divorced from Rene, has been diagnosed as suffering from bipolar disorder. Before her sentencing for drug dealing, Lana's sister Jennifer had been diagnosed with post-traumatic stress disorder. In this, as in so many aspects of organized crime, *The Sopranos* has replaced *The Godfather* as the Mafia's cultural handbook.

The final year of Lana and Porky's marriage was not pretty. They fought bout after humiliating bout. Lana recalls their last fight, in June 2000. "He was choking me. I got hold of a hockey stick and smashed his car lights. It was brutal. The children were in the house. But I do not back down. *I do not back down.*"

He drove away that night, and stayed away. They are now officially separated.

"He blames me," says Lana. "He says I'm vicious and violent."

Has she considered the possibility that John married her because she was the boss's daughter?

"I have to face it that maybe I was used."

Having often called on her father to support her in arguments against her husband, Lana believed that her father would back her all the way, through her most outrageous extremes of temper. She wanted him to be present at their divorce hearings, to fight in her corner. But at some point Lana's ultimate sanction, her threat to tell Daddy, lost its power. Even after an acrimonious split from the boss's daughter, Porky's light was undimmed. "My father loved John. Still does," she says.

It may be the effect of confronting some harsh realities, or the result of therapy, but Lana is surprisingly self-aware. She admits that she has given John a rough ride, and that she learned parenting skills from her bullying father. She's learned to be tough all her life, until she hardly knows how to access any softer feelings—and yet she can still make fun of herself. When she talks about how the children are coping with their parents' separation, she refers to a complaint made by her eldest son: "Who the hell needs a father? I need a mother."

Nine months after he left their Jersey home, in June 2001, John Zancocchio was arrested at his mother's house in Staten Island, charged with tax fraud and loan-sharking. Lana, to her dismay, was named on the same indictment, for tax evasion. John pled guilty and was sentenced to seventy months. Lana could have been facing a year in jail.

By the time her troubles were getting serious, the restaurant became Lana's lifesaver. The work got her out of the house, supplied her with friends, a little local family for her to boss around and people to go out with after closing on a Saturday night.

On a warm Friday evening, Lana's middle sister, Rene, was waiting on tables. She was friendly and pretty, with black hair done up in Bjork-style bunches. Lana arrived, wearing all black as usual. As the tables starting filling up, Lana let the manic coming and going wash around her. She ordered seafood salad and crab cakes, and picked at plates of tuna and veal. Every so often she had to go to the phone to settle arguments between the children at home. Rene's son had had a fight with one of Lana's children. His father is a boxer, and the boy, though tiny, is a fearless minipugilist, and often takes on his much bigger, and older, cousin.

Lana got up from the table at one point and returned with a huge bottle of bourbon and a jug of soda. "My mother says you gotta let loose once in a while," she said, pouring two massive drinks.

Rene had a great rapport with the customers, older couples with leathery tans and highlights, who loved her exuberant manner and imitated her Brooklyn accent: *Get me a fwork!* "MTTM, that's what my friends call me," Rene joked. "Married to the Mob." When *The Godfather* theme came on the PA, Rene threw up her arms and yelled: "They're playing my *sawng!*"

The youngest and most clever of the Graziano sisters, Jennifer had always seemed the one who would lead a different kind of life. Everyone who observed the family as the three daughters grew up claimed to have been shocked when Jennifer got into trouble. She had made an effort to get away from her father's world. She was just a couple of credits short of a master's in educational psychology when she was busted for dealing marijuana. At sentencing, Judge Sifton had given her a strong talking-to about not wasting her life.

"You took over a drug operation of a probably fairly scary person. You seem—I mean, I guess you grew up in a fairly scary family and you certainly surround yourself with frightening people. . . ."

As a teenager Jennifer had money and privilege, and was very taken with the organized crime scene. She was going to school with two or three hundred dollars in her pocket and spending time with other children of mobsters; she had a gang, a mini-aristocracy of

Mafia rich kids, who would hang out in a schoolyard in Bulls Head on Staten Island, smoking, drinking, and boasting about their fathers. Sammy "the Bull" Gravano's daughter Karen was her best friend. She hung out with Chris Paciello, a member of a new, younger Bath Avenue Crew who later dated supermodels and dominated the club scene in Miami Beach before being arrested for murder.

In her twenties, Jennifer dated some rough characters, including one man who beat her up repeatedly and so viciously that she was later diagnosed as suffering from post-traumatic stress disorder. Then she got pregnant. According to court records, the father, Ramon Cross, spent some time in custody after a shoot-out following a nightclub brawl. It was not what her parents would have hoped for their clever daughter.

Anticipating her family's reaction to the unexpected pregnancy, Jennifer delayed telling them about the baby. She was afraid her father would cut off her allowance and try to stop her mother and sisters from speaking to her, but, although tensions were high, they supported her. Indeed, while she was awaiting her own trial for selling marijuana, Jennifer moved into the house on Arbutus Way with the baby, and when she went to prison, the two-year-old infant was given into his grandparents' care.

Of Jennifer's troubles, Lana would only say she didn't know the baby's father.

Lana and Rene reminisced about Lana's own laughable boyfriend choices—the bikers, the tattoos, the mushroom-munching hippies who liked to drive while tripping. They talked about their Sicilian grandfather, who used to put Rene on his knee and give her five dollars ("Fidolla! Fidolla!" she roared, imitating his accent). Apparently he still gives her five dollars every time she visits, even though she is now thirty.

"Let me tell you," Rene shouted as she rushed past, "there's no money in crime. If there was, I wouldn't be waiting on tables!"

Lana just raised her eyebrows.

She talked about her long-suffering mother, who might complain when her husband punched a hole in the wall, but she never threatened to leave. "I tried to mother her," says Lana. "I used to say, 'Why don't you hit him with a frying pan and leave him?'"

Of course Veronica never left him. A wife doesn't leave a mafioso of Anthony Graziano's status and temperament. She would be unlikely to survive the attempt. He, on the other hand, is free to come and go. This is a fact of life for Mafia wives, part of the whole package: it's a trade-off between an affluent lifestyle and status in the community and a frequently absent, and serially unfaithful, husband.

Not Lana. She wouldn't put up with that stuff from her husband. She talks about how she cut up John's suits and put sugar in his gas tank. Now he has gone, and she is left with the unfinished house and bills to pay. Malicious gossip suggests he has requested a transfer to a prison as far away from her as possible. Lana may yet get the last word. Some people say she won't give him a divorce.

And yet, Lana has had her own troubles with the law. After years of protecting her husband's illegal activities by banking his earnings in her name, she became the target of an IRS investigation. Although she had always complained to her husband that she did not like being excluded from his Mafia business, now, ironically, she was very much involved. He had made a guilty plea and was handed the maximum sentence for his crime. How would the courts deal with her?

ALTHOUGH Lana Zancocchio has been surrounded by members of organized crime all her life, it was never her expectation to be in trouble with the law. Like other women in her position, she assumed a kind of filial immunity. And when she married a mobster bringing in millions of illicit dollars, she just signed the papers, made the monthly mortgage payments in cash, and spent the money.

The money was, on the face of it, hers to spend. Everything her father and husband possess, in the way of cars, houses, apartments, restaurants, bank accounts—all of it is owned, on paper, by the women. Her father's million-dollar Staten Island mansion is officially owned by his three daughters; her husband's New Jersey restaurant was registered to Lana and her mother-in-law. The big house near the Jersey Shore is in Lana's name; the property they plan to develop, in their daughter's. It was a simple, and much practiced, expedient. Lana was never supposed to get into trouble—that wasn't in the rules of the game.

A false tax return caught her out. The IRS had been scrutinizing the paper trail that led from John Zancocchio's gambling and loan-sharking businesses and seemed to vanish into thin air. While acquiring and rebuilding the large house in New Jersey, and making thousands of dollars a week from illegal activities, John had nevertheless failed to show any income for three years. Meanwhile IRS agents discovered $15,000 of Lana's money had not been declared on her 1995 tax return. She was arrested on June 21, 2001, charged with tax fraud, and released on bail.

The boss's daughter is not supposed to go on trial. Neither is his wife. Such an indignity is just not in the vocabulary of Mafia business. The big guy can't protect his own family? It's a humiliation that a boss cannot allow. Nothing enrages a Mafia capo as much as the threat of legal action against his wife and children.

Assistant U.S. Attorney Ruth Nordenbrook, who harbors no doubts about the financial acumen of her gender, believes it unfair that a Mafia woman should be off-limits if she is providing cover for her husband's illegal earnings and spending the proceeds at Armani. Forcing Mafia women to take moral responsibility for the illegal provenance of their wealth has become something of a mission for Nordenbrook. But first she has to convince judges that women are not helpless bystanders in the Mafia enterprise.

Nordenbrook made herself very unpopular in 1984 by prosecuting Marie Attanasio, wife of Louis "Ha Ha" Attanasio, who was identified in court as a member of the Bonanno family, for tax fraud. Nordenbrook was accused of "playing dirty" by the defense lawyers, who were appalled at her determination to go ahead with prosecuting a mafioso's wife. According to mob rules, Louis "Ha Ha" was supposed to take the rap for his wife, but he let her go to court. Marie was acquitted, but her husband's reputation suffered as a result of the episode.

Aware of this reluctance to expose the women to legal proceedings, prosecutors occasionally threaten to indict a mob wife unless the husband pleads guilty. It very often works. It worked in Lana's case in 1990, when, in order to escape the ignominy of having their women dragged into court, John Zancocchio entered a plea bargain that involved letting the women off. Anthony Graziano hung on for five months before finally capitulating.

This time, a plea wasn't an option. Zancocchio offered to serve a longer sentence if his wife could be exonerated, but Nordenbrook wasn't cutting a deal. She wanted to see Lana do jail time. The apparent immunity of the Graziano womenfolk had begun to get on Nordenbrook's nerves. "Nowhere is it written in the law," she said, "that women have a right to commit a crime if their husband is prepared to go to prison."

In March 2002, disaster struck. Following investigations in Florida and New York, after years of illegal activity comparatively untroubled by the law, Lana's father was arrested on charges of drug trafficking, loan-sharking, extortion, illegal gambling, and conspiracy to murder. Aged sixty-one at the time of his arrest, Graziano was denied bail, in spite of his failing health, as a long-term member of organized crime and a potential danger to witnesses. (Graziano would eventually plead guilty to racketeering and tax evasion, and was sentenced to 11 years in prison. He cracked jokes during court proceedings and insisted that, had he been a younger man, he would have fought the charges. He consistently denied being a member of organized crime, and even refused to admit the existence of the Mafia.)

Her father's arrest had attracted a great deal of publicity because of his senior position in the mob. Meanwhile, as Lana's sentencing approached, stories about her case appeared in the local press. If Lana Zancocchio's neighbors didn't know who she was before, they certainly did now. At the restaurant, her young, local staff were beginning to ask questions. Realizing she had to tell them something, she gathered them all together for a meeting and told them about her legal troubles. She had to tell them she might be going to jail.

The night before Lana had been due to appear in Brooklyn's federal court for the first time, in 1990, she got drunk on Southern Comfort martinis. She broke down and cried hysterically, begging to be allowed not to go to court. She had to be dragged forcibly from the shower, her fingers unlocked one at a time from the side of the door.

On the day of the sentencing, Lana had to get out of the shower by herself and drive the children, and their therapist, Cheryl Daniels, to Brooklyn on a warm day in May.

Although she stands a little under five feet five, Lana is an imposing figure. For this occasion, she wore black trousers and a black shirt, and not much makeup. There was nothing of the classic Mafia princess about the way she looked—her hair was black, not bleached blonde, for a start, and worn loose down her back. Her appearance and demeanor demonstrated that she had made no particular effort.

Sitting on the polished wooden benches of the near-empty court-room before the proceedings started, she and the children chatted about *The Osbournes*—sixteen-year-old Anthony's favorite TV show. Lana was particularly disgusted by the scenes of the Osbournes' dogs messing in the house. (This wouldn't be the last time *The Osbournes* was mentioned in connection with Lana's family: local investigators later described life with the Zancocchios as every bit as bizarre as MTV's best-loved reality show.)

Lana's father loomed large over the proceedings—his influence, if not his presence, very much in evidence. His incarceration was a source of some relief to Lana's lawyer, who had banned him from a previous hearing on the grounds that his reputation would do noth-ing for Lana's cause. (Detention does not prevent Anthony Graziano from making his feelings known to his circle of dependents. From prison he makes regular phone calls to his own, and his family's, at-torneys, demanding information and barking orders in his rasping, sixty-cigarettes-a-day voice.)

Ruth Nordenbrook, for the prosecution, was seeking a period of incarceration of between five months and a year. The judge, Jack Weinstein, had requested Lana to bring her three children to court so he could speak to them directly. Lana had reason to believe that Judge Weinstein would look kindly on her and her family: at a presentence hearing, her lawyer had said he didn't want the court to think he was using the children to manipulate the court's emotions. "Why not?" said Judge Weinstein. "I don't find that objectionable."

The judge, who was not wearing robes in order to make the pro-ceedings less formal, gathered all those present, including the chil-dren and their therapist, around a long wooden table. Only a couple of bemused agents from the FBI and the IRS, who had done all the legwork for this investigation, were left sitting on the public benches. If Judge Weinstein, who has tried some formidable Mafia criminals in his time, was making efforts to be less intimidating, none of it made an impression on Lana Zancocchio. Throughout the proceed-ings she scowled at him under furrowed black brows, her prodigious sulk declaring her dim view of him, his court, and the process of law.

Asked what they would do if their mother went to prison, the children made their speeches about how unpleasant life would be.

John, aged eleven, said he didn't want to stay with his grandmother. "She's not like so great to be with, because she can't like tell you a lot of stuff and she's neurotic, she's very annoying at times."

"She's very what?" said the judge, either through poor hearing or incredulity.

"Annoying," John repeated, obviously in great discomfort. What else could he do?

As astounding as this display of disloyalty was, the therapist ultimately stole the show. A mousy-looking middle-aged woman with sandy-colored hair, Ms. Daniels dropped a bombshell. "I believe that Lana is a victim of emotional domestic violence for many years. Her mother was only fifteen when she had Lana, which I don't feel is an appropriate age to be a mother and take care of a child. . . . Lana and I have extensively worked on issues—"

"We refer to people by their last name in court," the judge interrupted.

"Mrs. Graziano . . . Lana Zancocchio's mother . . . Mrs. Graziano was fifteen when she had Lana and Lana's father is a man who Lana wanted to look up to and to be loved by him, however, that was very difficult. Until today, I don't think that Lana has been able to accomplish the love that she wanted from him."

"The defendant is a mature woman," the judge interposed again. "We refer to her by her last name."

But it was the immature woman to whom the therapist wanted to draw the court's attention.

"Mrs. Zancocchio has been hit by her father as a child, has been told she is fat and ugly, has been degraded time and time again. Mrs. Zancocchio and I have worked diligently with the children on parenting skills that greatly differ from what she was brought up to understand. I want to share this with you, because I think this is very important. There was one episode, Lana was in the backseat of a car, and she was a young child, about Sonni's age, and someone stopped her father's car and they had an argument and in front of her, her father bit off the man's ear."

In the informal courtroom there was a general intake of breath—not least from Lana, who remembered her father as the victim of this particular episode.

Anthony Graziano, always dominant in person, had taken over the proceedings in his absence. Graziano himself was on trial in this courtroom, accused by both sides: the defense charged him with ruining Lana's life by his continual abuse and his violent, criminal behavior, while the prosecution accused him of instructing his daughter in the life of organized crime and supporting her in illegal and preposterous behavior. If Lana had inherited his controlling, unloving ways, did that make her a victim, or an abuser? Ms. Daniels argued that it was her father's fault, that he had ruined her life and her children's lives. In private, she has confessed to her poor caretaking skills, recalling her son's words: *"Who the hell needs a father? I need a mother."* Perhaps this was Lana's revenge against her father: she put all the blame on him.

After Ms. Daniels had finished making her case, it was left to Ruth Nordenbrook to conclude hers: to portray Lana's father as a criminal, to present Lana as an accomplice who took advantage of her father's powerful position, not as a victim of his rough treatment. Nordenbrook represented Lana Zancocchio as the classic wealthy Mafia wife, living off her husband's ill-gotten gains while helping him to avoid paying taxes, the spoiled Mafia princess always threatening to tell Daddy: "She has used her father's position in organized crime to enforce her will, both against her husband and against outsiders."

Asked if she wanted to make a statement, Lana got to her feet and said haltingly: "This is the worst day of my life. I'm humiliated totally because of what I have put [the children] through. I'm trying my hardest, since I asked my husband to leave, who I loved very much, to spare them any difficulty in life."

Lana and her lawyer both maintain that she had made an effort to remove her family from the world of organized crime in which they had grown up, and that when her husband was released from prison she tried to persuade him to go legitimate. They each made references to starting afresh, to making a new life, and so on. They painted an almost absurd picture of a world in which daughters of Mafia bosses marry Mafia soldiers, then when the going gets rough, make a clean break from their criminal past, and consort only with straight people forever after.

This idea of a Mafia woman's freedom is scarcely borne out by reality. Anthony Graziano is not the type of man to allow his children to make their own choices in life—two of his daughters married his crew members. But that too is beside the point: Lana is not likely to ask her husband to go straight because she scarcely knows what straight is. Her father and husband have both pled guilty to offenses in the past, but she refuses to acknowledge that they ever did anything wrong. She has never accepted that her own role in her family's financial dealings was illegal. Following the classic Mafia woman's script, she accuses the prosecution of waging a decades-old vendetta against her family. She has challenged her father on countless occasions, but she has never rejected his way of life: she may rebel, but still she respects him.

Ruth Nordenbrook attempted to convince the court that Lana Zancocchio is not the sort of woman who changes her ways without a hard shock to her system. But the judge was of a benign disposition: Lana Zancocchio was granted a conditional discharge. Ordered to make restitution of $101,000, she was given a lecture on being a good mother, and fined an additional $100,000.

As he went through the usual drill about not associating with criminals, the judge established that Lana Zancocchio's whole family was at most only a couple of degrees of separation from a criminal. At a presentence hearing, Judge Weinstein had run through the same routine:

The court: You have no guns in the house?

The defendant (Lana Zancocchio): No.

The court: No drugs?

The defendant: No.

The court: No relationship with any criminal persons, except, I guess, your father and husband, but not in any criminal context?

The defendant: My sister.

Mr. Rabin: Her sister.

The court: Her sister is a criminal?

Mr. Rabin: She is in Danbury at the present time on a narcotics matter.

The court: And your sister.

The judge acknowledged that banning the family from associating with criminals would have been a problem: "I cannot cut them off from their cousins. . . . But you boys and young lady better recognize that these people, who have gone to prison, including your father, are not role models for you."

It was difficult to imagine how these children could disregard the influence of every powerful figure in their family. Since most of the grown-ups they loved were in trouble with the law, how could the law be right? But in that sunny, otherworldly courtroom, presided over by the benign personage of Judge Weinstein, anything seemed possible.

When the proceedings had ended, Lana, the therapist, and the three children strolled across the street to a diner that serves as the courthouse canteen. At one table sat about ten uniformed and armed police officers. At another sat the mobster's daughter and her little retinue. Lana was exhausted. "This year has been nerve-wracking, stressful. It sucks to wake up every day. I'm so tired, just waiting for the other shoe to drop. And it does. It seems never ending."

And yet, now that the immediate danger of imprisonment was over, the prospect of the summer stretching ahead looked a bit brighter. The problem of how to raise $201,000 loomed, but Lana was hoping to sell off some plots of land to cover it. Anthony would work at the concession stand on the boardwalk, John would ride his bike with his friends.

But just when it seemed as if a version of normal life might prevail, the violence of Lana's family's world intruded once again. While Lana spoke, Sonni, all dimpled innocence in a velvet hair band, appeared at her mother's side. "Mommy, can you tell me that story about Poppy biting off the man's ear?"

5

WOMEN actively involved in Mafia business can expect to confront the full force of the law, but, unlike Lana Zancocchio, most women who merely live on the proceeds of organized crime never come before the courts. Women exculpate themselves by claiming to be innocent bystanders—they are not planning scores or building a criminal enterprise. As Mafia women become followers of money and power, their devotion to their way of life tends to obscure any moral sense. Many exist in a state of willful ignorance—it protects them from the law, and it also prevents them having to acknowledge the evil deeds committed by their fathers or husbands. One such case of moral blindness was Camille Serpico, who married her husband's killer. She maintains she did not know her new husband was the murderer, although people around her had their suspicions at the time. If she did not know, apparently it was because she did not want to.

Camille Serpico looks like the classic Mafia moll: beautiful and stylish, she has progressed through a series of wealthy husbands—all but one reputed to be connected to the mob—accumulating jewelry, furs, and aliases. Along the way, she became increasingly involved in the men's work, until 2001, when she was arrested with her husband. If she started out an innocent bystander, experience has taught Camille to do what it takes to look after herself. Perhaps attracted by danger and easy money, in five marriages she has never strayed far from the mob and has been drawn in more deeply: silent complicity has transformed into active involvement.

Camille married her first husband, Joey Colucci, in the spring of 1963. A young builder from Bensonhurst in Brooklyn, Colucci was on friendly terms with Sammy "the Bull" Gravano. Until the late 1970s, Bensonhurst was an Italian enclave where Mafia wannabes would congregate and invent scams to catch the eye of neighborhood mafiosi. As up-and-coming mobsters in their mid-twenties, Gravano and his friends attracted attention, not just from older wiseguys, but from girls. Joey Colucci's sister, Jackie, who has lived in Bensonhurst all her life, knew Gravano and his crowd in younger days.

"I knew Sammy from the neighborhood here," says Jackie. "He was twenty-four years old when I knew him. He was always hanging around on Bath Avenue, and my brother was friends with him and Tommy Spero and those other guys. They used to come over and eat at my house. My brother Joey was a construction worker, and he was the only one who was married at that time, so everyone used to come over to our house; my brother and his wife, Camille, lived next door. The guys used to play cards, the girls used to hang out. . . . My brother went out to work every day, but they were already getting their money elsewhere."

Camille was "drop-dead gorgeous," as Gravano later described her, with long legs and black hair. According to Jackie, she and Camille were best friends. Camille and Joey had two young children, and Jackie doted on them. "At Christmas Sammy brought gifts for the kids, we were all friends together," says Jackie. "We were very close, we were all in and out of each other's houses without ringing the bell."

These were good times; life was never boring, and the young men's energy made it seem they might do something with their lives. Tommy Spero was already connected: his uncle was a ranking member of the Gambino crime family. The young guns plotted and schemed how they might get attention and rise through the ranks.

"We were all impressed by the mob thing," says Rosanne Massa, another Bensonhurst woman, who worked as Gravano's secretary in the 1980s. "I was impressed that I worked for Sammy the Bull. The people I saw coming and going were in the papers, there was a lot of buzz around them in the neighborhood: we all got off on it. At that time it wasn't even about money. It was just to see who could be more powerful. They were all grooming themselves for positions in the mob."

Girls were drawn to these young toughs, attracted by the scent of illegality, by their aura of power and danger, but most of all, says Jackie, by the money. Unlike most other young men in the neighborhood, Gravano and his friends often had money in their pockets; they owned clubs and bars, people took notice of them.

In 1970, their little entourage would be poisoned by a series of catastrophic events. Joey had a brief affair with another woman, and Tommy Spero, turning the situation to his advantage, told Camille. Joey and Camille's relationship was never the same again. Soon Joey moved out of their apartment and back in with his mother next door. Gravano later said he heard that Tommy was "making moves" on Joey's wife.

For the neighborhood gang, the aura of illegality became the real thing when Gravano committed his first major crime. Gravano, having been told that Joey Colucci was planning to murder him, and then Tommy Spero, in retaliation for Tommy's relationship with his wife, was ordered to hit Joey first. At four o'clock in the morning on February 28, 1970, the friends were all together, driving around in Tommy's car, when Sammy shot Joey in the back of the head. They dumped his body out of the car on Rockaway Parkway, and Gravano shot him three more times. Joey was twenty-six, his youngest child just eighteen months old.

"The cops came to the house and said they found my brother dead," Jackie recalls, "and a couple of hours later in come Tommy Spero and Sammy going: 'We're going to find out who did this to Joey,' crying, consoling me and my mother and my father. At that point you're so ripped apart, and these people, you think they're your friends, you go, 'Yeah, please, please try to find out. . . .' "

In the days following the murder, Jackie and her mother, Annie, began to have a feeling that Tommy Spero had something to do with Joey's murder, but there was nothing they could do about it. Annie Colucci has said that within weeks of the killing, she was wagging her finger accusingly at Tommy Spero whenever she encountered him in the neighborhood, saying: "You had something to do with it, you know who killed him. How could you do this?"

Within a couple of weeks of Joey's death, his widow, Camille, was openly dating Tommy Spero. This seemed to confirm Jackie's worst suspicions. "I told Tommy Spero: 'You murdered my brother,'" Jackie recalls. "I said, 'My brother's wife cheated on him. Don't you think she's going to cheat on you? You did it for nothing.' My brother died because Tommy Spero didn't want him around. He wanted to move in, be the husband, be the father of my brother's kids. So that's what he did."

In December 1970, ten months after Joey's death, Camille married Tommy Spero. Joey's family was heartbroken. And they wondered, since they had strong suspicions that Tommy was involved in Joey's murder, how could Camille be oblivious? If she had an inkling about how the mob worked, how could she sleep with the man who had probably killed her children's father?

There is a scene in *The Godfather* when Kay confronts Michael, who has succeeded his father as the head of the Corleone family, about the murder of his brother-in-law Carlo. To calm her down, Michael tells her she can ask him, just this once, a question about his business. "Did you do it? Did you?" she asks anxiously. He looks her in the eye, steady, unflinching, and lies. She is visibly relieved by his answer, and gratefully embraces him.

Perhaps Camille never asked Tommy whether he had killed Joey. Or, if she did, perhaps he lied. She has always maintained that she did not know Tommy had any involvement with her husband's death. But if Camille got away with lying to herself that time, the next time was even easier.

Camille's marriage to Tommy did not last long. A few years later, she left him for another man. Camille's next husband was not a mobster but a builder, a successful developer named Bob Stenrud. They met when Stenrud was working on the house she shared with Tommy, turning an average Staten Island family home into a mini-mansion. Bob had two children, who spent a lot of time with the couple. They owned a small country house, which Bob and Camille rebuilt and extended, and where they would entertain their friends and throw parties on weekends. When Bob died of cancer, there was an ugly tussle between Camille and his children over the inheritance. She claimed he had died intestate, but years later this was discovered to be a lie. Perhaps deception was coming easier to her. At any rate, Camille was becoming more skilled at looking after her interests.

The next man she married was Anthony Serpico, who had made a lot of money in the auto salvage business, and who investigators claim had links to organized crime. He was older than Camille, but kind, and rich—and although she would dump him after five years, she kept his surname. To find her next husband Camille had only to cross the street to another garage. Ernest Varacalli, identified by prosecutors as an associate of the Genovese crime family, was earning millions through his auto theft and salvage business. He and Camille moved into a multimillion-dollar property in Dresden Place on Staten Island with all the amenities, including a workout room and a tanning bed. Camille looked after herself—now a blonde, with a nip and tuck and plenty of pampering, she still looked striking.

Varacalli was working with a network of car thieves and salvage yards that stole cars for spare parts. Prosecution records show his specialty was air bags, which he sold wholesale to other garages in the network. Although his garage in Brooklyn had a permanent Closed sign on the door, the place was making a profit—according to a conservative estimate—of $106,000 a month. Camille was helping him with his finances, moving tens of thousands of dollars between bank accounts held in her various names—after so many marriages, she had plenty of ready aliases. By the time law enforcement tapped their phone lines, Varacalli was under a good deal of stress, bailing out his employees, dodging surveillance, and drilling them on their escape in case of a surprise visit from the police. One phone conversation taped by the FBI revealed Camille calling her husband at the garage, trying to navigate the complicated system of their bank accounts:

"What am I . . . with this money? Now where am I taking it out of?" she asked.

"Well, you gotta use your brain," he snapped. "You take it out of the new account."

"The one that has eighty thousand in it?" she asked.

"Yes," he said, exasperated, "say it a little louder."

Still confused, she said: "No, but that's how, Junior . . . that's how we got our mortgage."

"Okay, okay," he replied. "Good enough and just, just, jot it down and then I'll, I'll take it out of, I'll, I'll show you tonight what to do."

On another occasion, in December 2000, much to the amusement of prosecutors and agents who heard the tapes, they learned that Camille's beauty routine came before her husband's business:

"I'm on my way to go to the bank," she told him.

"You didn't go to the bank yet?"

"No, I had to do my nails first," she admitted.

"Camille," her husband pleaded, "don't walk around with all that money, today. It's the holidays, they're robbing everyone."

Camille exasperated her husband in other ways. An ambient bug picked up a conversation in which he joked with Camille's sister about her extravagant style. While he was in the middle of bankruptcy proceedings for one of his companies, Camille had walked into court resplendent in a mink jacket and jewels. "I'm going to jail here," he remembered thinking, and they laughed.

In some conversations, Camille could be heard gently prompting her husband to go legitimate, and he too expressed the desire to get his affairs in order, clear up his tax debts, and move into a different business. He said he needed a million dollars to get things straight; unfortunately, law enforcement got him first.

In early 2001, according to prosecution records, Camille was working a few days a week at her husband's garage, answering the phone. He instructed her in great detail how to avoid dealing with the public: they had to be sure not to sell their stolen parts to anyone they did not know, as the parts would not pass a vehicle inspection without triggering an investigation. One of Varacalli's friends who phoned the office when she was working teased her about being caught up in his illegal business:

"Don't tell me he left ya there to get locked up?"

"Yeah!" she replied.

"You know he's bailing out—ya know that, right?"

"Yeah, I know, that's why I don't want to be here," she said, laughing.

"He's probably going to rat you right out, Camille."

"Without a doubt!"

They laughed, but Varacalli was getting increasingly uptight. He knew the end was coming. On May 17, 2001, he and Camille, along with sixteen others in New York City, including Varacalli's son John, were arrested and charged with falsifying business records. The following week, Varacalli and twenty-three others, including alleged Genovese capo Fritzi Giovanelli, were charged with running a multi-million-dollar auto theft and resale ring. On July 12, Camille answered the door of their house in Dresden Place, Staten Island, to find a police detective serving her with seven further summonses: for herself, her husband, and the various auto companies involved in the salvage ring.

By this time, Varacalli's phone message had been changed to a sulky: "Don't leave a message, don't leave a number. I ain't answering any calls."

A state civil action was launched against the defendants for the return of over $1 million of their illegal earnings. Police seized the following items from the Varacalli residence on Dresden Place:

1 Brown ¾-length fur coat with "CMV"

1 Brown full-length fur coat with Lt collar

1 Brown full-length fur with "CMS"

1 Black and Brown ¾-length fur with "Camille S"

2 Movado watches

1 gold/platinum Rolex with clear stones

Cash in amount of $21,520

They also recovered numerous pieces of gold and diamond jewelry, charm bracelets, and many other baubles belonging to Camille, some of which had been sewn into the curtains. (Camille had always counseled her friends to keep some money stashed away for themselves.)

There was one surprise item that turned up in the search: the last will and testament of Robert Stenrud, Camille's third husband, who had supposedly died intestate. Because no will had been found at the time of Stenrud's death, Camille became his sole beneficiary. According to the prosecution, the alleged dispute over Stenrud's inheritance happened too long ago for any investigation to be undertaken.

The police seized the couple's assets and found various bank accounts in Camille's name containing a total of $160,000. There was just one bank account registered to Ernest Varacalli with money in it. The total amount on deposit was just $78.72. They took the keys to the couple's new Jaguar.

Ernest Varacalli's case would go to federal court in late July 2002. On the first day of the prosecution, the public benches were almost empty, apart from the defendant's wife. Camille's strawberry-blonde hair had been teased and puffed into a perfect halo around her face; her enviably straight nose and perfect cheekbones were marvelously bronzed and glowing, her eyelids gleamed with gold eye shadow. She was elegantly, and expensively, dressed and looked absolutely poised. Underneath her calm demeanor, she was seething: a story had appeared in the press the previous day claiming that she was seeking to work out a deal with the authorities. What seemed to annoy her most was not the implication that she was making a guilty plea, but the unflattering mug shot used to illustrate the story. "If they wanted a picture I could have given them a better one!" she said. Ernest Varacalli was found guilty of operating a chop shop, but his state prosecution was still pending.

The following winter would be a grim one for Camille. Apart from trying to negotiate herself a deal—the authorities were demanding over $300,000 to settle the civil case—she was also trying to sell the house in Dresden Place and visiting her husband in prison when she could. At a hearing in Brooklyn on a bitter January day, Camille appeared in court along with a number of assorted mechanics, car thieves, and other riffraff, as the judge issued trial dates. She was not in good humor—clearly, she had not expected it to get this close to the wire.

It would not be until March 2003 that Camille finally reached an agreement with the government. She pled guilty to a reduced charge of attempted money laundering and got five years' probation. With restitution and legal bills to pay, she finally sold the house on Dresden Place in April, and moved to New Jersey.

★   ★   ★

Despite her narrow escape from prosecution as an accomplice to her latest husband, Camille is still dogged by the troubling legacy of her first marriage, to Joey Colucci. Articles in the New York tabloids still refer to her as "the Merry Widow": for as long as she lives, the question of how much she knew about Tommy Spero's involvement in her husband's murder will always remain.

Such questions still bother Jackie Colucci and her mother, but they will probably never get a satisfactory answer, at least as far as Camille's conscience goes. They would, however, learn how Joey died, and why. In 1991, shortly after Sammy Gravano became a co-operating witness in the case against John Gotti, he admitted to murdering Joey Colucci.

Worse was to come for the family. In his 1997 biography, *Underboss*, Gravano described the killing of Joey Colucci in obscene, graphic detail: "Everything went into slow motion. I could almost feel the bullet leaving the gun and entering his skull. . . . I felt a surge of power. I realized that I had taken a human life, that I had the power over life and death. I was a predator. I was an animal. I was Cosa Nostra."

Joey Colucci had fallen victim to two distinct but mutually compatible ambitions: Sammy Gravano needed somebody to kill in order to become a candidate for membership of Cosa Nostra; Tommy Spero wanted Joey dead so he could marry Camille.

Gravano's book goes on to dismiss Tommy Spero out of hand: "After the Colucci hit, Tommy Spero wound up marrying Camille. It didn't last long. She saw him for what he was, a total nothing, and left him for another guy."

The day the news broke, Camille called up Joey's mother in tears. "I swear I didn't know," she sobbed. "I didn't know. . . ." Because of her marriage to Tommy Spero and her continuing friendship with Sammy Gravano, who gave her and Joey's son a job on one of his construction projects, Camille must have seen how it looked through the eyes of Joey's family: to them, it would seem as though she colluded with the murderers.

"You want to believe that she didn't know," says Jackie. "She had these people in her house and dinner parties for Tommy. . . . At some point in her relationship with Tommy she had to have asked him, 'Who was involved with Joey's murder?' And he probably would've left himself out, but he would have named Sammy."

If Joey had been a made guy, in Mafia terms, he would have had every right to have Tommy killed for making moves on his wife. Since he was only on the fringes of the mob, he had no muscle on his side and became an easy target for his more ambitious friends. Camille was no longer living with Joey when he died, even though, according to his sister, he had tried to make amends for his infidelity. She had, apparently, already chosen her path: her men would always be the ones with power.

6

LIFE for the daughter of a Mafia boss is not easy. She may have the character and disposition of her mobster father, but she is formally barred from taking an active role in his organization. In the more traditional Italian crime families, she is discouraged from aspiring to be anything other than a homemaker, and is thus unlikely to emerge from protective obscurity. Those who have wanted their own careers in the legitimate world have tended to distance themselves from their fathers by changing their names and moving away. For Victoria Gotti, daughter of the late Gambino crime family boss, convicted murderer, and racketeer John Gotti, going undercover was not an option. Her father was a celebrity mobster whose trials were reported on the front pages of the New York papers. If she wanted a career, Victoria had no choice but to live in the public eye. What makes her an extraordinary case is that she has had the wit to exploit the public's fascination with the Mafia and make a career for herself as the daughter of a mobster.

Growing up a Gotti, as Victoria has said, was no walk in the park. "All this conspiracy, all this innuendo, the Mob, the FBI . . ." she says. "It's like having the last name Kennedy."

Influenced, perhaps, by the persistent attention of both the media and law enforcement, the forty-two-year-old Victoria has ended up believing the hype and elevated her father's criminal career to the level of statesmanship. In a stunning perversion of the American dream, she has successfully launched herself in his footsteps; readers of *People* magazine might be forgiven for thinking Victoria Gotti is indeed the daughter of a former president.

In many ways, John Gotti defined the celebrity mobster. His media soubriquet, the Dapper Don, had nothing to do with rackets and everything to do with appearances. During his ascent to power in the mid-1980s, Gotti gave the mob a new image. His daughter calls him a "Pied Piper." He talked about "my people," meaning his loyal public in Queens, who could always be relied upon for a heart-warming anecdote about the boss buying gifts for babies or paying for fireworks. And he encouraged the media to spread the word. Unlike the glory days of glamorous characters like Lucky Luciano and Bugsy Siegel, mob bosses in recent history had become dreary industrialists—like Paul Castellano, isolated inside his castle, avoiding publicity. Gotti changed all that. Here was a heroic outlaw of the kind America holds dear. Gotti believed in his invincibility. It seemed there was nothing he couldn't do: fix juries, terrorize witnesses, kill a man and not get arrested. And the people believed his propaganda—getting one over on the law became a desirable thing.

In fact, John Gotti's criminal career was anything but stylish, and featured numerous arrests for hijacking, at least five murders of suspected collaborators, and summary executions (he was caught on an FBI surveillance tape raging: "He's gonna die because he refused to come in when I called"). His unsanctioned murder of mob boss Paul Castellano broke the rules of Cosa Nostra, which he claimed to embody. Gotti's dictatorial manner and ferocious temper, vanity and hubris led him ultimately to foolish lapses of judgment and a head-on confrontation with the law, which he could never win.

Nonetheless, Gotti knew how to manipulate popular opinion, and Victoria, growing up in Queens, internalized the public perception of her father as a local hero.

Public image is important to the mob: Carmine Galante had his cigar, Al Capone his white hat, Gotti his $2,000 Brioni suits. Gotti's daughter, too, created a striking persona. Unlike her mother, who sometimes appears rather dowdy, Victoria Gotti looks every bit the classic Mafia princess. She had a dramatic nose job and dyed her hair from black to blonde, adding several inches of hair extensions to create a Hollywood mane. She always wears huge earrings and colossal

diamonds, short skirts and teetering heels. Her plump lips are out-
lined in pink and her nails are perfectly manicured.

Many people have observed that Victoria Gotti is more intelligent than her younger brother John, a bull-necked thug who was
pushed toward life in the Mafia by his father despite the evidence
that he was not equipped for it. Victoria and her father were always
close; if she had been a boy, there is little doubt that she would have
played a part in her father's criminal empire. Victoria has said that
when she was born, her father was disappointed she was not a son.
She and her father were very much alike, she once told *People* magazine: "We have identical personalities. I fare great in the face of adversity. I will take you to task if you push me. It's probably one of
my bad traits."

"If she was a man," commented a friend, "she would be her father's clone."

In the more traditional Italian neighborhoods, girls are not
brought up to take an active role in a man's world. Victoria was
probably not privy to her father's criminal activities when she was
growing up—unlike her brothers, she was in all likelihood shielded
from what he was doing. All the same, she ended up marrying a
member of his crew.

In 1984, Victoria married a local tough, scrap-yard multimil-
lionaire Carmine Agnello. According to some commentaries, he
was her childhood sweetheart. In an interview, she said Agnello was
from the "other side of the tracks," that he "represented danger." If
Agnello was from the wrong side of the tracks, from which side, one
wonders, was her father, the former hijacker, degenerate gambler,
and murderer? On which side did she place herself?

She and Carmine were married shortly after she had appeared in
the Miss New York beauty pageant, an event sponsored by Agnello's
auto salvage yard. Her wedding was spectacular, but her heart always
belonged to Daddy. She might complain about the persistent attention that her name attracted, but she never changed it. She was always a Gotti. She and Agnello were married for seventeen years and
had three sons, Carmine, John, and Frank. They lived in a $5 mil-
lion mansion in Old Westbury, Long Island; her living room was

decorated with Corinthian columns and featured a massive carved jaguar crouching beside the fireplace.

These days, Victoria dresses in Alaia, owns a white horse and drives a Mercedes, but it has not always been so. In the beginning of Gotti's career, the family went through long periods of poverty. His gambling habits often left them penniless, and he was frequently arrested, leaving his wife alone to raise four children. More than once she was reduced to applying for welfare.

Tragedy struck the family in March 1980 when a neighbor, John Favara, accidentally hit their son Frank, aged twelve, with his car. The boy was riding a borrowed minibike around the streets near his home, and Favara, driving home from work, dragged him several yards before he even knew he had hit him.

Mrs. Gotti was distraught after the accident. Victoria remembers that her mother was beside herself with grief. In the days and weeks that followed, Favara received anonymous telephone death threats. "Murderer" was spray-painted on his car. Mrs. Gotti attacked him with a metal baseball bat.

Favara, who felt blameless, did not react as quickly as he might have if he had considered whom he was dealing with. He kept the car that he had been driving when the accident happened, which became a daily reminder to the Gottis of their loss. Eventually he realized he had to leave the area, but too late. Days before he was due to move out, Favara disappeared. John and Victoria Gotti were in Fort Lauderdale at the time, but when interviewed by detectives, Mrs. Gotti said: "I don't know what happened to him, but I'm not disappointed he's missing. He killed my boy."

Informants later revealed that Favara had been abducted and killed by a hit team of Gotti's men. Using a van and two cars, according to sources, eight men abducted Favara, stole his car and shot him dead. His body was stuffed into a barrel, which was filled with cement and thrown into the Atlantic Ocean; his car was crushed. "Gotti's wife has been completely distraught since the death of her son," sources said, "and Gotti had promised her revenge."

Every year on their son Frank's birthday, the family puts In Memoriam notices in the paper—even when Gotti was featured on the front pages for killing the head of the Gambino crime family, his moving little notice appeared in the classifieds.

Victoria has faced her own share of troubles. At fifteen, she enrolled at St. John's University in Queens. But while she was exercising with the college track team one day, she developed stabbing chest pains and was diagnosed with mitral valve prolapse—a debilitating heart condition that can cause dizziness and palpitations. She now wears a heart monitor, and has undergone open-heart surgery. She wrote a book to publicize the disease, and raises money for the American Heart Association.

Her problems would continue after her marriage to Agnello. Not long after their wedding, Victoria found she was pregnant, but nine months later, the baby girl, named Justine, was stillborn. Victoria was devastated. For weeks, she slept on the floor in the nursery she had prepared for the baby, refusing to see anyone or answer the telephone. Her father ultimately pulled her out of her paralysis of grief and encouraged her to get on with life. She told *People* magazine: "'Look,' he said, 'you're doing what your mother did after Frankie was killed.' I realized that he was right." Within a couple of months, she was pregnant again, with a son, Carmine Junior, who would be born healthy.

When she was nineteen, Victoria graduated from St. John's and decided to pursue a career in law. This was a characteristically brave move, since most of her father's friends would never have accepted a female defense counsel. The law would have been an excellent path for an ambitious woman disqualified from her father's profession by gender: everyone connected to a Mafia family becomes expert in many aspects of criminal law, it goes with the territory. Quite a few sisters or daughters of criminals and victims become so proficient they end up training as paralegals. Once she was married with children, however, Victoria decided to become a writer.

"In light of her father's celebrity, she wanted to put something substantial out there," one friend says of Victoria's decision to become a novelist. "She's not just John Gotti's daughter."

Being John Gotti's daughter inevitably helped. The news that a mobster's daughter was publishing a novel caused a sensation. It was unheard of for someone in her position to enter the limelight, but it was typical of John Gotti's revolutionary style that his daughter should aspire to public life. She later wrote that when, as a student, she announced that she wanted to set up her own fashion business, her parents had been flustered and perplexed. "What does she have to prove?" her father reportedly asked.

"I was raised with the notion that women belonged in the kitchen with a slew of kids tied to their apron strings," she comments. Considering her father's overbearing nature and caustic put-downs, it is greatly to Victoria's credit that she successfully launched a career.

For the daughter of a mob boss, novelist was a clever choice. If she couldn't write, it wouldn't be a problem: she could always hire a ghost writer. Because of her name, people were bound to buy her books to search for some insight into her life. Her publishers certainly traded on the connection: the very first line of the blurb on her book jackets boasts: "Victoria Gotti is the daughter of John Gotti."

"Most publishing houses expected a tell-all on John Gotti," she admits. "But that's not what they [were] getting."

Victoria later claimed that the only thing that might hold her back from fulfilling her literary ambitions was her fear of media exposure. On the eve of publication of her first novel, she says she told her agent: "It'll be like walking into a hail of bullets."

In spite of the anxiety conveyed by this ill-chosen phrase, Victoria Gotti has shown an excellent understanding of how to handle the media. She published her novels under her own name, and never shrinks from an opportunity to publicize her books. What's more, her novels are full of knowing references to her family background. The first novel, *The Senator's Daughter*, opens with the aftermath of a gangland-style execution. The murder victim is described as both a good guy and a ruthless thug. The female prosecutor is a demonic figure—corrupt, sexless, and ruthless in her drive to pervert the course of justice. The heroine, an attorney named Taylor Brooke, has the looks of a model, with long blonde hair and green eyes. At one point, she picks up a photo of the supposed villain's three children, and muses: "Cute kids, ordinary kids. But how ordinary could they be living under the same roof as him?"

The Senator's Daughter is, like her next book, *Superstar*, full of sadistic violence, particularly against women. In *Superstar*, the heroine's stepfather is a murderer. Both books contain an undercurrent of men's fear and hatred of beautiful, powerful women.

Ms. Gotti and the media played an elaborate game: TV channels and weekly magazines invited her to talk about her novels and then questioned her about her father. She agreed to give interviews on the pretext of publicizing her novels and used the airtime to deny that her father was ever involved in illegal activity. Her steadfast public refusal to accept the mountain of evidence amassed against her father turned her into a figure of great curiosity. Depending on whom you ask, she's either a master of deception and denial or a shining example of filial loyalty.

Victoria has insisted that as far as she was concerned, her father was a "contractor." She claims not to have read coverage of his crimes in the press. But if she wasn't paying attention to his business activities, she was certainly taking note of the way he exploited the media. On *Larry King Live* she appeared cool and collected, with her long platinum-blonde hair and sculpted nose, smiling ruefully at the outrages committed by the press and painting a family portrait as wholesome as *The Waltons*.

"What was it like growing up a Gotti?"

"Regimented, warm . . . it was instilled in us that we were a close-knit family. . . . My father was home for dinner every night."

On the subject of her father's profession, she says, "He was a contractor growing up and that was fine." She says she never accepted the government's version of events. This line is harder for Victoria to get away with than for other mobsters' children—since her father has actually been caught on tape saying incriminating things like "I am Cosa Nostra"—but she sticks admirably to the script.

"He had to be doing something illegal?" asks Larry King.

"No. He was making a living."

Her lines are well rehearsed. At school, she says, her sons are not bullied—quite the contrary: "They get praised. I'm not going to say respect." The cause of her unease growing up a Gotti, she claims, was not her father's profession but the media exposure—which smacks of irony, given that Gotti is probably the only mob-

ster ever to court the press, and Victoria the only mobster's daughter to work in the media. Sitting under the television lights, a picture of composure and charm, she has clearly mastered her fear of
the media firing squad. When asked her reaction to the news that
her father had ordered killings, she responds calmly that she has
never felt "the sense or the need" to find out about them. "I know
my father for my father. I know what he's all about and that's
enough for me."

This is a sentiment heard often from children of mobsters, who
judge their fathers by their own relationships with them and not in
the light of any acts they might have committed. Only in extreme
cases, when a mobster brings his murderous crimes into the home—
like that of Boston mobster Steve Flemmi, who abused and murdered his stepdaughter—do we find a child pushed beyond the limits
of filial duty, prepared to send his or her father to jail. And yet it is
impossible for a mob boss to keep his domestic and business lives entirely separate: his public role, which depends on being able to exer-
cise power and control, demands power and control in the private
sphere. A mobster's children may decide not to judge their father, but
they undoubtedly have an idea what he's capable of.

Victoria Gotti's public pronouncements leave one wondering: is
she merely delivering lines she has learned by heart, or is she convinced of her father's innocence? Certainly, Victoria used her exposure to fight in her father's corner when he was no longer able to
give interviews himself, and she did it to great effect. During one
appearance, Larry King read excerpts from a few of the hundreds of
fan letters Gotti regularly received from all over the world. Victoria
told the story of one Australian child who wrote a letter. This little
boy had his bicycle vandalized, and complained to his father. His father told the boy there is a good man he could turn to for advice:
an American named John Gotti. The tacit suggestion was that John
Gotti would know how to punish the vandals and get the victim's
bike back. The audience was familiar with John Gotti's style of pun-
ishment. Is this what we are being invited to admire? The terrible
avenger of bicycle thieves?

Such moments bring into sharp relief the potential contradictions
in Victoria's dual role of crime boss's daughter and media star. They

illustrate how the traditional Mafia woman's stance—of knowing nothing and asking no questions—can serve a useful purpose, even to a woman like Victoria Gotti, who claims in so many ways to be liberated from family tradition. Lana Zancocchio would love to have a media career; on one occasion, she told me she would be interested in producing a TV documentary about her life. But such an idea is impossible—Lana is the real thing, and there would be far too much risk of exposure. Her family would never permit it. Victoria Gotti, the novelist, like her father the popular hero, is a media construct, taking the limelight to deny everything; turning reality, like her hair, from black to white. Somehow, magnificently, she succeeds.

Victoria Gotti has exercised masterful control over her image and her career, but whatever her public assertions, the unruly, sordid reality of the mob was never far away. There were problems in her private life that no amount of careful PR could neutralize, and instead of being the princess, she found herself dragged back into the mire.

A S a man, John Gotti was never easy to deal with. In later years he was self-aggrandizing, vain, and mercurial. He mistrusted those around him and criticized everyone: friends, family, lawyers—especially lawyers. Although Gotti was devoted to Victoria, he was very tough on her. She uses euphemisms like "regimented" and "disciplined" to describe her father's rule at home, but his bullying and insulting behavior toward his family has been caught on tape.

Conversations in the prison visiting room were recorded as a matter of course, and one tape of a 1998 visit with Victoria and her uncle Peter was released to the media. Gotti could be heard railing at various members of his family: he called his son a "babbling idiot" for mishandling the family's business affairs and insulted Victoria's husband to her face. "He's gonna get indicted any day, this moron. He's built himself a gallows. He's bought the noose." Gotti ranted on: "He's an imbecile. And you gotta see the charges. Malicious mopery. Possession of brains with intent to use. Malicious mopery. Malicious mopery. Stolen bumper. Hubcap."

Gotti even mocked his son-in-law's depressive illness. He asked Victoria: "So what's the story with Carmine?"

"What do you mean, what's the story with him?" she asked.

"Is he feeling good? Is he not feeling good? Is his medication increased? Decreased? Is it up? Down? Does he get in the backseat of the car and think someone has stolen the steering wheel?"

As his father-in-law predicted, Agnello was arrested in January

2000 and charged with racketeering, extortion, and numerous other crimes, including threatening police officers. While he was awaiting trial, the authorities froze his assets. Victoria put up the advance for her second novel for his bail—a move that one New York paper described as a publicity masterstroke.

However, Agnello would repay his wife with rank treachery. In preparation for the case against the junkyard king, the government had recorded thousands of hours of Agnello's conversations. The tapes revealed he was having an affair with Debra DeCarlo, the bookkeeper at one of his scrap yards, and was seeing two other women on the side. Debra, described as "acid-tongued" and "gutter-mouthed," apparently had her lover's face tattooed in the small of her back, with his name written across the top. Had he been a better-looking fellow, one might have forgiven her, but Agnello looks like a boxer's punching bag with sunglasses on.

On the tapes, DeCarlo comes across as a wannabe mobster, aggressively promoting her lover's interests, berating him for not collecting debts, and advising him on business deals. She reveals a detailed knowledge of his hidden interest in a number of companies. In one conversation she criticizes Agnello for being soft on an associate who had fallen behind with payments. "I would have thrown him out a fuckin' month ago, the sick motherfucker. You put that man in business. It did not cost him a fuckin' dime, then he fights you for payoffs. They all fucking get over on you. The ones that fucked you, you keep letting them do it. You keep getting fucked. I get so pissed at you."

"Yeah, yeah, yeah," Agnello replied.

In one conversation, he refers to DeCarlo as "that fuckin' whore." In another, Agnello berates a friend for bringing his girlfriend to a social event, embarrassing his pregnant wife: "Everybody fucks around. But your wife is a good woman and you got two kids and one kid on the way. Have a little class for your fucking wife."

Having spectacularly failed to heed his own advice, Agnello found himself on the receiving end of a divorce suit. After the very public and humiliating revelation of his affair, Victoria filed for divorce in January 2001 and fought him over custody and visitation rights to their three sons. Again, she demonstrated that she was not the traditional Mafia wife: most have no choice but to accept that their husbands have mistresses on the side. In return, he is expected not to humiliate his wife in public, but in any case, the mob wife is supposed to put up with her husband's infidelities as part of the deal. Not Victoria. She made her own living, she could exist outside the marital home, and this enabled her to dump her cheating husband. She had never changed her name, and now her family background became her rallying point: nobody treats a *Gotti* that way. After the divorce, however, the strain began to tell: she experienced a recurrence of dizzy spells as her heart condition deteriorated, and she underwent emergency open-heart surgery. She recovered but remained under medical supervision.

The *New York Post* obtained copies of the tapes produced as court evidence, and the episode of Agnello's unfaithfulness was played out in painful detail in the press. Victoria and the family's lawyers complained vociferously. This wasn't the first time the family had locked horns with the media. Just after the murder of Paul Castellano, in 1985, *Daily News* reporter David Krajicek was posted outside the Gotti family house in Howard Beach, Queens. Gotti had been fingered as Castellano's murderer, but none of the papers yet had a picture of him. After a few days of sitting outside the house, the reporter and his photographer saw John Junior, then aged about seventeen, coming out of the house and getting in his car. After they had trailed him around the neighborhood for half an hour, John Junior pulled up next to the reporter's car and opened his window. "Youse keep coming round here botherin' my mother and I'm going to start chopping off heads," he said. His friends giggled in the back of the car. "Youse come back here you'd better bring a lot of friends cause you're going to fucking need 'em."

There is generally an understanding that reporters have a job to do, and mobsters, when their paths cross with the media, try to foster good relations. John Junior's outburst was not the way the son of the boss was supposed to conduct himself. Krajicek wrote a mildly mocking piece about the confrontation and got a ferocious response from the boy's outraged mother.

In a letter to the paper, which she apparently sent without her husband's knowledge, Mrs. Gotti defended her son, taking particular offense at the implication that he was not very bright. The boy had attended New York Military Academy, she said. "My son doesn't speak in *dese dem dose,*" wrote his mother. She also strongly protested the reference to her son as a "baby bully."

The letter was most unusual in that mobsters' wives at that time never emerged into the public eye; for the most part, nobody even knew their names. But Mrs. Gotti boldly crossed the line that separated mob business from the family and attacked the press for its crass behavior: "Now I know why people like Cher despise the media. You are tantamount to vultures that will print anything, no matter how inaccurate." Why she chose to single out Cher is perplexing, but she had, perhaps unwittingly, hit upon the very thing that was different about John Gotti. Wanting to be treated like a celebrity, he courted the media—and then complained about the coverage.

Gotti was not, all things considered, a successful mobster, but he was a good self-publicist. One should remember that this was before the Mafia had become a marketable commodity, before known mobsters started appearing in television dramas, playing themselves. Gotti's relentless attention seeking would ultimately destroy him and the rest of the Gambino family. That he placed himself and his family so glaringly in the limelight still baffles many observers; he behaved exactly as though he were famous for some legitimate activity, and invited scrutiny of his affairs.

Victoria followed her father in his pursuit of publicity, exploiting—but never satisfying—the public's curiosity about organized crime. In 2001 she was offered a newspaper column at the *New York Post,* a celebrity-mom slot that would very likely have suited the wife of a Kennedy.

The column was a clever move by the *Post,* but it was perhaps better as just an idea than in reality. Her weekly musings on motherhood and morality made, for some, bizarre reading: In one of her first columns, Victoria wrote, with breathtaking chutzpah, about how her father had been a taskmaster and "traditional patriarch," laying the foundation of rules and regulations, and building his children's characters. She may have been making a veiled reference to his bullying behavior, but it read like praise for traditional family values.

"Excuse me? John Gotti taught her rules and regulations?" an irate reader responded. "The man broke almost every federal felony law ever written. After all that, he had enough time to teach her character? Like how to watch some poor, hard-working schmuck build a business up only to have it taken from him by a bunch of two-bit thugs who couldn't do a day's work? Your whole life has been funded by the theft of the people of this city. Yet you proudly write about it like you earned it."

When the direction of Victoria's column changed and it became a celebrity gossip slot, her own celebrity status was never far from the surface. She, or possibly her editors, made constant play of her status as a mob boss's daughter, having her write frequently about *The Sopranos*, getting quotes from members of the cast as though she had an inside track. "I might be violating the code of *omerta* for telling this," she wrote, a propos a cast change, "but secrecy can be a casualty of this job." The Mafia princess had made numerous show-business contacts—people excited to get a phone call from the daughter of a famous criminal. Certain actors and singers will allow themselves to be courted by mobsters. Such connections lend them an air of dangerous glamour, and Victoria always treats her celebrity friends with care.

While her career was established on her connection to organized crime, she was careful never to reveal any information about the people close to her, or to traduce her father. Her primary role was to provide an upbeat counterpoint to the endless negative stories about her family. At times, Victoria's column seemed penned in an alternative universe, and on more than one occasion she clashed with the editor of the Sunday *Post* over what she was prepared to say in print. On February 17, 2002, the *Post* reported that Carmine Agnello's junkyards had been shut down by the police; in her column that day, Victoria confirmed that her divorce was final, and then whizzed off to the New York fashion shows, where she sat next to Lorraine Bracco (one of the stars of *The Sopranos*). On the day her husband was given a nine-year prison sentence, Victoria wrote about the unexpected victims of September 11—people like herself who couldn't get a hospital appointment.

In one memorable interview with *Entertainment Weekly*, she dismissed the mountain of evidence the FBI had collected against her father (which, as we know, includes wiretaps on which he discussed his crimes). "When you live under a microscope for fifteen years," she countered, "Mother Teresa would have a hard time."

Her critics say that if Victoria Gotti wants to exploit her father's celebrity, she must accept some responsibility for the reasons he is famous—or, at the very least, acknowledge them. She has done neither, batting away questions about organized crime and enraging the admittedly small sector of the public still unmoved by the world's fascination with the mob. But having taken the position of absolute ignorance about her father's crimes, she sticks to her agenda.

Victoria Gotti's column, however illusory, did portray a Mafia family at home, with the glamorous, hands-on, working mother at the forefront. In this, she could have been hired as the Gambino family's publicist. A lot of mobsters lack confidence and savoir faire outside their own neighborhoods; after *The Godfather*, they discovered the value of a strong public image. Gotti took this a step further. He realized they needed good lines, and good suits. He saw that it helps to have the public on your side, especially if they are picking up the tab for your crimes, and that, during a big trial, the popular press could be persuaded to put across a positive message. He also understood that the media had an insatiable appetite for mob stories.

Gotti was not the only boss to use such PR tactics. Like their Sicilian counterparts (and disgraced politicians everywhere), American mafiosi have been known to let their women speak out when things get tough. Vincent "Chin" Gigante, the boss of the Genovese family who stayed out of jail for thirty years by pretending to be mentally ill, relied on his daughter to talk movingly to the media about his deteriorating state of health. But it was Gigante's elderly mother who made the most dramatic impression: here was an old woman struggling to take care of her poor sick baby: "He's too thin. The doctors say they must put more pounds on him before he goes into the hospital. But how? I wasn't there to cook for my son. With-out me, he doesn't eat. Only a mother knows a son."

After it was discovered that Gigante's mental illness was all an act to avoid standing trial, the U.S. attorney's office charged him with obstructing justice and threatened to prosecute his family members for bolstering his "crazy act" all those years. In the end, Gigante pled guilty to spare his family.

Rosalie Bonanno, wife of mafioso Bill Bonanno, wrote an ac-count of her married life that contains no information about the criminal activities of her husband or father-in-law, mob boss Joe Bonanno, and mentions nothing about the career of her father, Joe Profaci. Instead, she portrays the women of the family as unsung martyrs struggling to cope with infidelity, penury, and long ab-sences. Joe Bonanno's wife once had to go into hiding to evade a subpoena, and Rosalie praises her constancy: "She lived for three months in a basement room, sort of like Anne Frank had lived in an attic . . . his mother never voiced a complaint . . . All she ever said was, 'What can I do to help?' "

On June 10, 2002, John Gotti died of cancer in prison. After his death, many commentators praised his achievements, noting in par-ticular the impact the Dapper Don had on popular culture. But it fell to his daughter, Victoria, to remember him as a national hero. At Gotti's funeral, on a gloomy day in June, a crowd of curious local well-wishers gathered to ogle the assembled mobsters at the ceme-tery in Queens. From the crowd, one could hear comments shouted out about how Gotti didn't deserve to be in jail, and about what good work he had done in the community. "How do you know the man done bad?" one man asked rhetorically. "I knew him, my fa-ther knew him . . . he was a good man."

One man, who pushed the crowd back and said, "It's not the Pope coming, it's a murderer," would quite likely have been lynched had he not been wearing an NYPD uniform.

For all their support of the dead man, the crowd was really wait-ing to see the women. They craned and whispered as Mrs. Gotti emerged from the chapel and climbed into a limo. They gasped as Victoria, stick-thin from grieving and wearing little makeup, stepped out in front of her teenage sons, escorted by a bodyguard. She wore a tight black suit, her hair hanging down almost below the hem of her skirt, and shielded her face from the crowd.

Victoria's editors at the *Post* had requested a column in her dead father's honor, and she duly composed a tribute fitting for a senator. "This man of strength and character raised me with old-country values to be a good person, a good wife and a good mother. . . ."

"A legend does not die. It merely grows with the telling of each act of courage and display of strength. . . ."

"The media coverage of my dad's death over the last week and his funeral yesterday has been what it was because my father was the man he was. To some, it was excessive, to others, scant tribute."

Reading this column after the event, one wonders why the *Post* had the bad taste to publish it. In fact, at least one person at the paper found it excessive: an editor inserted the words "convicted murderer and mob boss" into a description of the author's father. When Victoria Gotti was informed of the change, she insisted that the *Post* stop the presses and remove the offending phrase.

Less than a year after her father died, Victoria's uncle Peter, who was identified by the government as boss of the Gambino family, was convicted of racketeering, joining his brother Gene and Victoria's brother John Junior in prison. Within a month of the conviction, the editors at the *Post* judged that Victoria's usefulness was at an end, and her column was dropped. But Victoria has retained her star value in America's tabloids: within weeks her column was snapped up by the *Star*. She has also been named among the potential editors of the U.S. launch of *OK!* magazine. And she has joined the lineup of a new all-female talk show planned by Sony Entertainment, along with assorted TV personalities and divas.

Victoria's mother, too, previously reluctant to enter the public arena, has exhibited her artwork in a New York gallery. The show, entitled "In Praise of Older Women," featured naïve paintings of skinny ladies, naked apart from high-heeled shoes, accompanied by tigers and lions. She included a portrait of her husband set against the New York skyline, half smiling, emerging as though from a pothole in the ground. Mrs. Gotti showed she knows a thing or two about public relations too: part of the proceeds from the sale of her husband's portrait, priced around $5,000, went to a local hospital. Mrs. Gotti professed, through a handler, to be too shy to speak to the press, so her daughter stepped in.

"She comes from the old school," explained Victoria. "I think with that antiquated belief that a woman belongs in the home, guilt accompanies any desire to morph into a professional person."

Victoria herself has handled that "morphing" process with great skill. She judged the mood well: by launching herself onto the celebrity circuit generated by tabloid journalism and becoming one of the gang with her "bold-face" friends, she gained entry to a world that cares nothing about her background, only about her fame. As far as her own career is concerned, she has turned her father's legacy to good account and kept her dignity intact, rebutting inquiries about his past with icy aplomb.

The mystery remains as to what Victoria Gotti really thinks. Some people maintain that she clings steadfastly to the belief that her father was innocent, and anticipate that, at some point, the truth will eventually burst through, in all its ugly, painful reality. Others, aware of her talent for turning the past to profitable use, believe the mobster's daughter is planning a tell-all memoir, which will finally, explosively, reveal what life was really like growing up a Gotti. Only Victoria knows for sure, and for now, she is content to pursue her high-profile career, exploiting the public's sentimental attachment to her father's memory, without allowing the dirty reality of the mob to spoil the picture.

8

FAR from dominating in a man's world, most women in the mob have to work hard to earn themselves a footing. A man connected to the mob must be seen to exert authority over his women: if he can't control his wife, he may appear unreliable in other ways. This does not leave much room for an ambitious woman to maneuver. A Mafia wife with more than a little larceny in her heart is limited to operating through her husband: covering his tracks, concealing his assets, blocking police inquiries. And yet, some women find a way to play a part in their husbands' world, to make a place for themselves in the masculine hierarchy. Such was the case with Brenda Colletti.

From the moment she met him, Brenda knew her husband, Philip, was a bad man—it was one of the things she liked about him. Having grown up in a hick town in Massachusetts, she found the criminal world he inhabited thrilling. Philip's parents were Sicilian, and she envied in him that sense of belonging, of being chosen by birth. Philip understood the rules of the mob, he knew how to talk to connected people. Although he tried to teach her how to read people, and how to behave around made guys, she never felt she had his level of street smarts.

"There was always that side of him that was always really mysterious," she says, "because he's a hard case. You can look in his eyes and see there's that danger there. He always did things for people, he would always help somebody shovel snow, or change a tire, but there was always that little glint of danger in his eye. I guess some women like bad boys, you know."

When I met her, Brenda Colletti had lost everything because of her connection to the Mafia: her husband was in prison, her son was living with her in-laws, she had no home, and no money. After testifying against the Mafia to try to win her husband a reduced jail sentence, she had no friends. Still, she could not bring herself to condemn the mob for laying waste to her life. As far as she was concerned, the mob was still the most exciting thing that had ever happened to her.

She first met Philip in a Dunkin' Donuts in Philadelphia in 1989. She was twenty-three, pretty, with long auburn hair, and worked as a go-go dancer. He was a plumber. After work, he would go and lift weights at the gym to build up his skinny frame, and they would drop by the Dunkin' Donuts for coffee and cigarettes at about the same time each evening. They smoked the same brand. She had married very young, to a guy in the navy whose idea of a workout was to beat her up, so she was in no hurry to settle down again. It was nearly a year before Brenda and Philip moved in together.

They got married in 1990 and lived in suburban south Jersey, a short drive from Philadelphia. For a while, Brenda carried on dancing; she was earning good money and it paid the mortgage. She had seen something of the criminal underworld while working in the sex industry: she danced in porn shops and brothels owned by a family with mob connections. As she writhed around a pole in a bikini, she began to understand the power of men in that world, and realized she wanted part of it. Since she was good with numbers, her boss let her count the takings. "In that kind of world, for a woman to be allowed to do anything was a big deal," she says. "I think that's when I first started getting my thrills being around people that I knew were connected. That's when I thought 'I want to climb higher and higher—I want to be in the mob.'"

Such ambitions were outrageous for a stripper, but as it turned out, her husband provided her with an opportunity to join the ranks of the criminal underworld. Philip had grown up around the South

Philadelphia mobsters and was well known to them. He had a criminal record for killing a man in a fight, but having claimed it was done in self-defense, he had served only eight months. He stayed out of mob circles for a while, but by the time he and Brenda were married, they were hanging out at mob-owned places, and soon Brenda was familiar with the cast of characters.

For the most part, she was not impressed by Philip's mob friends. They had seen too many *Godfather* movies and acted the part so self-consciously she wanted to laugh. Some of them were not very smart; one was a drug addict who fought constantly with his wife, also an addict. But the boss was different. She coveted the honor of being introduced to John Stanfa, known to prosecutors as the boss of the Philadelphia mob, to his underlings, respectfully, as the Old Man.

"He didn't say anything to me because I was a wife. A woman," Brenda told me. "Women are low class . . . they're like . . . they're the next thing to your pet dog. When we were all out together it was like 'Hey, how ya doin'?" and then all the men went out to talk. And the women got to stay behind—and they were bimbos! They were only interested in talking about the beauty parlor, talking about their nails. . . . Most of them were older than me anyway and I just didn't fit in. . . . Afterward I used to ask my husband, 'What did you talk about?' I told him I'd love to get involved. He'd say, 'You can't, you're a girl.' I said, 'I'd love to, it'd be a thrill.' I really wanted it. I've just never been a regular girl. Never interested in getting my hair all fancy, never interested in clothes. I always hung out with guys."

Direct involvement with Mafia business might have remained a fantasy for Brenda Colletti, if the Philadelphia underworld had not gone to war. In 1993, Stanfa's leadership was challenged by a faction led by "Skinny Joey" Merlino, and the boss needed hit men to go after his enemies. That's when Stanfa's crew came calling for Philip Colletti.

The Collettis' suburban family home became a regular meeting place for mobsters. The couple's three-year-old son, Paulie, would be playing under the kitchen table while Philip's associates discussed tactics. Brenda would cook for the men as they plotted how to kill Merlino and his sidekick, Michael Ciancaglini, known as Mikey Chan. Guns were brought to the house to be hidden, out of reach of the little boy. A pipe bomb was constructed using four pounds of explosive, and Philip's partner, Sal Brunetti, would fiddle with the wiring at the kitchen table. The bomb proved to be a temperamental instrument. Rigged with a remote detonator, every time the men tried to deploy it under Merlino's car, it failed to go off. Three or four times the men got the device into position and waited for their enemy to climb into the driver's seat. They would press the detonator button—and nothing happened. Stanfa himself gave Colletti a talking-to. The men were frantic about getting this thing to work. At one point Brenda suggested she should go out and set the thing off herself, since the men seemed incapable.

Philip bought Brenda a gun and taught her how to use it; they set up a few crude targets in the basement and used it as a firing range. "I dread to think how many bullets the people who bought the house from us must have had to dig out of the wall," she says. "We were just bad people."

As Philip and his associates continued to bungle their assigned hits, the murder plotting around the Collettis' kitchen table became more outlandish. Sal Brunetti suggested that Brenda get dressed up in her slinkiest outfit and go to a nightclub with Merlino and his friends. While he was distracted, she would slip a vial of cyanide into his cocktail. A syringe of cyanide was duly procured and hidden on the couple's porch. The plan sounded like something out of a third-rate gangster film, but it fired Brenda's ambition. "If I had got him, as far as the family would have seen it, I'd be like . . . hey—I'd be an untouchable woman," she told me. "Then I'd have said, 'Now you've gotta hire me, I'd be one of those contract killers.'"

Philip's reaction to the plan was more traditional: he was furious that his friends should try to involve his wife, and that was the end of it.

Brenda's ambitions weren't so easily dampened, and as the mob war intensified, Philip increasingly relied on his wife to get him out of trouble. With a previous record, he could not afford to get caught in possession of a weapon, so when police searched his car and found a handgun, he could have been looking at serious charges. Brenda was asked to take the rap and pretend it was hers. It was a step that earned her the grateful acknowledgment of the boss himself.

"John Stanfa's son had been shot in the face, so we went to find him at the hospital. He called me aside and we went to a corner in the hallway and I told him what I was considering doing, and he just thought it was the greatest, and he patted me on the cheek and told me I was a smart girl.

"I left the hospital, and I was just on cloud nine. That's the first time I ever got to have a meeting with the Old Man. And that was it for me. 'Cause I've never known a woman who was able to have a private meeting with the boss."

Brenda and Philip focused all their time and energy on his murder assignment. If he succeeded, he would be in line to be made a member of the mob—an ambition husband and wife both hungered after. "Philip really wanted to get made. And I wanted it for him. There's just that power trip, you get a lot of respect . . . it's really hard to explain but it's no different from someone from the DEA going under cover. They go out on a job and they know that someone could shoot them at any second. It really is that thrill—just from a different side . . . it's a rush."

The Collettis' rush came on the afternoon of August 5, 1993. Philip and one of his associates, a wild man called John John Veasey, had gone out "hunting," cruising the streets of South Philadelphia armed with handguns, looking for their prey. Hunting was an imprecise method of assassination, but this time they got lucky. At about five o'clock, Brenda received a breathless phone call from Philip, telling her to "clean the house" and get to his mother's place in Philadelphia right away. From the excitement in his voice, it was clear that he and John John had encountered their target.

Brenda took all the weapons out of the house and hid them out in the back garden, then drove into town, where she met up with the two men. "Turn on the radio!" said John John. Brenda turned on a news station and heard that there had been a gangland shoot-out in which Michael Ciancaglini had been shot dead and Joey Merlino wounded. Philip motioned to her to follow their car, and she waited as they set fire to it on a deserted stretch of road. In his excitement, Philip threw the match into the gas-soaked car just as John John was reaching in to pick up some loose change. Brenda watched helplessly as John John flapped his burning hand in the air, setting fire to his clothes, before Philip ran over and patted out the flames. The men got in Brenda's car and they sped away from the scene. Veasey was in agony—his hand was badly burned—but was forbidden to go to a hospital in case he should be linked to the torched car, which had been leased in Philip Colletti's name. The three all talked at once as they figured out their alibis. Philip would go home and pretend to have been working on the house. Brenda was to phone the police and report the car stolen.

Veasey bore the pain of his burnt hand as long as he could, then went into the back garden, poured lighter fuel over his hand and set it on fire again, screaming for the neighbors to help. At the hospital, he told doctors he had been lighting the barbeque.

When the police came to question Brenda about her stolen car, they took her straight to Homicide. She realized they had made the link between the burning car and the murder of Mikey Chan, but she knew that if she stuck to her story, they could not prove it.

Brenda's face lights up at the memory of her interrogation. "I thought, Whoa! This is too deep for me! But in all honesty it was a thrill. I stuck with the story and had a good time, I enjoyed breaking their stones. They had a good cop and a mean cop, just like on TV—all the psychology head trip. I loved every second."

When she emerged after four hours of questioning, Philip nervously asked if she had let anything slip that would implicate him in the murder. "Nah, I handled it," she said.

This would become Brenda's big moment. Protecting her husband and his associate made her feel like an honorary member of the mob—and people treated her as such. She was no longer stuck with the wives at mob dinners, but greeted by all the guys with new respect. "When we went out to dinner, I was introduced to people. There was like . . . these big union reps, they're powerful people. And I'm getting introduced to them, and all the other wives are just stuck at the table talking about their fingernails. I'm meeting all these connected people. It was really cool."

Brenda's excitement at being accepted in the macho world of the mob meant she felt nothing but admiration for her husband's actions. She understood that when mob factions went to war, the other guy would kill you if you didn't get him first. Since the targets were mobsters who had gone into organized crime awake to its dangers, they were fair game. By this reasoning, she and her husband, too, were fair game—and this was part of the thrill.

"It was fun. In all honesty, I don't believe there's anything wrong with the mob," she explained to me. "The only thing that makes it bad is that people get killed. When they do shakedowns, they're only collecting money off people that are doing illegal things. They're doing illegal things and they can't go to the cops for protection so they come to us."

Referring to the mob as "us" is just one of the ways Brenda revealed that she believed herself a member of the mob: by covering for her husband, she had become part of the system, one of the guys.

Brenda wasn't alone in enjoying a boost in status after the hit on Ciancaglini and Merlino. Whenever Philip took their little boy, Paulie, to a bar, or when he went to place a bet, old mob guys would stuff twenty-dollar bills into his little hand. Paulie got one-hundred-dollar bills on his birthday. Brenda and Philip never paid for a meal. For a while, they floated on this wave of recognition, and both were convinced that it was just a matter of time before Philip would get made.

As the fighting intensified, the Collettis started taking evasive action: traveling in separate cars, and sleeping with guns under the mattress where they could reach them in a hurry. After the murder, FBI agents were constantly on their tail, following them and monitoring their movements. Brenda was instructed to keep a sharp eye out for any car that passed by the house twice. Even this dangerous time was thrilling. She loved teasing the FBI agents, giving them the finger as they executed U-turns and sped off down the road. The only thing that worried her was that Philip had still not been made.

She knew that with this much heat on them, if Philip were out of favor with the mob, he would be finished.

In September 1993, Philip was arrested on a gun charge, and after he spent a leisurely nine days cooling his heels in jail, the mob raised his $5,000 bail. The FBI was eyeing Philip as a suspect in the Ciancaglini murder; they also threatened to indict Brenda for a number of crimes, including illegal possession. Even Philip's father was a suspect, for helping him conceal weapons. With her husband facing a possible life sentence, and the likelihood that she would encounter heavy charges, Brenda's loyalty to the mob boss melted away. The respect he commanded, the tradition he represented—none of it meant anything if she and her husband had to be sacrificed.

Over the fall and winter of 1993, Brenda and Philip discussed cooperating with the FBI. "This is something we talked about for weeks and weeks, just fighting in our own minds about what to do. Philip would say, 'They ripped me off, well, how about if I became a rat?' But it was more to test my reaction. He wanted to know that I would still love him because a lot of wives leave their husbands when they become rats. I wanted him to do it, but it wasn't like I could suggest it." On February 3, 1994, Philip and Brenda turned themselves in and offered to cooperate.

"It's hard to explain because these people had been good to us," she said. "But it's like when you're a kid, you don't think about who's right and who's wrong, you just think about whoever treats you the best, they're the ones. These people treated us great, we used to hang out, we had barbeques, their kids played with our kid, compared to what? A bunch of Feds. We hated Feds! We still feel bad for them all, they didn't deserve to go to jail, but we did it because I didn't want Philip to go to jail for life and he didn't want me to go to jail for life. In the end, it's a choice."

John Stanfa, his underboss Frank Martinez, and six capos were arrested in March 1994 and charged with murder and racketeering. Brenda and Philip Colletti, and John John Veasey were all slated to testify against them, along with Sicilian-born hit man Rosario Bellocchi, who had once been engaged to marry Stanfa's daughter Sara.

Testifying in court was a terrifying prospect. In the second week of the trial, on October 5, 1995, the morning John Veasey was due to take the stand, his brother was murdered. This felt like a chilling message to Brenda and the other witnesses, but she did not back down. Although she was sick with nerves, once she took the stand and confronted the lineup of mob bosses, she felt powerful again. All those little mob wives were seated quietly on the benches at the back, and the judge, the lawyers, and everybody else was listening to her. She described how many times her husband and his associates had failed to hit their target with the useless pipe bomb; how she was going to murder Joey Merlino herself with a syringe full of cyanide; how she had covered for all of them with the police. Even when the court heard a recording of Philip threatening to kill a man with whom Brenda had a brief affair, she seemed to relish the attention. Afterward, she was praised as a more articulate and reliable witness than her husband. Brenda Colletti's testimony helped convict John Stanfa and all seven of his codefendants. Stanfa got a life sentence. Philip pled guilty to murder and his cooperation was taken into consideration. He was given twelve years.

Giving evidence against her husband's associates meant Brenda, her son, and her parents-in-law would all go into witness protection together. This was a difficult step for Brenda. Typically, the marshal service relocates people to places where they are unlikely to encounter others from their criminal past, in remote, rural areas. Brenda, who had fled the horror of small-town life, found herself stranded in a small town in the middle of Arkansas. She rebelled. "I'd be walking down the street and people would say to me, 'Hi, how are you doin' today?' I'd go, 'Who the fuck wants to know?'" She battled with the marshals whose job was to protect her, and eventually returned to Philadelphia, without her son.

Having fought the mob system and testified against the boss, Brenda took on law enforcement. She battled to be allowed to visit Philip; she fought them over money, over accommodation, over everything. She gave an interview to the local TV station, which was against the marshals' rules. When she was arrested for shoplifting a bottle of sleeping pills, the marshals, who had had enough of her smart mouth, changed the locks on her apartment and kicked her out of the witness protection program.

Brenda eventually moved to the South. Her son remains with his grandparents, who have also left witness protection. And yet, after all this time, she is unrepentant about her involvement with the mob, which gave her life so much excitement.

"If it wasn't for the mob," she concludes, "South Philly would suck."

9

FOR Antoinette Giancana, growing up with a mafia boss as a father was a lot like being in a political family. Her father, the violent mob boss Sam "Momo" Giancana, also known as Mooney, was a top figure in the Chicago crime syndicate from the mid–1950s until his assassination in 1975. His activities were continually reported in the press, and while Antoinette and her sisters were growing up, they were under constant pressure to behave well and not disgrace him. It was a role for which Antoinette was ill-suited, and she frequently rebelled. Antoinette had her own ideas about how she wanted to behave. Her father had spies everywhere, which forced her to live much of her life under cover, sometimes with the secret collusion of her mother. Her father would not permit her to model, so she did it under a pseudonym. If she went out with a man of whom her father did not approve, again, she used an assumed name. "I couldn't live with the name Giancana," she observes bitterly.

Although Antoinette enjoyed the glamour that went with her father's position, the treacherous nature of Mafia celebrity was clear to her from an early age. Like Victoria Gotti, she draws a parallel between the worlds of politics and organized crime, and claims that being the boss's daughter was worse than being a Kennedy. If a member of America's first family had been an alcoholic, she argues, they would only have the press to deal with. If it became public that one of Sam Giancana's family had a breakdown, it would cast doubt on his mental capabilities and his decisions. When Antoinette was suffering from alcohol-related problems, she had to go into the hospital under a false name to prevent the media from finding out.

Sam Giancana's criminal career started while he was still a teenager, when he was indicted for murder. Before he came to trial, the main witness was killed. Giancana belonged to the 42 Gang, a group of violent young hustlers who were trying to attract the attention of Chicago mob boss Al Capone. Sam's skill as a getaway driver and his eagerness to undertake violent jobs got him noticed, and he quickly rose through the ranks. On his way up, he was constantly targeted by the police and was arrested no fewer than seventy times.

In the mid-1950s Giancana became the operational head of the Chicago crime syndicate, but he was always kept in check by his seniors, Tony Accardo and Paul Ricca. As boss he was unpopular and ruthless, but he made money for the mob. He had gambling interests in Mexico and Las Vegas, and took over the Chicago numbers operation by force from the black gangs who ran it. He was also involved in a CIA plot to assassinate Castro—a move that did much to discredit Giancana within the mob.

If Giancana's violent history, his ruthlessness, and political connections weren't enough to ensure him a high profile, he also had high-profile friends, including John F. Kennedy, Marilyn Monroe, and Frank Sinatra. Although his behavior always attracted attention, he was enraged by the constant presence of the FBI and the media. He wanted to control his public image even when he had brought tremendous heat on himself. His family would suffer in two ways: first from the media, then from Sam's fury.

Antoinette could hardly have done more to anger her father. "I was a source of frustration because I defied him," she writes in her memoir, *Mafia Princess*, published in 1985. She describes their fights when her father learned that she was seeing men of whom he disapproved: crazy, violent battles that raged around the house, both of them hurling lamps, plates and, on one occasion, brandishing knives. Her father would wait for her to come home and then yell at her as she screamed back. She seems to have been one of the few people who was not afraid to confront him—perhaps the only one. When he was under intense scrutiny from government agencies, she threatened to inform on him to the IRS—which led to their worst fight ever.

When I asked her about her stormy relationship with her father, it was clear that she still relishes playing the Mafia princess. Now sixty-five, Antoinette is good-looking, in spite of a drastic nose job she had done when she wanted to be a model. She wore a dash of silver-green eyeliner and red lipstick, and her blonde hair was pulled back into a youthful scrunchy hair band. We met in a former mob hangout in the western suburbs of Chicago, where, as she swept into the restaurant, impressively tall in a fur-lined coat, she was greeted effusively by the staff. When she traveled to England and Ireland to publicize her memoir, she was told: "You're almost like a queen here." Certainly, in this neck of the woods, she is royalty.

Her happiest memories, she told me, are of when Sam would take her to drink cocktails in the most glamorous bars and night-clubs in New York or Las Vegas. She talks affectionately about the "boys," meaning her father's assorted hoodlums and tough guys. After her mother died, she often accepted the role of first lady to Sam's Mafia boss. She writes, "I always played the role of a lady so as not to embarrass Sam. I dressed in the finest clothes . . . and I wore expensive jewelry . . . I never overdressed with the jewelry, but I wore the right amount for the occasion . . . enough for people to know that I was *somebody*. Sam liked that."

Antoinette always felt ambivalent about Sam's wealth. While enjoying her designer dresses and cocktails in gorgeous surroundings, she also resented Sam for spending money instead of giving her love and affection. "I had riches, luxuries, a nice house, fur coats, cars, private schools—but I paid for it all in one way or another. I am still paying for it."

More often than playing the part of Sam's first lady, Antoinette was his alter ego, a competitive, mean hoodlum. Strong-willed and stubborn, she is very much like her father; she constantly challenged and enraged him with her insubordination. "I am similar to him," she says. "I got his looks, I got his meanness. I did defy him constantly. He was very nasty to me, and I really had to defend myself."

Police reports from his early days describe Sam Giancana as "a snarling, sarcastic, ill-tempered, sadistic psychopath." She remembers his coldness, the way he tried to buy people instead of gaining their affection—and his control. Sam required complete submission from his family. He checked out his daughters' classmates and dictated who would be acceptable as friends; when they were older, he decided whom they could date. Antoinette repeatedly disobeyed his orders, often simply to prove to her father that she could defy him.

With their similar streaks of willfulness, father and daughter were bound to clash. "I was never afraid of creating a confrontation," she says, "but as I look back, the confrontation was primarily to let him know I'm an adult, to let him know I have a mind, because as you know, in the Italian heritage, women don't have minds, women can't think for themselves, it's just the guys. He never gave me credit for anything. Not once. He was never proud of anything I did. And that really bothered me.

"I wanted a response from Sam, but not because I needed his attention. I wanted to be recognized because I thought I was so strong. For me, being strong was very important."

Antoinette's need to project a strong image was not limited to her relationship with her father. When a TV miniseries was made from her book, she criticized the actress who played her. "She played me as a weakling. It bothered me. I'm not like that," she said.

With her fixation on strength, Antoinette sometimes comes across as more mafioso than her father. In 1963, Sam was carrying on a much-reported love affair with singer Phyllis McGuire while publicly seeing other women on the side. During this time he came dangerously close to losing the respect of his underlings and being replaced as the head of the syndicate. Antoinette admits she lost respect for him when he allowed his love of women to distract him from business and diminish his status. But there are numerous other incidents about which she effuses. In 1965, Sam was summoned before a federal grand jury investigating the Chicago syndicate and refused to answer any questions. He was cited for contempt and sent to jail for a year. She was proud that he had not given any information against his mob associates, and praised his "honorable" conduct.

Although she says her father never gave her any credit, she does record just one occasion on which he showed some admiration of her character. When Antoinette was a young woman, she attended a barbeque at mob boss Tony Accardo's house. At one point Antoinette took a dip in the pool, and Accardo bawled at her in front of all his guests for forgetting to shut the pool door. Hiding her humiliation, Antoinette got out and calmly dried herself, giving her host a "Mafia look . . . a look I suppose I had inherited from my father," and closed the pool door without a word. As she did so, she caught a look of amused approval on her father's face.

"She has said publicly," her coauthor, Thomas Renner, writes, "that if she had been born a man, she would have followed in her father's footsteps and become a leader in the mafia." The problem for Antoinette was that becoming a leader is not an option for an Italian-American girl—and if it's true for today's women, like Lana Zancocchio, it was even more the case for women in the 1950s. It seems the curse of mobsters' daughters, particularly eldest daughters, that they inherit their fathers' natures and are brought up in the ways of the mob but without any useful outlet. Being fearless, aggressive, and adventurous are all useful qualities for an up-and-coming wiseguy, but in a girl they're considered inappropriate and unmanageable.

What Antoinette was supposed to do was make a good marriage to help the family—that is, the Mafia family—by binding the Giancanas to another dynasty. Several families are tied to each other by intricate relationships—the Gambinos and Castellanos of New York were linked by several marriages, while the Bonannos and Profaci families, also of New York, were conjoined by the marriage of Bill and Rosalie, which strengthened their hold on the rackets. These relationships protected the links to the old country, and the old traditions.

Antoinette Giancana's father wanted her to marry an ambitious young lawyer who would one day be useful to him. Initially, she went along with the plan. The period of this courtship was, she says, the only time her father really paid any attention to her. But the relationship didn't work out, and Antoinette subsequently rebelled against the idea of making a good match for her father's sake. She wanted to make her own choices. Her more biddable sister Bonnie married the lawyer instead, and Antoinette upset everybody yet again by refusing to go to the wedding. She ended up marrying Carmen Manno, a bartender, among whose defects as a son-in-law was the fact that he was divorced.

In *Mafia Princess*, Antoinette (she was christened Annette but changed her name with a view to a career on the runway and the stage), laid bare some ugly aspects of life in the family of a notorious mobster. Smashing the picture-perfect image the boss demanded of his family, she unflinchingly reveals her lowest moments: submitting to bloody backstreet abortions in her early twenties made more frightful by the terror that her father would find out, undergoing electroconvulsive therapy for depression, spending her children's college money on booze. In one of the worst episodes she describes her disintegrating marriage, frequent beatings from her husband, and her father refusing to come to her defense. Not only did Sam tell her to put up with the beatings, he also forbade her to get a divorce. "Divorce among the children of Mafia members was unheard of," she wrote, "and among bosses it was sacrilege." After all the fights with her father, it was her eventual divorce in 1974 that marked a permanent rift between them. He swore he would never speak to her again. He even had a new will drawn up that would disinherit her, but apparently he hadn't the heart to sign it. They never spoke to each other again. Within a year, he was dead.

As much as Antoinette Giancana has tried to be effective in a male-dominated culture, to earn some attention in her own right, her efforts have mostly been crushed. Undaunted, she is determined to have the last word on her father, not necessarily to vindicate him, but herself.

She achieved this to some extent by publishing *Mafia Princess*, a book that offers some valuable insights into domestic life in a Mafia family. In it, she describes what she calls the "last supper syndrome": Sam was arrested so many times during his life and imprisoned for such long stretches that, when he was home, his wife and children were like the family of a soldier going off to war who may not return. Every day the family gathered around the dinner table, fussing over the head of the family and waiting on him hand and foot. Before the plates were cleared, he would be back out risking his life on the streets.

She also describes the extent to which a Mafia boss can become a fantasy figure, inventing himself in a number of roles. As a career criminal and tough guy, he has to construct a hard-man image to strike fear and respect into both friends and foes. He has the public, to whom he must appear philanthropic, well connected, and beneficent: hence the importance of being seen arm in arm with Sinatra or Dean Martin at a charity event for poor Italians. He has the family at home, who must be nurtured and attended to if they are to do him credit as an obedient and respectful brood.

"Mobsters are all great actors," she says.

Her father had another side to him that he tried to use to counter the persona of the violent hoodlum: Sam Giancana was a sophisticated art lover. In later life, he developed a keen appreciation of the finer things in life. Although he came from humble beginnings—as the son of a Sicilian immigrant who peddled ice and fruit and vegetables from a cart—Sam made a fortune from gambling and protection rackets and was able to move his family into the wealthy neighborhood of Oak Park. There he furnished the house with beautiful things. "There was this strange thing about my father that made me feel that he might be human," says Antoinette. "His sensitivity to art and love of finery, art, china, crystal, jewelry, cars, houses . . . any man that is so sensitive, and likes cultural things, can't be all that bad." What others might perceive as the mob boss's desire to show off his ill-gotten wealth, his daughter, touchingly, sees as evidence of his fine sensibilities.

Sam Giancana's refined lifestyle would come to an abrupt end in June 1975, when he was shot dead by an unknown gunman in the basement of his house. He had recently been issued a subpoena to give evidence before a grand jury, and the immediate assumption was that he had been murdered to prevent him from testifying.

After his death, Antoinette became a jealous guardian of her father's flame, not least because it represents part of her income. Over the years, she has fought to retain her status as the ultimate authority on Sam Giancana, but she has never escaped the shadow of his reputation. It's a career path that does not leave much room for personal development. Neither is it particularly lucrative. When her father was shot dead in his Oak Park mansion, he left his daughters nothing. Antoinette spent years trying to disentangle his financial affairs, and it was during this process that she uncovered his criminal history. She gained access to his FBI files, and read hundreds of pages of FBI surveillance notes on his, and her own, daily activities. But she never found out where the money went, which is still a source of bitterness. These days, when she should be sitting poolside at a nice condominium in Florida, the princess works on the shop floor at a home design store.

More than anything, being left without any financial security is what makes Antoinette resent her father. "I feel anger, because he didn't take care of his children, because I'm doing what I'm doing at my age. I love it, but it's exhausting physical work, and the hours are brutal. I could have a heart attack. Sam didn't take care of his family and I resent him for that."

Antoinette Giancana was never meant to be broke; it wasn't part of her plan. Even now, she fantasizes about a life in which she would be married to an immensely wealthy old boy and spending his money on philanthropic works.

As much as Antoinette criticizes Sam for being a bad father, she never tries to paint herself as a good daughter. Paradoxically, after suffering so much at his hands, she now often feels it necessary to defend him. It's become a mission. Since his death, she has spoken out many times on his behalf—less to proclaim her father's innocence than to stop other people claiming their own guiltlessness. When Frank Sinatra, under questioning by the Nevada Gaming Control Board, denied being linked to Sam Giancana, Antoinette was disgusted by his treachery and tried to contact the board to say Sinatra was lying. No one was interested in what she had to say. Recently, when the mayor of Rosemont, Illinois, boasted that he had pushed Sam Giancana's mob out of his town, Antoinette gave an interview to the Chicago *Tribune* in which she repudiated the claim as "preposterous."

"There's a resentment in me today that I feel very strongly about," she says. "I'm trying to right some of the wrongs people are doing to him and saying about him—but it's not for him, it's to make me feel more comfortable. It's been a rough few years. Psychologically I've been through a lot. And every time one of these books comes out I get more panicky. They're not telling the truth, and it just goes on. I'm very upset."

In *Mafia Princess,* she referred to Sam's intimate knowledge of the art of murder and terror; now she seems intent on downplaying his crimes. "I'm convinced there were some off-color things going on, some off-the-record type of things going on, but if Sam committed those murders, why wasn't he put in jail? They didn't have enough to accuse him. I rebel over that."

Critics say that Antoinette just can't let go of being Sam Giancana's daughter, that she's merely interested in hanging on to whatever scraps of celebrity are left to her. She's certainly made an open play for celebrity—at times defiantly so. Although her father hated the idea of her modeling, in 1987, twelve years after his death, she posed bare-breasted for a bathtub sequence in *Playboy* magazine. It may have been a deliberate insult to Sam: whatever else a Mafia princess is supposed to do, she is not supposed to strip for a porn mag. She joked in the interview that if Sam had been alive, the photographer would have been killed.

In recent years, she has tried to branch out by launching her own brand of marinara sauce. It's something of an in-joke for the Mafia princess to be selling pasta sauce, but she has enjoyed a certain amount of success. She keeps coming back to her father's story, however, perhaps drawn by the need for reconciliation, looking for resolution after the final rift. She is planning another book, linking the unsolved murders of her father and John F. Kennedy. It may be that she has something of interest to add to the history of those turbulent times. The press still return her calls when she wants to make a comment on the latest "revelations."

Ultimately, Antoinette is still grappling with her father's violent end, still puzzling over conspiracy theories. She acknowledges that Sam's reputation has benefited from the public's love of a good outlaw—second only, perhaps, to its enthusiasm for violent death. When these factors are combined, the victim is accorded almost mythic status. Perhaps this is the most that a Mafia boss's daughter can hope to gain from his legacy. "He was like a cult hero," she says. "He still is. He's become so great in his death."

FROM its earliest beginnings, Las Vegas promised the fulfillment of dreams. In the 1940s, a handful of entrepreneurs and mobsters looked at this tiny, dusty town in the Nevada desert, surrounded by mountains, and had visions of creating a resort playground. Las Vegas was an entirely man-made invention, an expression of those pioneers' wildest ambitions, where America's private vices, illegal almost everywhere else, were permitted. It quickly became a place where ex-convicts and gangsters could reinvent themselves and become legitimate—and rich.

In that wild frontier town's early days, the Jewish gangster Davie Berman had his own dream. Berman went into partnership with notorious New York mobster Bugsy Siegel and became one of the founders of the new Las Vegas. With his Mafia partners, he ran the luxurious Flamingo hotel and casino, and later, the even grander Riviera. Berman had escaped a desperately poor background in snowbound North Dakota. After serving eight hard years in prison for his part in a shoot-out with cops, he had finally found his place in the sun.

In this illusory world, dubbed the "neon oasis," Davie Berman's daughter Susan enjoyed a fantasy childhood—she was a princess with free run of her daddy's fancy hotel. In her eyes, her father was a hero, a matinee idol. Susan spent her early years frolicking in the Flamingo's fabulous swimming pool, ordering shrimp cocktails from room service and trying on the chorus girls' lipstick and high-heeled shoes. She worshipped her father, who cut a glamorous figure in the casino—

sharp-suited, pacing the pit, watching everything that went on at the tables, extending or severing a gambler's credit with a scarcely perceptible nod of his head.

Vegas was a place built on unreality, and Susan's upbringing was similarly unreal. She saw her early life refracted in the kaleidoscope of neon lights, a vision that never altered as she matured. Susan Berman would always be, in part, a princess in her shimmering castle.

In her memoir, *Easy Street*, Susan Berman paints an irresistibly charming and romantic picture of her father. He would come home from the casino to read his daughter a bedtime story, then return to the counting room until the early hours. He helped with her homework, teaching her to count with casino chips. He taught her to play gin rummy at the age of four, and soon she could beat the hefty bodyguards who doubled as babysitters in the Berman household. She was a smart little girl; he always encouraged her to do better and she strove to please him. If he was a taskmaster, his world was also bountiful: as a boy he had gone to work without a coat on his back through the bitter Dakota winters; as a wealthy man, Davie Berman took pride in a wardrobe full of tailored suits and topcoats. Always immaculately dressed himself, he wanted his little girl to be seen in beautiful frocks, which were made specially for her. He once commissioned a portrait of her wearing a hand-tooled pair of cowboy boots and little embroidered jeans, her hair in ribbons. The painting hung in the lobby of the Flamingo. Susan quickly became the hotel's mascot.

Davie Berman thrived in Las Vegas, proving dependable to both his mob bosses and local politicians. Historian Hal Rothman describes him as one of the most powerful people in Vegas: "He was the *de facto* manager of the town. Everybody respected him, and feared him." In his book *Neon Metropolis*, Rothman notes that Berman was exactly the sort of man the fledgling Las Vegas needed. "Established, forthright, and as true to his word as a man who spent eight years in Sing-Sing could be, Berman represented the best of illegal culture."

Las Vegas journalist Ed Becker worked for Davie Berman as the entertainment director at the Riviera. Becker didn't need to know what crimes his boss had committed to see that Berman was tough. "He was a man that you'd never step over the line with. You wouldn't want to get him angry. But he had a certain mob honor about him. I wrote a check for $25 once and cashed it with the hotel. My wife had taken money out of the account and the check bounced. The manager started bawling me out on the casino floor. Davie walked over to him and almost picked him up with one hand. He said, 'If you've got a problem you take it outside. But you've got no problem with this guy.' He was very fair."

Becker contrasts Davie Berman's demeanor with that of his partner, Bugsy Siegel, a man of uncontrollable rages, whom you avoided if you could. "Davie knew he had the strength to do anything but he didn't show it. He realized that the life he had lived was wrong, and he cultivated a pleasant manner. If you met him you knew he was tough, but if you talked to him you'd start to like him. He had learned to have a nice personality. We all liked him, but we were all wary of him."

In his newly respectable role as a founding father of a growing city, Davie Berman contributed to local charities, particularly to Jewish ones. The son of an immigrant Russian rabbi, he and his family had been abused and refused employment when they arrived in America. Susan would later observe that, at that time, Jews in the Midwest had few choices if they wanted to get ahead: "they could bob their noses and change their names and pass for gentile, they could go into men's wear, or they could go into gambling."

After the hardship of his youth, Berman had told a friend he was determined to "make it as a Jew." Sure enough, it was the Jewish gangsters Meyer Lansky and Moe Sedway who gave him his biggest breaks, and he remained powerfully attached to Judaism. Before Las Vegas had a synagogue, he delighted his daughter by celebrating Passover seder in the casino showroom. As Susan grew up, she was always passionate about her Jewish roots.

Susan's mother, Gladys, was another exotic creature. She was very attractive, and Susan loved to watch her get dressed up for an evening out. She would take Susan to the beauty parlor while she had her nails done, or show her a few dance steps. Gladys had been a dancer when she met Davie Berman and had toured the United

States with her cousin in a successful double act. After a long courtship, Davie eloped with her in November 1939, but almost as soon as they were married he enlisted to serve in the Second World War. As an ex-convict he was barred from joining the U.S. Army but, characteristically, he would not be deterred: he traveled to Canada, where he had no criminal record, to join up. Growing up in the Midwest, Berman and his brothers had suffered constant taunts for being Jewish, and Davie would always respond to anti-Semitic jibes in the playground with his fists. Now he was determined to go to war against the Nazis. He distinguished himself at the Allied invasion of Anzio in Italy, and was honorably discharged at the end of the war.

Returning in triumph to America, Davie Berman made a lot of money for the mob running a gambling ring in Minneapolis. While he was negotiating himself a part of the great future of Las Vegas, Gladys became pregnant. Although she stayed in Minnesota to have the baby, unlike many wives of the mobsters in this frontier town she joined him as soon as she could, and they began their great Vegas adventure together, as a family.

Las Vegas might have remained an adventure for all of them, except that Davie's work took up a great deal of his time. Gladys spent many nights bored, tense, and lonely, waiting for his brief, reassuring phone calls, until he returned in the early hours after counting the casino take. And what little time they spent together at home wasn't free of anxiety. However respectable his position in Las Vegas, Berman's life in the mob was never far below the surface, its symptoms plain to see: the windows of their house were all above eye level so no one could shoot them from outside; Susan's father never carried house keys in case something happened to him—one of his bodyguards always got the door. And he gave her strict lessons on what to do in case anyone tried to kidnap her.

Susan's memoir recalls a halcyon childhood, but there were also times of upheaval when she and her mother were whisked off to Los Angeles. For Susan, a veteran of room service at the age of five, these little vacations at the Beverly Wilshire Hotel were fun: like a Californian Eloise, she sat at the counter and ordered ice cream sundaes. For Gladys, not knowing what sort of trouble was brewing for her husband, or when they would be able to return home, these trips were torture.

In another book, *Lady Las Vegas*, about the history of Vegas and her relationship with her hometown, Susan Berman tries to recapture the joy of family life when she was a girl. But the gilded superlatives of her description and the picture-perfect family scenes she conjures are almost disturbing: willing the past to be idyllic, she sounds desperate. "I lived in Las Vegas, the center of the world, and my dad owned it. Our home filled with song and laughter." At breakfast time, she would find her mother and father seated at the piano, playing and singing together. Susan had a room filled with "hundreds of toys," and was given her own slot machine at the age of four. It all sounds too good to be true.

In fact, the truth about Susan's mother was much darker. The story of Gladys Berman as told by her daughter gives a rare insight into the plight of mob wives. The rule preventing wives from being told anything about the business often saved them from subpoenas, but it caused constant worry. Not knowing, but suspecting, the risks to which their husbands were exposed in their violent world must have made normal relationships almost impossible.

One of the problems Gladys had to contend with was boredom. The charm of a holiday resort, after all, is its temporary, unreal quality, which, year-round, must have worn pretty thin. Other mob wives took to drinking or gambling to pass the time, but Gladys had little interest in either. The one thing that had consumed her before she met her husband—dancing—she had given up. Gladys had been a professional tap dancer since the age of thirteen, and when Davie asked her to marry him, he asked her to stop, and she did. This willing sacrifice robbed Gladys of her joy, and an outlet for her pent-up anxiety. When she lost her love of life and fell prey to depressive illnesses, her old dancing shoes and dresses remained a source of private solace.

Gladys had her first breakdown when Susan was three. She was taken to Minneapolis for electroshock treatment, the first of many such trips. Often she stayed away from Las Vegas for weeks at a time. For much of her childhood, Susan remembers her mother as a frail, sick figure who took to her bed for days on end and lay there, weeping. When she was home, she rarely had the strength to play with Susan.

Susan later realized that the violence of her father's life had begun to destroy her mother. Gladys was not free to make friends as she chose, or to go where she pleased. Davie told her nothing, but she understood enough to know that her adored husband and child were not safe. Susan wrote: "She knew we were living on the enchanted edge of a dark reality."

Mafia members tend to marry women from organized crime families, partly to consolidate their position, but also because these women are prepared for the psychological battering they will endure: they are trained to be tough. Davie Berman, like most of his Jewish mobster friends, married a woman from a totally different background—a nice girl from a respectable East Coast gentile family. Nothing had prepared Gladys for a life fraught with unseen danger.

In 1947, the Vegas Mafia would enter a period of uncertainty with the murder of Bugsy Siegel, the East Coast mob's front man in Las Vegas. Davie Berman and his associates quickly announced they were taking over the Flamingo. Siegel's violent death created a shift of power, and some of Berman's friends, perhaps even Berman himself, received death threats. Gladys could not deal with it.

Gladys suffered a series of nervous breakdowns that would increasingly disable her, and she was eventually institutionalized with depression. Susan believed it was the danger and unpredictability of her father's world that had made her mother ill.

"My mother had no support systems, no security, no assurance that tomorrow would come for any of us," Susan wrote. While other, tougher wives were able to survive the mob lifestyle, "my tortured, sensitive mother could find no release."

The fairy-tale existence in the Nevada sunshine—days spent playing with her mother by the pool, then watching her get dolled up for a night out—became fragile as the reality of her mother's condition inevitably began to impinge. Susan's father had taught her to play "The Sunny Side of the Street" on the piano, and dressed her up as a butterfly on the Flamingo's float in the Las Vegas parade. But the noise of merrymaking could not drown out the unhappiness beneath.

Davie Berman sent his wife to live in Los Angeles, where she could be treated by a series of psychoanalysts in whom he had faith. One of the doctors who knew Gladys was married to a mobster was of the view that nervous disorders went with the territory, and made no attempt to treat her. Susan stayed, for the most part, with her father in Las Vegas, living an oddly isolated existence, dancing at the edge of her father's vision, trying to get his attention.

Berman was trusted and respected in Las Vegas and by the mob bosses who pocketed the profits skimmed from the casino take. Perhaps it is a sign of his high standing that he was almost the only one among his associates of that era to die a natural death. But the great, cruel irony of Davie Berman's life was that while he was willing to spend everything he had on the best doctors available to treat his wife, he would not, or could not, give up the very thing that threatened her well-being the most—the mob.

In *Lady Las Vegas* Susan recalls her father saying to her, "Susie, with these hands I'm going to work and work until we get that girl well." But those very hands held the awful secrets of his violent past. One of the many myths connected to Davie Berman the mobster was that he could kill a man "with one hand tied behind his back." Susan never discovered what crime gave rise to this awesome reputation, but the fact was unavoidable: those same hands were killing Gladys.

While her mother faded away in Los Angeles, Susie remained at her father's side in Las Vegas, where she enjoyed the run of the Flamingo, and later the even grander, more sumptuous Riviera. She saw a good deal of her father's associates, strong, glamorous mobsters who commanded respect—"my men," she calls them, "glossy men, vibrant men." These men, like her father, held her attention as a child, and retained their fascination for her as an adult. She recalls one, "Icepick Willie" Alderman, who got his nickname because "he allegedly killed people with an ice pick. Willie was my favorite." (Favorite what? One is tempted to ask. Favorite uncle, or favorite ice-pick murderer?)

Susan's character was shaped by this period of her life, in which she spent most of her time with her father and his middle-aged friends, internalizing their mannish assertiveness. By the age of ten she was plump, precocious, and spoiled. When a new family moved into the neighborhood, she recounts in *Lady Las Vegas,* the children were invited to her house to play, but Susan, busy with her new slot machine, paid them no attention and they never came back. "Susie is just like an old man," they complained. "She's very bossy and she chews cigar stubs."

Most of the children who grew up around Las Vegas hotels were spoiled, remembers Ed Becker. "They could ask for anything and they would get it. Kathryn Grayson's daughter Patticake walked up to me one day and bit me. What could I do? Her mother was the star of our show. Susan was a little kid when I knew her; her father was very protective of her. He was scary with everyone else, but he was really a softy when it came to her."

Little Susan took a dislike to one of her father's associates, a fearsome mobster who wouldn't pay her any attention, and whose face never changed from a scowl. One day she kicked him hard on the ankle, to see if she could get a reaction.

The mobster didn't howl, or laugh. He just said: "She takes after you, Davie."

As her mother faded into her fearful world of shadows, Susan's father also moved out of reach. He too had his demons: depressed by the failure of his wealth and success to make him happy, and afraid that he had ruined his wife's life, he was increasingly ill with stomach ulcers and polyps. He even traveled to Israel on a spiritual pilgrimage. At the same time his business world was in turmoil and fraught with danger. One of his partners, Gus Greenbaum, was a heroin addict increasingly out of control, and Berman was ordered to keep him out of trouble. If he failed, both their lives would be on the line.

Susan recalls her desperate bids to get her father's attention, or to cheer him up, but even she knew the fantasy he had created for her was cracking at the edges. By this stage he needed an operation to remove obstructive polyps in his gut, but postponed it until after her twelfth birthday party, a lavish affair at which Liberace performed "Happy Birthday," just for Susan.

The birthday party would be Davie Berman's last sparkling tour de force. A few days later, he checked into the hospital and never came out: he suffered a heart attack after surgery and died. His death sent a wave of panic through his mob associates, who feared he had been murdered and swore to take revenge. The papers published respectful tributes to David Berman, philanthropist and war hero, whose vision and industry had created Las Vegas.

At the funeral, Susan, hysterical with grief, tried to throw herself into the coffin. Her father had been the center of her world. Susan knew that with his death, her charmed existence in the neon oasis was over, and that whatever lay ahead looked bleak and threatening.

11

A FTER her father's death, Susan's mother was too ill to look after her, so her beloved uncle Chickie, Davie's younger brother, took her to live with him at his estate in Lewiston, Idaho. Chickie, charming and glamorous, was also a career criminal, but he lacked Davie's class. He was a degenerate gambler whose debts threatened to destroy him; protecting Chickie from his creditors had become one of the major stresses of his brother's life. Chickie once gambled, and lost, a million dollars Davie had raised from mob sources to take a stake in the El Cortez hotel in Vegas. He went to prison several times, notably for a major stock-fraud operation in which he sold $400,000 of nonexistent shares. Chickie was one of those people whose faults are unfailingly redeemed by his charm, and Susan adored him. In later years, when Susan visited him in prison, he asked her to wear Chanel No. 5, "so that I can smell the real world."

Susan's mother died less than a year after her father. Like so much of Susan's early life, her mother's illness and death were shrouded in mystery. She was never told what was wrong with her mother, or why she couldn't live with her, only that she was "not strong." She was told her mother had died from a heart attack. Years later, she read the death certificate, which stated the cause had been suicide from an overdose. Susan was also aware of rumors that just before her death, Gladys had been pressured by the mob to hand over her husband's money but had refused to give up Susan's inheritance, and so she was murdered. Her mother's death became one of the unresolved elements of her past that would gnaw at Susan's peace of mind as she grew older.

When Chickie ran into difficulties with the law, which was often, he would send his niece to an exclusive boarding school, the sort of place where mobsters' children mixed with Hollywood offspring. Though her father had tried to protect Susan from his mob business, he had inculcated her with a sense of "us against them"—*them* being the law. She could never see the justice of her sweet uncle Chickie being taken from her and thrown in jail. Her moral guidelines were already clear: she sided with her loved ones, "no matter what."

Before long, that "no matter what" would be thoroughly tested.

In his later years, Chickie suffered from a heart condition that threatened to kill him. As his health declined, he offered Susan glimpses of her father's criminal past: he told her proudly that he had been involved in kidnapping bootleggers ("they all did it"), and robbing banks; that one of the officers who arrested Davie said he was "the toughest Jew that ever lived."

These inklings of her father's life as a hoodlum, before he reinvented himself in Las Vegas, lay dormant in Susan's consciousness for a long time, but would later be pricked into life by other acquaintances' questions about her father the famous mobster. The process took several painful years before she was able to confront what he had been.

In the meantime, Susan had been to college. Between her father's inheritance and her uncle's choice of schools, Susan would receive a good education. What's more, her father had instilled in her a faith in her own abilities and the desire to succeed. Unlike her mother, the poor passive creature, Susan launched herself on the world with a passionate ambition to make her mark. She graduated from Berkeley in 1969 and, while doing postgraduate studies in journalism, started publishing articles. Her first big story was a rather risqué outing of San Francisco as a gay city, long before it was acceptable to mention such things. The article, titled "Why I Can't Get Laid in San Francisco," made the cover of the city magazine—and was picked up by the national press.

Susan was smart and funny, and even if her prose was imperfect, she always got access to the people she wanted to interview. Former colleagues remember that Susan, from the moment of her sensational debut, always behaved as though she were a world-class operator. Although a lot of the time this attitude worked, she also antagonized a lot of people. One of her teachers at journalism school later described her as arrogant and lazy—she had good ideas, he said, but would never put in the legwork. A fellow student commented acerbically: "She was a spoiled little girl who didn't know how to deal with life. She was marginally talented and didn't like the fact that she had to research topics." Susan dropped out before finishing her master's degree.

Her father had taught her to do whatever she needed to survive, what he used to call "getting along," and Susan became very focused on getting ahead. She would turn up in editors' offices, usually with an acolyte in tow, to introduce herself, and she would seek out people who looked as though they might be going places and make friends with them. Some unsuspecting media types found themselves drawn into Susan's inner circle without quite knowing how it happened. Julie Smith was one such person. A reporter at the *San Francisco Chronicle* in the 1960s who enjoyed a fair amount of success, Smith recalls the rookie journalist walking up and introducing herself. "Susan courted people. She saw what she wanted and went for it," says Smith. The two women became friends.

Susan was never shy about talking of her father the mobster, but she also revealed her background in more subtle ways. Like her father, who always kept a closet full of good suits, Susan dressed, if not quite fashionably, at great expense. During the height of San Francisco's hippie days, when everyone else was wearing patched, embroidered denim, Susan wore a red fox fur jacket. She didn't care if it was unhip, she just loved that jacket. As a graduate student at Berkeley, she drove a white Mercedes—a dreadfully unfashionable status symbol for the times. She also loved to wear chunky gold jewelry, and always wore a huge medallion with a Star of David on one side and Davie Berman's name inscribed on the other. "Too big," said a friend—although not to her face.

A friend recalls visiting Susan a few years later, after she had moved to New York. They were shopping at Saks when Susan saw a navy blue Ralph Lauren silk blouse she liked. Although it cost $300, Susan ordered it in every color. Another time, she took off the boots she was wearing and instructed a friend to throw them out while she put on another pair. This combination of extravagance and imperialism appalled and fascinated the people around her, who never really knew where all the money came from.

In fact, she was still receiving money from her father's original 4.5 percent stake in the Las Vegas Riviera, and was later bought out with a lump sum. She never told anyone how much she was paid, but however much it was, she certainly burned through it.

In some ways, before she was even properly aware of her father's Mafia connections, Susan had already become the classic Vegas mobster's daughter. She went to the hippest restaurants and bars, and always made an entrance. She wanted people to know who she was. If a new restaurant opened, she made a point of meeting the owner, so he would know she was somebody. She gathered brilliant people around her who were intrigued by her unconventional behavior, drawn to her wit, and absorbed by the endless theatricality of her life.

"They were fun times," says Berman's friend and fellow journalist Stephen M. Silverman. "She had more energy than anyone and she would use it for good or evil, depending on whatever she desperately needed at that very second. She was never boring. She could spread gossip faster than anyone—always to her advantage."

"What was great about Susan was she was a lot of fun," says Julie Smith, "she had a great sense of humor, a rapier wit—not always kind, but very smart. She had incredible confidence; that was her charm. She thought she was queen of the universe."

But behind Susan's brazen pursuit of professional and social success, she missed the wonderland of her childhood, her happy Vegas home, which no longer existed. She didn't dare go back because she knew no one would recognize her as the daughter of the great Davie Berman, and no one would care. She wrote: "It was all just a blank of sadness and loss, loss of family, loss of power, loss of self."

The link between family and power, so essential to Susan's Mafia roots, is something she would spend her whole life trying to restore.

In California, Susan acquired a vast range of allergies and phobias. She described them as the physical symptoms of the trauma of her parents' deaths, her uprooting and isolation, as emotional scars that would never heal. She suffered from anxiety attacks, and described herself living with a dread that "apocalyptic events" could strike at any time.

She couldn't stand to ride in an elevator or cross a bridge—she was afraid that she would throw herself off. A meal in a restaurant would begin with a long lecture to the waiter about what foodstuffs would trigger her potentially fatal allergies. She saw death threatening, or perhaps inviting her, from every corner. When she moved to New York in 1977, her fear of heights intensified. She could never go above the third floor of any building. Typically, she dramatized these phobias to her friends: she could only go in an elevator, she claimed, accompanied by a "big strong man to hold her." After a childhood as the Flamingo's darling mascot, with a father who was often too busy to be with her, Susan craved drama and attention. These phobias, although increasingly maddening to those around her, were not mere attention seeking. According to Julie Smith, who saw her through one suicidal crisis, they were real, and devastating.

In the 1970s Susan worked at *New York* magazine, where fellow reporters would occasionally ask if she was related to Davie Berman the mobster. Until then, she had not been overcurious about her father's past; she wanted to preserve her perfect family image, her "house filled with music and laughter." Gradually she began to realize that not knowing the truth about her father was becoming more threatening than what the truth might hold. Like her mother, Susan was pinioned by unseen terrors.

Many Mafia daughters grow up not knowing exactly what their fathers do for a living. Antoinette Giancana's father never told her or her sisters that he was in the mob, but they all knew. There was a constant murmur of hushed voices and a parade of suited men coming and going: her father's criminal activity buzzed like white noise through family life. Even though they were taught not to believe what they read in the papers, there it was, in black and white, day after day.

In the Mafia's secretive world, it is much harder for a child to confront her father's criminal actions once he is dead, since no one will volunteer the information. Babette Hughes's father was a low-level hoodlum who was shot dead when she was only three. She was told that he had died in the hospital, of an illness. In her memoir, *Lost and Found*, Hughes describes an existence knocked off-center by ignorance of her father's life and death. The family was unhinged by its terrible secret, which seemed to create unvoiced enmities and bitterness. She grew up in a moral and emotional vacuum, clinging to a half knowledge of who her father was. But when Hughes uncovered her father's story and learned how and why he had been murdered—he had been killed in a turf war between bootleggers—she instantly and unequivocally took his side. Having arranged events in her mind to her own satisfaction, she was able to reconcile herself with her past.

Sam Mendes's film *Road to Perdition* questions the relationship a boy can have with his father when he knows very little about what his father does for a living, except that it involves killing. The boy's conclusion is this: "When people ask me if Michael Sullivan was a good man or if there was no good in him at all, I always give the same answer. I just tell them: he was my father."

Susan Berman was thirty-two before she began to research her father's history in earnest. Slowly, and cautiously, she explored her father's past, negotiating for months with the FBI for access to their files, going back to the bleak hick town in North Dakota where his parents, Russian émigrés, had acquired a piece of pitiless, barren land. It was a frightening, lonely journey which for years Susan had instinctively avoided making, for fear of what she might find. She described the "treacherous journey" she made, afraid she would find out something that would make her love her father less, that would interfere with the "idealized, romanticized view" she had of him. She wrote: "I was afraid I would find out he had a barbarous nature."

Through FBI reports, Susan learned that her father had grown up in extreme poverty and became an enforcer for local bootleggers in his teens. If a debtor failed to pay, Davie Berman and his gang were sent to beat him up. He started gambling, and learned the tricks of the trade, running rigged games of poker and craps. Then he became a bootlegger himself, which brought in serious money (his mother, glad to be able at last to buy a new coat, didn't ask where the cash came from). He also started carrying a gun. To cover his gambling losses, he robbed banks, and at the age of nineteen went to prison for eight months for robbing a poker game at gunpoint.

If Susan was shocked by these revelations, in her mind she managed to turn them into heroic capers. She describes his "daring escapades," in which Davie always put himself in the front line to protect others, and never gave anyone up to the police. The language in the FBI reports is unequivocal: Davie Berman is "a most dangerous type of law violator . . . tough . . . vicious." But for Susan there was a parallel narrative, of Davie Berman the outlaw. One of his fellow bank robbers reportedly said: "Davie was scared of nothing. I never saw courage like that. . . . He was calm and steady."

In 1927, Berman, then twenty-five, was sent to New York to open up the territory to bootleggers from the Midwest, and was arrested after a shoot-out with police. He refused to give up his associates, even when he was offered his freedom. "Hell, the worst I can get is life," he said. The remark was reported in the newspapers and earned Davie Berman popular acclaim. Susan writes in *Easy Street*: "it was the perfect gutsy gangster phrase, and people everywhere in bars elbowed each other and repeated it."

Berman spent eight years in the notorious Sing-Sing prison, but when he eventually got out, the mob rewarded his silence. Meyer Lansky agreed to let him run the Mafia's gambling and prostitution racket in Minneapolis. This was a time when mob shootings were commonplace, as gangs defended their territory with extreme savagery. However, the picture of Davie Berman that emerges from his daughter's pen is glamorous and heroic: a man who never cracked under pressure, never killed anyone who didn't deserve to die, and whose black hair glistened.

After such an idealized account of his hoodlum years, Susan's view of Davie Berman's role in Las Vegas, as a founding father, an upstanding pillar of the community, is equally romanticized. Ed Reid, in his history of the Las Vegas casino industry, *The Green Felt Jungle*, accords Berman a minor role in the history of the city, describing him as a hoodlum and a tough—a mere muscle man for the mob. But according to historian Hal Rothman, the only reason Berman makes a poor showing in the annals of Las Vegas is because of his innate dislike of the limelight. He was smart enough to avoid appearing before the Kefauver Committee, the public inquiry into organized crime that was broadcast across America. In any case, publicity seeking in general was not Berman's style.

"In the late 1950s and '60s, things fell apart without Berman's steady hand," says Rothman, who worked with Susan on a TV documentary about Las Vegas. He concurs with her vision of her father as a local hero: "He was a career crook, but he had done his time, and was a man of some considerable rectitude."

By researching her father's background in the mob, Susan Berman had taken a tremendous risk and it paid off. She discovered her father had been an outlaw, but the best possible kind: a stand-up guy, a good racketeer. She discovered that he had committed crimes, including murder, but it did not make her love him any less. So what, she wondered, did this make her? She admitted she ended up with more questions about her own ethics in not being able to judge her father for the crimes he committed, than she had about his actions. She observed it is rare for children to judge their parents by how they conduct their business, but she was still bothered by the fact that her new knowledge about her father did not alter her feelings toward him. "Why doesn't it make a difference to me emotionally," she wrote, "and should it?"

The daughters of mobsters who try to examine their fathers' legacies from the perspective of civil society usually find it can't be done: their moral sights are set from an early age by the gulf between "us and them." Most pay dearly for their fathers' criminal pasts, and yet, like Susan, they remain passionately loyal. Antoinette Giancana, who comes closer than most to confronting the reality of her father's bloody reign in Chicago, now claims he could not have committed crimes for which he has become notorious in Mafia lore.

The daughter of an enforcer and hit man for the mob who did not want to be identified described the moment when, as a grown woman, she confronted her father about murders he had committed.

"I asked my father, 'How could you kill somebody?'

"He said: 'Would you rather I left them paralyzed?'

"And he's right. It's business. They know what they're signing up for. If they can't handle it or if they've done wrong, they have to take the consequences. Those people got what they deserved."

This woman was clearly relieved to find that she concurred with her father's logic. Susan, too, was happy to exonerate her father. In a culture that glamorizes outlaws, it wasn't hard to do. In a curious passage in *Lady Las Vegas*, Susan Berman wrote about her father being "reincarnated and cleansed"—nowhere was this more true than in his own daughter's work. In her chosen career as a writer, Susan set out to recreate her father's history, turning him into a hero of his age. She also rewrote her own life, returning to Las Vegas as her subject again and again, in an attempt to recapture what was lost and transform the darker times. But no amount of revisionism would forestall the violent end that lay ahead.

12

UBLISHED in 1981, *Easy Street,* Susan Berman's book about being the daughter of a mobster, was a hit. Seven years in the writing, the book made her name. Since she couldn't escape her past, she did the next best thing and turned it into her stock-in-trade. She sold the film rights to *Easy Street* and, flush with success, and cash, in 1983 she moved to Hollywood to become a screenwriter.

When she had money, Susan spent it effortlessly, like someone accustomed to bottomless wealth. She rented a house in Benedict Canyon and filled it with friends. Two months after moving to LA, she met a man in line for script registration at the Writers Guild who said he recognized her from her author photo. He was from Las Vegas and knew all about her; his father used to work for Davie, and adored him. For Susan, struck with fame and still obsessed with her hometown, this meeting was magical. Mister Margulies was twenty-five and good-looking, a tortured artist with intense brown eyes, who shared Susan's dream of being a writer. Susan Berman, thirty-eight, longing to recreate her Vegas family and drawn to anyone who had known her father, fell in love. The following year, in June 1984, they were married, and so began one of the darker periods of her life.

Susan laid on an extravagant wedding at the Hotel Bel-Air, a lavish Vegas-style do, glittering with ice sculptures and friends, including film producer Robert Evans and music mogul Danny Goldberg. Her old friend Bobby Durst, the real estate heir, gave her away.

Friends were ambivalent about Susan's new husband; one remembers the relationship brought out the worst in her. Just six months after they were married, Margulies, who had given up drugs when they met, started using again, and abusing Susan. Unusually for her, the breakup was not accompanied by marathon phone calls, agonizing over what she should do. She just called a friend one day and said, "It's over."

Even though she was quick to let go at the time, two years later she told friends that she and Margulies were getting back together. Always a romantic, Susan apparently believed the marriage could be saved. And then Mister died of a heroin overdose.

His death was a terrible blow: she had been convinced things would get better, and Mister's suicide sent her spiraling into a breakdown. She persuaded a friend to drive her across the country to visit the therapist she used to see in New York, and she spent the next few weeks crying every day, talking of death and refusing to take her Xanax. Susan knew she had inherited her mother's depressive streak and, like her mother, struggled with suicidal feelings at various times in her life. It was only in later years that she discovered her mother had violent and suicidal episodes: in between all that song and laughter, her father had been hiding the knives.

Susan had always depended on her friends, and people were loyal to her, even though she tested them. She would have tantrums: if she fell out with people they'd be out of the Rolodex. Some people, tired of the endless phone calls and constant demands, were secretly relieved to be out. People who have at one time or another been in the Rolodex have said some nasty things about her over the years. Her intense relationships seem to have been fraught with power struggles; friends remained bound to her by ties of generosity and debt. Susan was like a mafioso in her demand for loyalty. Her friends had replaced her family; they were her own mob, and she expected to be treated like the boss.

She was not above playing on her father's mob background to get her way, either. Stephen M. Silverman remembers: "I once heard her talking on the phone to a relative, and they were having an argument about her uncle Chickie's ring. She said, 'Don't forget who my father was. I can fight just as dirty as he could.'

"I just sat in wide-eyed amazement. Then she put the phone down and gave me her little-girl smile. She played at being sweet and demure. She was about as sweet and demure as a Mack truck."

There is no doubt that Susan exploited her father's mob background to further her own career. *Easy Street* was a triumph in many ways, both a literary success and a vindication of her father, in which she was able to question her own moral position. But she was unable to move on. In later years she became a kind of rent-a-quote on the Vegas mob of the 1950s.

A year after Mister's death, in 1987, Susan met Paul Kaufman, a financial adviser who wanted to work in Hollywood. He and his two young children, Mella and Sareb, moved in with Susan and gave her the family she craved. She was a wonderful mother to the children—even after she and Paul later split up. Sareb would tell a reporter from *New York* magazine: "She held my hand through everything difficult in life. She was the only person who was always on my side and never judged me."

Susan and Paul had grand plans: they collaborated on a Broadway musical about the Dreyfus Affair, financed by Susan. It was a typically ambitious notion and it proved ruinous, financially and in every other way. In 1992, Paul and Susan split up, Susan went bankrupt, and the bank repossessed her house. It was the beginning of years of frightening penury.

During this time, Susan was locked in an ongoing feud with her landlady, who was fed up with not getting the rent and many times threatened to evict her. Susan hated not having money, but would never consider taking a part-time job to tide herself over—it simply wasn't her style. Instead, she borrowed money and sold anything of value—even her mother's jewelry—to pay it back. Her friends, who include extremely successful publicists, producers, actors, and editors, sent her $100 now and again.

One friend would send her considerably more than $100. When she got desperate, Susan contacted property millionaire Bobby Durst, one of her closest friends, whom she had known since college—she used to call him her "brother." She had not spoken to him for some time, and tracked him down through his family's property company.

He sent her two checks for $25,000, telling her he didn't expect to be repaid.

This generosity solved Susan's immediate crisis, enabling her to repay her debts and clear the slate with her landlady, but it was the kind of generosity that most people find hard to take at face value. Apart from being extraordinarily rich, Bobby Durst was not a well-liked man. When his wife, Kathy, had disappeared in New York years before, investigators heard tales about their unhappy marriage, his abusive behavior, and their fights about money, and Bobby, although never charged, was suspected of murdering her. Some of Susan's friends always disliked Bobby. He was, in their eyes, just the kind of violent type to whom Susan was attracted.

Susan's childhood fascination with her father and his mob cronies remained strong when she grew up: she was always drawn to dangerous men. This fascination ruined her life, and probably caused her death. At some level, she was aware of her father's violence; she perceived power and violence as a kind of fatherly love. "She would talk about a man and say, Oh, he's such a lovely guy," Julie Smith remembers. "Then you'd meet the guy and your skin would crawl. You wouldn't believe she'd have such positive feelings toward people who were crass, and even cruel. Her father would probably have seemed crass to someone outside the mob."

Just before Christmas 2000, Susan was feeling unusually upbeat. She was full of plans for a new book and a TV documentary about Vegas. She also told one friend she had made a tremendous discovery, although she didn't say what it was.

She never found out. On December 24, Susan was murdered at her home. She had been shot in the head; it was described by her agent, Nyle Brenner, one of the first to arrive on the scene, as a "mob-style execution." The papers reported that a former mobster's daughter had been shot, gangland style, and speculated that the mob must have wanted to silence her. The *London Observer* reported: "An unnamed 'entertainment industry executive' told the UPI news agency: 'I heard initially that she was doing a tell-all and naming names and stuff. I think the mob got tired of hearing about her.' "

Such speculation was short-lived. In fact Susan's death was probably staged to look like a mob hit to throw investigators off the scent: it was pointed out that Susan only ever wrote about the mob in flattering terms. "There was no mob connection to Susan's murder," says Hal Rothman, "absolutely not. She knew nothing about the present-day mob. It's all changed here now anyway: I bumped into a couple of mob people she had known—they must have been eighty years old. The industry has changed: look at Vegas today, only Wall Street could build that kind of thing."

Another clue surfaced when it emerged that investigators had recently reopened the nineteen-year-old investigation into the disappearance of Kathy Durst. Police had contacted Susan Berman in November, saying they wanted to interview her. Suddenly that $50,000 gift from Bobby Durst took on a new light.

In October 2001, almost a year after Susan's death, Durst was arrested and charged with the murder and dismemberment of a neighbor with whom he had been having a feud (he was eventually acquitted in November 2003—the jury said they did not have enough evidence in the absence of the victim's head). Attention again turned to Durst's possible involvement in Susan Berman's unsolved death. Police found a 9mm handgun in Durst's car, but did not find any link between the gun and Berman's murder.

Friends say that if Durst was trying to buy Susan's silence with those checks, he was wasting his money. Even if she knew something, she would never have talked. Back in the 1970s, Susan had become Bobby Durst's unofficial publicist, defending him against accusations that he had murdered his wife. Susan privately admitted to a friend that, even if Bobby had done it, "that doesn't mean we don't love him." He should have known that, as a mobster's daughter, she would have defended her loved ones *no matter what*. She refused to see what others saw in Bobby Durst: a crazy psychopath, a sick and dangerous man. As she pursued her friendship with him, leaning on him for money, she remained loyal.

Sareb Kaufman, having learned the value of unconditional love from Susan, refused to believe that Bobby Durst killed her. He banned the media from her funeral so that Durst could attend without being harassed by reporters (in any event, Durst did not go), and said: "I want to give him the benefit of the doubt." That small phrase, "benefit of the doubt," conveys a great leap of faith: deciding someone is not guilty because you love them. This is the moral foundation on which so many relationships in Mafia families are built, and for some, including Susan Berman, it creates an uneasy peace.

Those who gathered for Susan's funeral agreed, not entirely seriously, that she had made enough enemies to implicate a dozen suspects. What made them most uncomfortable was the fact that whoever it was, Susan very likely knew her killer. With all her fears and phobias, she would never have opened the door to a complete stranger.

When she died, Susan was still hoping for success in Hollywood, still believing that her big breakthrough was just around the corner, with her next investigation into the mob's history in Vegas. In death, Susan Berman has acquired a fame that she craved in her lifetime. Her friends appreciate this irony, and point out that Susan would have adored all the drama.

13

LAS Vegas was always a man's town. Susan Berman knew it, growing up around her father and his cigar-chewing partners. Women were for entertainment only; showgirls and singers kept everybody happy, but they never had any say in how things were run. Only one woman, Virginia Hill, the drop-dead gorgeous, big-spending red-haired mistress of Benjamin "Bugsy" Siegel, could hold her own in Vegas. Throughout their highly public liaison in the 1940s, Virginia lent glamour and style to her lover, but she was also street smart and tough—a perfect foil for one of the most violent mobsters of her time.

A mob mistress is more likely to be let in on her man's business arrangements than a wife: he might use her apartment for meetings, she could keep books, or deliver messages—activities that would be considered compromising for a wife. But Virginia was unlike other molls: she didn't run errands for her lovers; she worked for the mob in her own right, and proved herself as shrewd an operator as the next man.

Virginia Hill was the first celebrity Mafia moll. She had highly publicized liaisons with several top mobsters, and lived extravagantly on the proceeds of organized crime. Her glamour, wealth, and attitude made her the tabloid fodder of her day, and the press followed her adventures with great interest. But the popular press could not invent half so many fantastical stories about Virginia Hill as she made up for herself, and she became a figure of mob mythology.

For much of her life, she seems to have moved from the arms of one lover to the next, whenever it suited her, or whenever she got bored. But she was not just surviving on handouts from admirers. Throughout her career, Virginia worked as a courier and money launderer for the mob, placing massive bets on fixed horse races and transporting cash or jewelry. Unlike almost any other woman in the Mafia's history, she kept her emotional independence, and pocketed her own income from illegal activity.

For many years, investigators had her in their sights as a "suspected racketeer," but they would never prove that she earned anything apart from gifts from grateful lovers and wealthy ex-husbands. Although she was obviously street smart, Virginia exploited the stereotype of the kind of dumb broad that usually hung around gangsters. She was, according to a commentator of the time, "more than just another set of curves. She had a good memory, a considerable flair for hold-in-the-corner diplomacy . . . close-lipped about essentials and able to chatter freely and apparently foolishly about inconsequentials." Government investigators considered her an active member of the mob, carrying information between people who could not talk on the phone or hold meetings without being subject to scrutiny. Reporter Theresa Carpenter writes: "Virginia enjoyed an independent power base within the Syndicate."

Like other women in her world, and most men, Virginia had grown up in a poor, rural backwater. Born in 1916, one of ten children of a mule trader in Alabama, she was raised in considerable hardship. Her father was a degenerate drinker, and one day, after one of his drunken tirades, Virginia's mother walked out and never came back—an act that must have impressed the young Virginia at some level, for as she grew up she would walk away from one relationship after another. In one of the stories she later told about herself, she claimed that she had seduced the son of a wealthy plantation owner when she was just fourteen. The couple eloped, and it was only by paying her a large sum, she said, that the boy's parents persuaded her to accept an annulment. This was just the first of many improbable tales Virginia told to explain her un-earned wealth.

At seventeen Virginia left home to go to Chicago, where the Century of Progress exhibition was attracting vast crowds, and where, according to various reports, she got work as a showgirl, a waitress, or a stripper. In Chicago she met Joe Epstein, who ran a massive bookmaking operation, laying off bets for mob bookies all over America. Soon she moved into Epstein's luxurious apartment overlooking Lake Michigan and began to enjoy the lifestyle she craved. He was a good deal older than she, and she became his protégée: he taught her to dress well and socialize with big spenders. He wanted her to look convincingly wealthy and to move confidently among the rich, so he could put her to work for the mob, transporting money, furs, and jewelry across state lines. Hill's working relationship with Epstein lasted for the rest of her life, and although she was repeatedly questioned about the work she did for the mob, she always maintained that the old man sent her a monthly allowance in cash, simply because he still had a soft spot for her.

Virginia spent enough time around mobsters to pick up their conversational habits, but her style was all her own. Her sex appeal was Virginia's most effective weapon; she would go back to former lovers when she needed them and none of them turned her away. Epstein once remarked: "Once that girl gets under your skin, it's like a cancer, it's incurable."

As long as she was bankrolled by the Chicago mob, Virginia wielded considerable power, which allowed her to transport information and assets between Chicago and New York. She had affairs with a series of top-echelon mobsters—Joe Adonis, Frank Costello, and Tony Accardo, to name a few—but as far as anyone knew, she never wanted to marry any of them. According to one of her biographers, she despised mob wives: "she called them 'dumb fucking dolls,' foolishly waiting to accept whatever love or money their husbands threw their way. She also saw the way the wives were abused, verbally and physically, and how mistresses were flaunted."

Flaunting herself was what Virginia did best. She was a hit on the New York nightclub scene, dancing the rumba barefoot, drinking hard liquor, and making outrageous propositions to the tough guys who caught her eye. She was not only unafraid of mobsters, she dared to pit them against each other in a continual game of sexual one-upmanship. She also had a more serious role, double-dealing between the New York and Chicago mobs, who had entered a tentative business arrangement. According to one account, she was originally sent to New York by Joe Epstein to spy on Joe Adonis, and ended up sleeping with him.

While working for different mob factions, Virginia Hill always looked out for herself. When they gave her money to invest or transport, she would always hold on to a few notes for herself. She also began to keep a record of the money she laundered for Adonis and Luciano, and kept track of bribes paid to politicians and other illegal transactions. The diary she compiled was, she claimed, her insurance policy, a highly incriminating document with which she planned to extort money from her mob associates should the necessity arise. No such diary was ever found, although it was the subject of frenzied negotiations at one stage. Certainly, Epstein carried on sending her money for years, perhaps because he knew she was an unsentimental type, capable of ruining him.

Virginia was constantly moving in search of new ways of making money or a more glamorous scene, and different people to amuse her. In 1938, Virginia moved to Hollywood. She invented a background for herself, pretending to be the daughter of an oil tycoon. She quickly got noticed, splashing money around and schmoozing with movie producers, but the event that brought her instant publicity was a fight in a restaurant in which—either accidentally or on purpose—she threw a drink at Errol Flynn. The local press loved the story. While she partied in Hollywood, Virginia continued her work for the Chicago mob: carrying money across the border into Mexico, and bribing customs officers along the Mafia's drug route.

At Christmas 1939, she made a memorable visit home to her family in Alabama, driving a Cadillac, bringing presents, handing out cash to everyone. Around this time she made a brief marriage to an Alabama boy she usually referred to as a football star. The couple got engaged during a night of spectacular drunkenness, and the marriage was annulled after about a week. In another bid to explain her limitless income, again she claimed her husband had given her thousands of dollars.

After living for a time in Mexico City, where she made useful connections among customs officials and diplomats for the Chicago Mafia, Virginia moved back to New York, taking with her her latest husband, a Latin dancer named Carlos Valdes with whom she loved to dance the rumba. When the Chicago mob invested in a nightclub called the Hurricane, she was employed as the front woman, drawing crowds of celebrities and glamorous mobsters and generating a constant flow of publicity.

Virginia Hill's life now made headlines, and she had become a celebrity in her own right, her flame-colored hair and movie star eyes well known to readers of the gossip columns. In 1941, she decided to ditch her rumba dancer and went back to Hollywood, launching herself in style by leasing Rudolph Valentino's mansion in Beverly Hills. She made a play for Sam Goldwyn and got a bit part in a Gary Cooper film playing a "free-spending playgirl"— herself, essentially.

Soon after returning to Hollywood, Virginia went to a party where she met Bugsy Siegel, the New York mobster who had been sent to open up operations on the West Coast. Legend has it that they repaired to the Chateau Marmont that very night, after which Bugsy memorably described Virginia as "the best piece of ass I ever had." This unromantic review was the prelude to a grand passion: Bugsy and Virginia had an intense love affair that continued until his death in 1947.

The two made a glamorous couple: he was handsome and charming, she was beautiful and funny. They also argued furiously, in public; both had a hell of a temper, but Siegel's rages were legendary. He once confided to a friend that he had killed twelve men, and no one who had seen him get angry could doubt it. He hated the name Bugsy, preferring to be called Ben, and anyone who used the nickname was liable to get punched in the face. One friend said: "He was like a pistol when he got mad. His rages were pure and incandescent." But he was crazy about Virginia, and some of his associates considered this passion his downfall. His friend Doc Stacher later said: "Bugsy was totally under Virginia's influence and we all knew she had a huge appetite for dollars. He was so much in love with her that he did anything she asked him."

Unable to resist danger, Virginia had an affair with Siegel's great friend, the actor George Raft. Although Siegel became suspicious, she got away with it. By this time Bugsy and Virginia were seen everywhere in Hollywood together, arm in arm at Hollywood premieres, hosting glamorous parties. In 1946, Siegel's wife, Esther, begged his partner and friend Meyer Lansky to persuade him to drop Virginia, but Lansky had to admit that nothing would tear Siegel away. Esther sued for divorce and went back to the East Coast without him.

In 1945, when Los Angeles entrepreneur Billy Wilkerson bought a piece of land in the cowboy gambling town of Las Vegas on which to build a luxurious casino resort, Siegel saw a brilliant opening for the mob. When Wilkerson needed investors, Siegel persuaded his East Coast backers to buy into the venture. The Flamingo Hotel and casino became Siegel's project, named in honor of the flame-haired, long-legged Virginia Hill. But Siegel was totally ill-equipped to oversee such a massive building project, and was too vain to let somebody else take control. His ill-judged extravagances and insistence on the best materials and workmen the mob's money could buy put the resort way over budget and deadline. He and Virginia moved into a luxurious penthouse at the top of the building before the structure was finished and, to the dismay of his associates and project managers, the pair of them swarmed over every detail of the place's construction and decoration. They had frequent, blazing arguments and often retreated to the penthouse when they were needed on-site.

During this time Bugsy, never a popular man because of his temper, became power-obsessed and delusional. The men around him, as so often happens, blamed Virginia, but even she found her lover difficult during this period and frequently left him to return to Los Angeles. She was also making regular flights to Zurich, where she would deposit bundles of cash in a bank account—she and Siegel were skimming money from the mob's investment in the Flamingo, and putting it aside for their own use. Siegel's friends later said she was stealing from him, or that she persuaded him to rob his friends, and both theories are entirely plausible: Virginia was constantly scheming to ensure her own long-term security. She stole tens of thousands of dollars of the Chicago mob's money, later admitting she had always stashed away part of whatever Joe Epstein sent her to be laundered or invested. It gave her pleasure to prove she was smarter than the mob.

The Flamingo's opening, between Christmas and the New Year in 1946, was a disaster. The weather was so bad that planes bringing celebrities did not take off from Los Angeles, and the guest rooms were not finished, so gamblers took their money to other hotels. Patrons were winning against the house night after night. After two weeks, the Flamingo closed.

Somehow, Siegel persuaded the mob to stay with the project and their multimillion-dollar investment, and they backed him for another launch. This time, the place was going to have to turn a profit, and Siegel worked around the clock to get everything ready for a grand opening in May 1947. The Flamingo opened on schedule, this time with fully appointed guest rooms and an all-star turnout. But it continued to lose money while other casinos were raking in dollars, and the mob wanted an explanation. Time was running out for Siegel.

By this point, Siegel's fights with Virginia had become increasingly violent, and the pair often bore the marks of their last bout. She had always been attracted to dangerous men: like so many women drawn to mobsters, she saw their violence as passion. But Bugsy's rages were frightening. She began drinking hard and making a spectacle of herself. She attacked a hatcheck girl she suspected of having an affair with her man, after which Siegel dragged her back to their suite and gave her a beating. Shortly after that she took a bottle of sleeping pills. Bugsy and a friend drove her to the hospital, where she had her stomach pumped. It was the first of many suicide attempts that were dismissed as bids for attention.

In June, a meeting of mobsters was held to discuss the problem with Siegel. Besides stealing money from the mob, he was considered dangerously out of control. Virginia had fled Las Vegas after another violent fight and returned to Los Angeles, where she had leased a mansion styled like a Moorish castle on Linden Drive. Just as Bugsy's life appeared to be in danger, she flew to Paris, making stops in Chicago, where she took a few thousand dollars off Joe Epstein, and in New York. While she was in Paris, Siegel and a friend went to stay at her house on Linden Drive. On June 20, 1947, Ben Siegel was shot dead as he sat on Virginia's sofa, reading the paper.

Epstein immediately contacted Virginia in Paris, told her to stay there, and sent her more money. Shortly afterward, Meyer Lanksy went to see her and persuaded her to return all the mob money she had salted away in her Zurich bank account. Virginia put on a brave front after Siegel's death; she told reporters: "I was in love with him, but there wasn't all that romance between us as some people believe. Ben had a terrific temper. He would jump down people's throats and shout at me in front of other people. It got so we couldn't live together for five minutes without arguing."

Commentators have said that Virginia Hill knew that Bugsy Siegel was going to be murdered at her home, even that she had some part in it. Even if these allegations are true, Siegel's death floored her, and she attempted suicide four times before the end of the year.

Her next move may have been an effort to get her life in order: she married an Austrian ski instructor, Hans Hauser, whom she had met while skiing in Idaho. By 1950, at the age of thirty-four, she was expecting a baby. Just as her life seemed about to stabilize, however, Virginia made her most spectacular appearance in American public life. She was subpoenaed to give evidence before the Kefauver Committee on Organized Crime—a rolling inquiry that was taking evidence from people suspected of involvement with the Mafia all over the United States, and broadcast on national television. Americans were captivated as figures like Frank Costello answered questions in his gravelly voice; after his lawyer requested that his face not be shown on TV, the camera remained fixed on his hands.

Virginia Hill made an entrance described by one reporter as "pure Hollywood pandemonium," and though she had put on weight from drinking, she looked as striking as ever in a wide-brimmed black hat and fur stole. True to her Mafia credentials, she stonewalled questioners about her involvement with the mob. "I made it a point not to know anything about anybody," she replied to the judge's questions. "I don't know the first thing about politics." Asked how she came to possess $50,000, she replied, truthfully, for once: "I know how to take care of myself."

During the inquiry, a senator asked her repeatedly why Joe Epstein continued to send her money long after she had moved on and was living openly with other men. At last she lost patience. "You really want to know why?"

The senator said that he did.

"Then I'll tell you why. Because I'm the best cocksucker in America."

Lines like these ensured her notoriety and intimidated many of the milder men who came into contact with her. One of Siegel's associates in Las Vegas later remarked: "She was worse than most men. When she let go she had nothing but foul language, just like the hoodlums around her."

Virginia caused a sensation. Her televised performance made her a national celebrity. The *New York Times* correspondent was breathless: "Smooth-browed, blue-eyed, with a classic profile framed by luxuriant, chestnut colored hair, she was easily the most photogenic witness to occupy the stand since the hearings started."

Outside the courtroom, Virginia was less composed. As journalists pressed for a comment, she slapped a female reporter, lashed out with her handbag and screamed: "I hope the atom bomb falls on every one of you!"

Although Virginia got away without divulging any information about her dealings with the mob, the government was not about to let her off the hook. She and her husband were not allowed to settle in America: he was denounced as a Nazi sympathizer, refused U.S. residency, and threatened with deportation; she was hounded by the IRS, who demanded $161,000 in unpaid taxes. In a humiliating denouement, the house Virginia had bought with Hauser in Spokane, Washington, was confiscated, and she arrived one day to find a huge lock on the door.

On a stifling hot August day in 1954, in one of the final, degrading acts of her life, Virginia's worldly goods were sold at a public auction. Her kitchenware, her coats, her jewelry, even her underwear were exhibited and fingered by a scandal-hungry public (the ever-crafty Virginia had already sold or stored the best furs and valuable jewelry). One man bought a cheap pair of earrings and a paste-covered ring for ten dollars. Virginia realized this was one of her wedding rings—she had lost it when she had taken it off while baking—and she begged the agents to get it back, but the man churlishly refused to return it.

She later told a friend that she and Bugsy had finally gotten married in Mexico in 1946, and this was the ring he had given her. If Virginia did finally marry her mobster, it's interesting that she had kept quiet about it for so many years. Perhaps she did not want to be united with him in the mob's eyes: if he became a target, she wanted to be able to walk away.

The auction of Virginia's house and contents raised a fraction of the money she owed the government, and a grand jury indicted her for tax fraud. Wanted posters went up all over the United States, describing her as a "paramour and associate of gangsters and racketeers." Before the indictment came down, however, Virginia and Hans had fled to Salzburg with their son, Peter. Hans eventually found work in Klosters, Switzerland, where Virginia grew increasingly bored and continued to drink heavily. Desperate to return to the United States, she tried to strike a bargain with the State Department. At the same time, she was trying to extort money from her former friends in the mob, threatening to tell the government what she knew.

In the end, she overplayed her hand. Even Joe Epstein no longer returned her calls. After more than ten years living in exile, her body was found by walkers beside a mountain brook on March 24, 1966. She had died of an overdose of barbiturates.

In contrast to so many women connected to the mob, Virginia Hill lived most of her life as a player in her own right. Despite her relative freedom, her power games became increasingly frenzied and in the end she became a marked woman, always having to look over her shoulder. Her love of dangerous men led to a grand passion, but no peace.

Society is not kind to ambitious women, particularly those who try to beat the system, and Virginia Hill was punished for her crimes by being banished from the country that had given her wealth and notoriety. The mobsters she had robbed and threatened with exposure would probably have liked to silence her. In this, as in everything else, she didn't need their help: she did it herself.

"I FEEL very fortunate with the life I've had," says Caroline Branco. "I feel very fortunate with the husband I've had. It's been exciting."

"Exciting" is one way to describe thirty years of marriage to a mob enforcer; years in which they have been shot at, bombed, sent to prison, framed, wooed by the FBI, testified against the mob and then gone into hiding. Her husband is described by one of his best friends as "a hard-headed guy with a hell of a temper," who used to beat people up for a living. Caroline just adores him.

John Branco was raised in Cleveland, where his father ran gambling houses; he perfected the art of making a man fear for his life in the back rooms of casinos. Hired to discourage stealing at Cal Neva, the nightclub and casino formerly owned by Frank Sinatra, Branco would take over the celebrity room, and the head of security would bring suspected thieves to him. "I'd get my leather gloves on and I'd smack 'em around, tell 'em, 'Look at you, you're robbing this place.' They'd get scared to death. And I'd tell them, 'Don't let me see you at the club again or I'm going to kill you. Do you understand what I mean when I say I'm going to kill you? I'm going to kill you.'"

When Branco describes these incidents, in the clipped patter of a Hollywood mobster, his wife listens, and laughs. He might just as well be describing his part in a movie.

I met the couple at their small, tidy home, a spotless arrangement of beige furniture and carpeting about as far as possible from one's notion of a Mafia mansion. John Branco, now nearly seventy, had been diagnosed with cancer, and was recently involved in a major motorbike accident, so he was no longer the imposing physical presence he once was. Still, he talks like Robert De Niro in his awe-inspiring gangster prime. His wife, seventeen years younger than he, with long dark hair and a trim figure, was as homey and sweet as any housewife you could find in a TV commercial. They are devoted to each other.

They talk of the old days with the Sicas, nine mobbed-up brothers operating out of Sun City, California, who employed the young John Branco in the 1950s as an armed robber and enforcer. In the early years, Branco also worked for Guido Penosi, a senior member of the Gambino crime family, and LA mob capo Mike Rizzitello.

"These were men," says Branco. "These were tough guys. These were the first guys I was with that had mob connections, and when I was with them we were strong."

"In the beginning I liked every one of them," Caroline effuses. "I thought the Sicas were just the nicest people I'd ever met. The mob guys I met were very friendly and nice and very respectful and a higher caliber of men than I had met before: very family oriented, very respectful and considerate."

"Back in them days," says Branco ruefully.

Like most women who spend time with violent men, Caroline was impressed by the way mobsters conducted themselves when they were around her. "I've always found true tough guys don't draw attention to themselves, they're very nice people. In my lifetime I've met a lot of tough guys, and they are the most gentle souls. They didn't have to prove a thing to anybody. They knew in their heart what they were. If they needed to be tough, it would come out."

John and Caroline met at the Cal Neva Lodge on Lake Tahoe, in 1971. Branco's job title was bar manager, but he was actually working as bodyguard to Bob Peccole, a prominent gambling figure who was running Cal Neva at the time. Peccole had left Las Vegas in a hurry after a dispute with another casino manager and, in fear of his life, he hired Branco for protection. Caroline, who was twenty-one and bored of her hometown, Sacramento, longed to see a bit of the world and find a bit of excitement. Soon after she arrived in Tahoe she asked Branco for a job. She had little idea how much excitement lay in store.

Branco never did give her a job, but he asked her for a date. By their separate accounts, they were both smitten. His first wife had died, and he was on his own. She had already heard about his reputation as a tough guy. Just before she arrived in Tahoe, Branco had been involved in a shoot-out in the middle of the club, when an unseen assassin took a shot at Peccole and Branco had returned fire. The gunfight was the talk of the resort.

"I heard horrible stories about him," says Caroline. "People would talk about Branco, 'Boy, you better not cross him,' and that kind of stuff. Well, I didn't know anything about casinos, I didn't know anything about the mob . . . I couldn't begin to comprehend what he was doing there. If anybody had told me he was Mafia, that would have gone right over my head, I didn't know what that meant. Anyway he asked me out to dinner. He was so polite, so respectful, so considerate, and we kept going out to dinner, and we had so much fun. I was just so impressed and overwhelmed."

Branco, the urban tough guy, fell for the young Caroline, an ingénue seventeen years his junior. "I was so impressed with her because she was not like all the casino girls I was used to. And she was so good-looking. I didn't want to take a bad shot, but I didn't want to lose her either."

She says he wanted to protect her from other mob guys who would take advantage of her adventurous spirit: "He saw me as very vulnerable, and thought I was going to get used and hurt."

"Well, everyone was hitting on you," says Branco.

Caroline decided to ignore whatever her new boyfriend was doing at Cal Neva, and just let it wash right over her head—but at the same time, she enjoyed being under the protection of a man with such a tough reputation. "I felt so secure with him. I just knew he wouldn't hurt me," says Caroline. "He made no demands on me, he kept saying 'I'm too old for you. You just stay as long as you want, and any time you want to go, you can go.' I told him I wasn't going anywhere."

By the time the season ended in Tahoe, Branco asked her if she would go with him to Vegas. She already knew she wanted to be with this man, wherever he went. "I used to joke with him, I said, 'Life is never dull with you.' And I never wanted a dull life."

They had a great life in Las Vegas. In those days it was smaller, and there were far fewer tourists; she remembers it being much classier, with more Italians running the hotels and casinos, and a more open-handed approach to customers. Unlike today's corporate entertainment, when only the high-rollers are comped, everyday gamblers would be wooed with free meals and drinks to pull them into the casinos. Caroline thought it would be fun to learn to be a dealer, so Branco set her up through a connection at the Golden Nugget Casino downtown, where she learned to deal twenty-one. But it was impossible for the mob enforcer's girl to be just one of the guys. Branco was working as head of security for the Royal Las Vegas Casino, breaking the noses of cheats and troublemakers; he was also collecting debts for a loan shark. His reputation for violence spread across town. The pit boss at the Golden Nugget was so terrified of Branco that he gave Caroline every possible perk: weekends off, long lunch breaks, whatever she wanted, and the more experienced dealers grew resentful. Other mobsters eager to curry favor with Branco would hang around the casino, watching for any perceived slight or overfriendly approach to his girl. The whole thing became too complicated, and Caroline quit.

Even if she couldn't work, she enjoyed herself in Vegas. She liked his mob friends and their lifestyle. As John Branco's girl, she was treated with the utmost respect. Caroline knew the business her man was in, and his modus operandi. She says it did not bother her. "I wasn't that stupid. I knew the money was coming from ill-gotten gains and I was enjoying every minute of it. And I wasn't saying 'Don't do that, I don't want to touch that money.' It was a wonderful life. I have no complaints."

She claims Mafia violence is blown out of proportion in the popular imagination; she sees the mob, in Vegas at least, as a kind of police force for the criminal fraternity. She reasons that the kind of people her husband was beating up justified his actions: "These people are bad people to begin with. They're cheaters, they're liars, they're thieves. They've stolen from somebody else, but before they've stolen, they knew what would happen to them if they stole.

"These are guys that you would never like. And they've committed a crime and now they're trying to rip off someone else, and someone's found out where they were, and now my husband's going in there and telling them you've got to pay. They don't have to get hurt. But they're still trying to get out of it. And that's when push comes to shove, and harm comes to them. So in my mind I can rationalize that. He would never hurt a person like yourself. I couldn't imagine him doing that, he's too good a person."

Branco unflinchingly describes himself in his former days as a bad guy. "Sure I got diamonds, I got things." He chuckles, spreading out his fingers bearing chunky gold and diamond rings. "Because I took 'em away from people. I took 'em away from bad guys. I didn't take 'em away from decent people."

When he describes incidents like the time he broke a man's finger because he pointed at him, or kicked another man so hard under the table that he broke his own toe, Caroline laughs gaily. The effect is unnerving, but these tales have been so often repeated, and he tells them so well, that they have become part of their colorful family history.

One thing that she did find shocking, Caroline says, is that ordinary people would come to her husband and ask him to commit murders for them. Several times, John Branco was approached by men who wanted him to kill their wives. That, she insists, was the real crime.

Branco never killed anybody's wife. In such situations, if he could, he would take the money and let the wife know her husband wanted her dead. Thus he became, in his wife's eyes, a champion of the defenseless. "He's always had scruples," she says. "I mean, a person's got to draw a line somewhere."

Some of the time in those early years they lived in San Diego, where Branco had business interests of his own. Caroline loved the place—it was more her style than Las Vegas, and it was there they got married.

After the wedding Caroline took him to meet her family back in Sacramento. Whatever they made of Branco's reputation, they saw how well he treated her, and they saw how happy she was. Caroline had been raised by her grandparents, and Branco became very close to her grandmother. He is a big practical joker, and he would often share a prank with the old girl. Her son had died when he was twenty-one, and Branco became like a son to her. Without a shade of irony, Caroline recalls her grandmother's wistful feelings about Branco, how he represented what her own son might have become. "He was her boy," she says.

"That was my girl," echoes Branco. "She was a sweetheart. She said she couldn't read anything bad about me. Sometimes I go and see her in the cemetery."

The couple's favorite thing to do was to jump on John's Moto Guzzi on the spur of the moment and take off somewhere new— to the mountains, or the sea. They both dreaded monotony, and in many ways the mob lifestyle was perfect: he had friends in different places, but he was not a made member of the Mafia, and had no ambitions to become one, so he was his own man. He took offers of work, but he did not have to answer to a boss. If he wanted to head off somewhere new, all it took was a phone call to one of his contacts.

"This is going to sound terrible," says Caroline, "but imagine not having to go to work . . . and if you want to go somewhere you up and go and the money's always there. I mean, I didn't ask, he didn't tell, but I'm not stupid, I knew something was going on, and the money was always there."

The couple's freewheeling lifestyle could not last. John was getting deeper into the counterfeiting rackets and making a good deal of money for the Los Angeles mob. With his forthright character and reputation for extreme violence, John Branco was becoming a well-known figure in organized crime and, inevitably, investigators would close in on him.

"We both paid a price for that wonderful life that we had," Caroline adds ruefully. "We paid with years of our life, and a lot of heartache."

15

CAROLINE and John Branco's easy life in the clubs and casinos of Las Vegas came to an abrupt halt in 1983, when Branco was arrested while arranging to buy $5 million in counterfeit banknotes. He had been convicted of counterfeiting before but had managed to get the verdict overturned. This time he was not so lucky, and he was sentenced to fifteen years, of which he served five. He was fifty-one.

While he was inside, his family fell apart.

He had a daughter by his first wife, Connie, an attractive young woman living in Chicago, and a couple of grandkids he adored. Connie had long been aware of her father's influence and impressed by his contacts. She saw the respect people showed her father. She cut out all the articles about his counterfeiting cases and kept them. She knew that if she ever needed a job, or a house, he could get it for her. In fact, he admits, she sometimes pushed him a little too far.

"See Connie used to go around telling everybody . . ." Caroline explains. "She liked that Mafia stuff, you know . . . she liked the attention."

When Branco was halfway through serving his sentence at Boron Federal Prison in California, Connie secretly married a much older man, a wealthy landlord who was not well liked in the community—nor, it seems, by his wife: she started an affair with a young cop, Ron Tellez, whose ambition was to be a hit man for the mob. Connie fanned his hopes by promising to introduce him to her father, the famous mob tough guy.

Connie visited her father in jail and told him she had been seeing an older man, who had beaten her (she did not tell her father she had married the old guy). He advised her to sit tight, that he would deal with it when he got out. About a year later, she visited again, and told her father the old man had been murdered. She explained about Tellez, the corrupt cop, and how she'd promised him an introduction to her father (without telling him her father was in jail). The cop, she said, realizing he was not going to get his introduction to the mob, was now demanding money. She was afraid he was going to harm her and her children.

Branco was terribly distressed. He had helped his daughter out of a jam once before by threatening to beat up a man who was ripping her off. Now he was in jail and powerless to help her.

"That was such a shock, to hear your daughter say something like that to you," he says, "that you say to yourself, did I make this happen to her because I'm a villain? And it bothers me a lot."

"He was watching all this crumble and he was locked up in the federal penitentiary and couldn't do a darn thing," says Caroline. "And I felt hopeless and helpless watching it happen and I didn't know what to do. I wasn't a real religious person but I used to drive by this church, and I went in, and thought if he can't tell me what to do, no one can. I spoke to the priest, and I told him everything. He said I don't know what you expect me to do. I said, well, if you can't give me guidance, no one can. What do you want me to do, walk out of here? And so he said, 'I think you should call the FBI.' "

Branco knew that his daughter could get life in prison if she was caught. He also knew that if this mobster wannabe cop continued to extort her, she could end up dead. Deciding he had no alternative, he offered the FBI a deal: he would record Tellez confessing to murder, and in return they would give his daughter a lighter sentence. For a man like Branco, turning in his own daughter must have felt something like cutting his own throat. He knew it was the only way to make sure she didn't spend the rest of her life in jail.

It took more than a year for Branco to convince the authorities, but eventually he was let out of jail for three days, and sent up to

Chicago. His wife was allowed to join him there for an unsupervised visit. "That was wonderful," she says. Accompanied by an undercover agent and wearing a wire, he met Tellez in a bar, and they chatted about the fellow's prospects of working for the mob. Branco acted skeptical, prompting him to boast about the hits he had done, and the man admitted to three murders. Branco went back to jail, and Connie and Tellez were arrested.

Connie spent five years in prison. After her release, she moved back to Chicago, and has not spoken to her father since. He hasn't seen his grandchildren since they were little, which hurts him terribly, but he believes it was a sacrifice worth making. Without that deal, his daughter could still be in jail. Sadly, she thinks she could have gotten away with it.

"I believe that girl had no idea what she was getting into," says Caroline. "After it happened, she called me up, and she started to say what happened, and I tell you this girl cried so hard she couldn't breathe. And to this day every fiber inside me says she did not believe it was going to happen. She was a very naïve girl who was playing with fire."

Branco's daughter was not the only family member to fall afoul of the law. When Branco had been in jail for about a year, Caroline was arrested for insurance fraud. The Brancos had opened a little shop, a tobacconist, in which they also sold jewelry: it was all stolen stuff, gems and trinkets he had taken off people who couldn't pay their debts. There had allegedly been an armed robbery at the store, and when Caroline claimed on the insurance, the company investigated and concluded it was a setup. While the investigation was in progress, Branco thought they must be going after Caroline because she was the wife of a convicted felon, and he figured it might help if he divorced her. This desperate move didn't work: she was charged anyway.

To this day, Caroline maintains her innocence, but says she was forced to plead no contest to avoid adding time to her husband's sentence, and because she had no money to fight the case. In a dramatic exchange in court, Branco announced that he had forced her to make the insurance claim. Caroline remembers: "He yelled out, 'I made her do everything. She didn't want to do it, I told her I'd beat her up if she didn't do it.' There's no way I was going to let him do that. So I stood up and I hollered, 'That's absolutely not true.' "

The court was electrified by this violent display of loyalty. "They had to take us out of the courtroom to calm us down."

Caroline was convicted and spent a year in the county jail, during which time she had to fight for the right to send letters to her husband, now officially her ex. It was an experience that left her feeling very bitter. "Believe me," she says, "there's nothing worse than sitting in jail and knowing you didn't do it. I can tell you from someone who sat there. Everything that happens to you, you know you don't deserve. I came out with a chip on my shoulder I had to get rid of.

"When we were asking for permission for me to write to my husband, the judge implied that I was going to run off with another man at the first opportunity. Things like that you've got to swallow and it just really, really irritates you—I mean, did the man call me a whore just then or did he not? I was so bitter. I told my husband I'll do the time and I'll come out with my head up, and I'll come out with the same personality and all the dignity I have—they're not going to break me."

When Caroline was released from jail, Branco's old friend Bob Peccole bought her a motor home. Whenever Branco was relocated to a new prison, she would just up and move with him, and get herself a lowly clerical or retail job in the local town—that way she could carry on visiting him at every opportunity. If she was not first in line at the visitors' gate, the guards would joke with her that she was late. "The way I see it," she says, "I didn't skeve the money when it was coming in. It was our thing, we do this together. We spent the money together, we'll do the time together."

The five years and four months that Branco spent in prison was without question the worst time of Caroline's life. And though it is her nature to put on a good front, he could see how much she was suffering.

"It hurt in my heart when we were apart," she says in her soft, lilting voice. "I can't tell you how much it hurt. I've never been hurt so bad in my life."

"Every time she'd come to visit," her husband adds, "I'd see it in her face what she was going through. And I wanted to ram my head through a wall."

When he finally came out of prison, in 1989, Branco was sure of one thing: he was not going back to jail. He decided to steer clear of his mob friends and go legitimate. For a while he worked repairing railroad cars, but before too long the Brancos found themselves drawn back to Vegas. He tried to get work through his old contacts collecting for casinos, but his probation officer would not allow it. So he and Caroline sat down with the local paper and scanned the classified ads. Finally, they found it: someone was selling a gardening business for $3,000. It sounded just right: no boss, no line manager, no grief with the law or any contact with mobsters. Around this time, they got married again.

John and Caroline bought the gardening business, and a modest trailer home, and started cutting grass for a handful of clients. The work was grueling under the Nevada sun, but they stuck at it, and expanded the business. After a couple of years they were doing landscaping, planting trees, and installing irrigation systems. For the hard man whose fingers were customarily encrusted in gold and diamond rings, working on other people's yards must have been a comedown. But Branco says he didn't mind it.

"We had a ball," he says, his deeply lined face creased in a smile. "We are both outdoors people. And all those people we worked for, they didn't know who I was. They'd come up and get a little cocky with me and I'd smile at them, and she'd look at me and she'd smile. We were thinking, boy, if only they knew. . . ."

Certain aspects of the new job did make Branco a little queasy. "I told her right from the start," admits the tough guy, "I'd have nothing to do with flowers."

While Branco was on parole, he deliberately kept away from any of his former mob associates in Las Vegas. If he saw them, he would say hello and pass quickly by. He and Caroline kept to themselves, making up for the time they had been forced apart.

Then, in 1994, disaster struck. Caroline started getting terrible abdominal pains that immobilized and frightened her. She did not know what was wrong, but the attacks were frequent and dramatic. When she finally saw a doctor, she was told she would have to have her gall bladder removed. The hospital wanted $5,000 up front before they would even admit her. The whole procedure was going to cost at least $10,000. They had no health insurance.

The Brancos had been making a living from their gardening business, but only just. They had no savings. Frightened by his wife's suffering, Branco felt he had no choice: reluctantly, he went back to one of his former mob associates, a loan shark called Herbie Blitzstein, and offered his services. It was a painful decision. Branco was an excellent man to have on your side, and Blitzstein jumped at the chance to employ him as a collector. He advanced him the money he needed for his wife's treatment, and set him to work.

"He gave us the money, she got into the hospital, and everything was fine," Branco recalls. "Then I was stuck. I was trying to pay the guy back, I was going around punching guys out for the money. That was about ten years back, I was a lot stronger then than I am now, and it went on from there, it kind of just grew."

Branco was in his early sixties, but his reputation had not diminished. As soon as people heard he was back in business, they came to him: someone was holding out on a payment and needed shaking up, someone else had reneged on a debt and needed a slap. Branco admits he did not make a habit of coming home and telling his wife how he had broken a man's jaw to make him pay what he owed: "I'd say, 'Well, I shook him up a little.'" He had good reason for not keeping her informed about his unpleasant business with the criminal riffraff of Las Vegas.

"I carried a lot of guilt," says Caroline. "He was there because of me. He didn't say it, and he would never let me say it, but I felt guilty knowing he was doing this all because of me. In my heart, I knew he wouldn't be in that mess if it wasn't for me."

What made matters worse was the lowlifes he was dealing with in Vegas. These were not mobsters of the stature he had dealt with in the past. The real "tough guys" that Branco respected were long gone, and in their place were punks and lowlifes, gambling addicts and cokeheads with no values and absolutely no class. He and Caroline would work at the landscaping business in the mornings, and when it got too hot, he spent his afternoons at a social club run by a short, obese fellow named Tony and his tall, skinny wife, Rose.

Unbeknownst to Branco and everyone else who used the club, but not to the investigators who had the place under surveillance, Fat Tony was a degenerate gambler who had run out of credit and was trying to dig himself out of trouble by informing for the FBI. Herb Blitzstein, for whom Branco was working as a collector, was a fat diabetic with serious health problems, and a weakness for strippers. His legs hurt so much when he lay down that he couldn't sleep, so every night he would go to a Vegas strip joint, slipping sweaty twenty-dollar bills to the girls until the club closed around dawn. Pete Caruso, another of Branco's associates, was a one-man crime wave who had to find somebody to rob every day, and was constantly picking fights with his friends. These men would sit around for hours talking about old times and planning scores, although most of the crimes they discussed never came to anything.

Around this time, Branco was also contacted by his former associates in the Los Angeles Mafia, who were still in the counterfeiting business. And he was shaking down the owners of the escort services in Vegas, a prostitution business known as outcall, taking a cut of their profits. Reluctant as he had been to get involved with mob business again, Branco found he was doing all right. The escort services were all paying, and although he had to share the money with his associates, he was taking the biggest cut. "We were making enough so nobody had to work. Things were going real good. I really got a big kick out of it. Then it started getting a little hairy."

Branco knew better than most that trouble was never far away in Las Vegas. One day he heard a knock at the door. He went over and stood back against the wall, and before he had time to ask who was there, two shots blasted through the door. One hit the TV and the other hit the wall. Branco dived on the rug, screaming as though he had been hit, and his would-be assassins drove off.

Since he had testified against the corrupt cop, Ron Tellez, Branco believed that Tellez, now in jail, had hired a man to get his revenge. The gunman soon learned that he had missed his mark. A couple of days later, he returned.

"We were laying in the bedroom," Caroline recalls, "and through the window comes a boom. There were holes through the walls, holes in the ceiling. We had to block the windows up as fast as we could and get in our car. We drove up to Baker, about a hundred miles out of Vegas. From there we went to Palm Springs. We managed to keep the business going: we told our customers we were taking a little vacation. But we lost everything. We never went back to the house. We lost it all."

Life with John Branco, as Caroline had observed in her first flush of love, was never dull.

Branco had been around enough criminals to know that his associates from Fat Tony's social club were trouble. They were constantly plotting against one another, scheming to rip each other off and set each other up, and Branco eventually lost patience with them. There was good money to be earned but they were too busy sabotaging each other. If there was legitimate money to be made, they weren't interested. "I told Caroline, I said, 'I gotta get out of this shit. These guys are all punks.'"

Unfortunately, he couldn't get out fast enough. One of the problems with mobster wannabes is that they feel the need to prove how tough they are all the time. If there is an opportunity for a fight, they are much more likely to get stuck in than defuse the situation. The other problem was that they felt threatened by Branco, who had more experience and a lot more street wisdom, and naturally dominated the ragtag crew.

When the trouble started, it was fanned by Fat Tony, who was always looking for something to report to his FBI handlers. Vinnie Bartello, who ran one of the escort agencies, decided he wasn't going to pay Branco anymore. One day Branco got a call from Fat Tony, saying Bartello was out with a bunch of men carrying baseball bats, looking to beat him up. Branco's reaction was typical: he drove straight over to meet Bartello, planning to fight it out, man to man. In Branco's experience, there were not many things that could not be straightened out with a good fight. Unfortunately, he found Bartello in a crowded steak house. Even more unfortunate, Branco was followed in by his crew, including the hot-headed Pete Caruso. As Branco tried to take Bartello out the back to settle the matter "the old-time way," Caruso pulled a gun. A scuffle broke out as Bartello went for his gun. Diners in the restaurant screamed and shrank back. As police sirens approached, Branco finished it by punching Bartello in the head, and his men fled the scene.

Three weeks later, Branco was arrested. He was charged with kidnapping and assault with a deadly weapon. Far more significant than the charges themselves was the fact that none of his friends had been charged with him, and no one turned up to bail him out. Hours passed, and he sat in jail. This was against all the rules of the mob.

"The bail was seventy thousand dollars," Caroline remembers, "and they needed seven thousand dollars in cash and the rest in collateral. I didn't have collateral. I mean there was no way that I could get it. We had just a small mobile home."

Branco continues: "I called up Herbie and said, 'Herbie, I'm in bad shape, you know I haven't got that kind of money to get out now.' I says, 'Can you come down and put up my bail for me?' Herbie hemmed and hawed me, and that got me hot. I says, 'Herbie, I don't want to stay in here, I'm innocent, you were there.' It was, 'Yeah, I'll get back to you.' I knew I was stuck."

"He said, 'I've got to get you my attorney, he's out of town now,' " Caroline goes on. "And I was telling Herbie, 'No, we want him out now, he does not want to sit in there.' I don't like to sound disrespectful—I don't like the way that sounds when a woman talks like that, but I was so frustrated trying to get my husband out, and angry and brokenhearted, that I said to Herbie, 'If it wasn't for my husband, you guys would be sitting in jail.' That's not something that you do . . . and I said that on the phone—I had gotten to that point. 'Well now, we shouldn't be talking like that,' he said."

It was left to Caroline to try to find a way to raise Branco's bail. She turned to Joan Nelson, a Las Vegas woman who had received a lump-sum insurance payout after her husband's death. She was an old friend of Herb Blitzstein's, indeed it was well known that she had been in love with him for years. She gave him money to put out on the street, and he cheated her shamelessly: he was charging 13 percent interest on the loans, of which he gave Joan only half. It was she who finally loaned Caroline $7,000 in cash to set against Branco's bail—to be repaid with interest.

"Joan was real decent about it," says Caroline.

When Branco got out, he was furious. Recalling the betrayal, ten years later, he clenches his fists and squares his shoulders. "I said, I can see the handwriting on the wall—it's all going to be Johnny Branco, and I'm going to wind up in the can for the rest of my life."

"Even before the arrest," Caroline prompts, "you wanted to get away from this. You were swimming around and you could see yourself going toward that drain and you knew you were going to get sucked under. You were thinking, 'How did this happen? All I wanted was to get the money for my wife's operation and this thing grew . . .'"

"Things were looking too bad then," Branco remembers grimly. "I couldn't earn. I couldn't work. I had a sixth-grade education. I come out of the can with nothing, my wife gets sick, all these things are going on . . . I can't take orders, I really had no other choice. I could see that this is what I had to be. I had to be a muscle for somebody."

Branco now had an alarming situation on his hands. He was facing serious charges, in the knowledge that his friends were not going to support him. One more time, he looked around for a way out of the mess he was in. Again, reluctantly, he found a solution. If his associates were selling him out, he would get them first.

It was late summer in 1996 when Caroline called the FBI and told them John Branco was prepared to give them information.

16

BECOMING an informer was a major step for a lifelong mob guy like John Branco: forty years of his life were put behind him. Unlike the last time he went legitimate, this time around there would be no turning back. Caroline, of course, supported him in his decision. She saw it as a way out of the current mess, an opportunity to start again, perhaps even a chance to return to their brief, happy period as free, law-abiding citizens. Besides, she was aware of the brutal alternatives: he was either going to end up in jail or, judging by the treachery of his current crew, get shot.

Branco found it harder to make the transition. He had never become a made member of the Mafia, but he knew its rules and respected them. For the first few months of his cooperation, Branco and his FBI handlers were wary of each other. "They didn't trust me, and they were right, I didn't expect them to say, Jeez, you're Johnny Branco, you're OK. No, I'm a bad guy. And I used to tell 'em, I said, 'Just let me prove myself, and we'll take it from there.'"

"Once he said he was going to do it," says Caroline, "he's a man of his word, and there was no backtracking later, or 'yeah buts' or anything, that's the way he is."

After a couple of months he had proved himself sufficiently to be teamed up with an undercover FBI agent. To his surprise, this agent turned out to be one of the people who used to drop in at Fat Tony's social club. Charlie Maurer had some twenty-four years' experience, and had spent most of his career doing undercover work investigating organized crime in Cleveland and Pittsburgh. He had been hanging out at Fat Tony's, posing as a businessman from out of town, making cases against the mobsters who hung out there, including Branco.

"Branco had a reputation of being a very, very violent person," Maurer says, "it's hard to believe when you look at him today. But he was strong, and he has no fear. He was a pretty big guy. He came up as a tough guy, his whole life he made money extorting people and collecting debts, so he had quite a reputation going."

Branco liked Maurer's bearing, the fact that he didn't curse every other word, that he seemed to know what he was doing in business, unlike the other mobster wannabes in Vegas.

"They told us the agent John would be working with was going to be Charlie, and we both laughed," says Caroline. "They said 'What?' We said, 'Because we always kind of had a feeling about Charlie. We always liked him.'"

"Didn't have a feeling he was a cop, though," says Branco.

The fact that they both liked Maurer made it a great deal easier for Branco to commit himself to being an informer. Maurer was a gentleman, which they both appreciated, and he was honest: they felt they knew where they stood with him. Besides, they joke around a lot, and Charlie Maurer likes a good laugh.

Maurer and Branco worked together, setting up scores and doing deals, expanding their operations to Los Angeles. They set up high-pressure meetings with mob bosses where at least one of them would be wearing a wire. A tiny slip by either of them would have given the game away. Trust became essential.

"We really made a strong team," says Branco. "Charlie conducted himself excellent. He was big, he looked good. Always talked nice, showed them he was a little below me. He would never say, 'Let's go,' he'd always say, 'Whatever you want to do, John.'"

"Charlie was open to learning," says Caroline. "He really wanted to learn and do it right."

Branco did have a few moments of regret about turning informant. After he and Maurer had their first major meeting with the LA mob, he was struck by the reality of what he was doing. "I was thinking, Jesus Christ, how could I do that? These people had done things for me. I felt bad. . . . There was a couple of times I wanted to walk away, but I knew if I did, they'd give me so much time, for Christ's sake, I'd be an old man when I got out."

Perhaps he didn't confide his misgivings to Caroline. At any rate, she had backed him in his decision and that was not going to change. As ever, she gives his story a positive spin. "He liked the challenge," says Caroline. "Some of these guys were little weasels. For them to get busted, that was all right. Taking that crew in LA off the streets wasn't sorrowful at all. But for people that had been right before, that bothered my husband. True, the mob wasn't what it was supposed to be, but he always handled his problems face off."

Maurer met up with Branco every day, and got to know his wife as well. Over the months, he became genuinely fond of the couple. Caroline says, "We found out later Charlie had said to people at the office, 'If anyone deserves a break, those two people do.'"

Maurer and Branco made a formidable team not only for the FBI, but also in the eyes of the mafiosi they were dealing with. The two men were setting up big counterfeit deals, and doing good business in Vegas. The LA mob wanted a piece of it, and proposed Branco as a made member. To have a made guy as an informer would have been invaluable for the FBI; it would mean they could have done business with mobsters all over the United States. Branco was working enthusiastically on the investigation: for his own safety, the more people he put away, the better his chances of survival. He had refused to become a member as a younger man because he did not want to be answerable to a boss. Caroline was never ambitious for her husband becoming a made member; she did not covet the status it would give her as a mob wife. "Financially it would have opened all kinds of doors," she says, "but that's not where we're coming from. It would have put restrictions on us." Now, ironically, Branco relished the possibilities for taking down the mob that getting his "button" would give him.

After Branco and Maurer had been working together for a few months, the FBI asked Branco to work with them full-time. This would mean selling the landscaping business he and Caroline had worked so hard to build, but if he was going to testify against the mob, they were going to have to sell it sometime. Then everything changed.

In January 1997, Herb Blitzstein was murdered. Branco knew that Blitzstein had become a target of the Los Angeles mob, who wanted to take over his loan-sharking business and run him out of town, but he didn't know they planned to kill him. Maurer and Branco had to abandon their carefully laid plans and concentrate on catching the murderers. Because Branco had not been told about the murder plan, he too could be in danger.

Branco and his wife were given three days to sell their trailer home and their business—trucks, equipment, tools, everything had to be sold to the first caller. They were moved into an apartment in a secret location, but kept the same phone number in order to allay suspicion. While Branco worked at getting the murderers on record, Caroline packed their bags, and waited.

The night Branco succeeded in getting one of Blitzstein's killers to confess on tape, the operation was wrapped up. Forty arrest warrants were issued, and in the middle of the night, as the police were preparing to kick in doors all over Vegas, Maurer and Branco drove over to the apartment where Caroline was waiting and loaded their few belongings into the car. They drove out of Vegas toward Sun City, where the FBI had rented them a small house.

Over the following months, Branco would be involved in preparations for trial. All but two of those arrested pled guilty, and in May 1999, Branco gave evidence over five days in the trial of Robert Panaro and Steve Cino. They were eventually convicted of extortion. After that, he was on his own.

Since the night they left Las Vegas, the Brancos have moved house several times. Because they opted not to go into the witness protection program, they had to bear the trouble and expense of moving themselves. "Witness protection is not what it's cracked up to be," says Caroline. "There are so many restrictions. Forget your family, for one. No contact with your family. They're just going to pick you up and move you, and your family, for all they know, you could just have died. They don't know what happened to you. Forget your pets. If you've got social security, forget that." Those who don't want to go into the program sometimes go their separate ways for protection. Not the Brancos. "Sammy Gravano disappeared from his wife for a time," says Caroline, "and for us that's not even an option."

"We're real close," says her husband. "We're real close. She's my buddy. We do everything together."

Caroline says that throughout their marriage they never wanted to be in one place too long—they would always get restless, they needed change. But what started as freedom to move around and see new places must have begun to feel more like running from danger.

After all the time and effort Branco had put into working with the FBI, and selling his business, he was expecting a small remuneration. "He told them, 'In the end, when all this is over, I need enough so that I can just buy a motor home and disappear for a year,'" Caroline says.

"I wasn't looking for anything special," says John, "I was looking to keep out of sight."

As it turned out, they didn't get enough for their motor home—Branco believed the FBI was dragging its feet over paying him, and once had a blazing row with one of his handlers. There have been times when he has felt exposed. "I've got to be available all the time, I've got to watch my back all the time, every time a car pulls up I've got to worry are they going to throw a grenade at me. . . . We still do the same thing now, and I'll be doing it all my life, because these guys are going to be getting out of jail soon. I put thirty-nine people in jail. These guys are all going to be getting out. Oh, but don't carry a gun, Mr. Branco. . . ."

Charlie Maurer has been a good friend throughout; he contacted one of his colleagues in the town where they now live and made sure they would get support if they needed it. "Enforcer for the mob" doesn't look great on the résumé, and the agent provided a much-needed reference for a job.

Caroline tells me about her decision to apply for a clerical job. "I put in a résumé," she says. "I have experience on computers and secretarial work that would more than qualify me for the job, but you know what? There's a lot of gaps. . . . If this agent hadn't helped us I don't think we would have got it."

These days they struggle to put money away and plan for the future. In the heady days in Vegas, when they spent all their time with rich people and never paid for anything, money never seemed an issue: it was always there, and more could always be gotten.

Vegas was not a place where people planned for the future; besides, men who live by violence don't, typically, have pension plans. "We lived every day for that day," says Caroline, "we didn't put anything away, we thought we were going to live forever. . . . We didn't think about the future."

Their future, for the moment, lies in this little beige house behind security wire. It's a long way from the bright lights of Las Vegas. The place seems too small to contain a personality as imposing as John Branco, but the couple are palpably grateful to be together, after all that has happened to them. The motorcycle accident was just the latest in a lifetime of potentially lethal turns. And yet, to hear Caroline talk, she could be married to a first-grade teacher.

"He shares with me. Most husbands don't share. I wish my sister had the kind of husband I have. It's so nice to have somebody that cares about you so much. He's my cup of tea."

17

DEBRA Scibetta was only seventeen when she met Sammy Gravano, then a twenty-five-year-old hustler and armed robber trying to establish his status in the neighborhood by running a nightclub. When he saw her, he says, she appeared to him like a Madonna figure. "I'm used to seeing a certain kind of woman and she's not that kind of woman," he told his biographer, Peter Maas, author of *Underboss*. "She seems so fresh, so innocent." Instead of going out for a Saturday-night date, she invited him for Sunday lunch: "I saw her in the kitchen. She had an apron on, she looked like a little house-mother, cooking away, cooking and tasting the sauce and the sausage and the macaroni. She was so different from the sluts that I'm dealing with every other minute at the club. Then and there I realized that she was for me."

It is typical of mobsters to choose a woman of discipline and reserve for a wife, and an outspoken, outrageous tart for a girlfriend. Sammy Gravano's choice of wife fitted this model exactly. Even so, Debra the innocent teenager did not go into marriage with Gravano blindly: her father, having checked into his background, discovered Debra's beau was a hoodlum, but the news failed to put Debra off. Perhaps her determination to marry Sammy goes some way to explaining how she stuck with him after all the terrible things he did. She loved him, and followed wherever he led. He depended on her to keep the family together when things were falling apart. And when he needed her, she became his accomplice in crime.

The wedding was held on April 16, 1971, in Bensonhurst, Brooklyn, a few weeks before Debra's eighteenth birthday. As Gravano recounts in *Underboss,* they invited three hundred guests from the neighborhood, mostly Sammy's aspiring mobster friends and some older wiseguys. The boss of the Colombo family, with whom Gravano was allied at that time, sent an envelope stuffed with cash.

Her wedding would give Debra a better idea of the life she was embarking on than anything she had previously seen: Cosa Nostra exerts its hold over its members symbolically by presiding at all the major family events. Weddings are excellent meeting places for mobsters—even when they are photographed by the FBI on the way in, the men always find an opportunity to get together and talk business. Weddings are an opportunity to show off, with each family laying on the most lavish reception it can muster. Family occasions are also useful for cementing loyalties, with the presentation of envelopes full of cash. Christenings are also politically significant: with the creation of godparents, mafiosi are bound to each other through the church. Such family events instill in the children a sense of loyalty to their people; when they get a check from the boss for their first communion, it gives them an unmistakable signal about where they belong.

In the early years of their marriage, Sammy's income seesawed horribly. Money would flow in a sudden rush—he and Debra would get themselves an apartment and start fixing it up and making plans for the future, and Sammy would feel free to insult her hardworking brothers, whom he despised. Then a venture would crash, or he would have to go on the lam; there would be no money coming in for months and Debra would have to crawl back to her family for help. This pattern repeated itself throughout their life together.

Gravano describes in *Underboss* how he and his friend Tommy Spero started selling reject merchandise—jeans and handbags with slight irregularities that the major stores would not take. Debra and Tommy's wife, Camille, would come in and help out, and they were turning a huge profit on the goods. All of a sudden, Sammy pulled the plug on the store. Debra suspected it was because he couldn't stand earning an honest wage. "Don't you ever want to start a family and become legitimate?" she asked. Despite her questioning, it is doubtful that Debra thought Sammy would ever seriously consider going legitimate—she knew his ambitious, predatory nature better than anyone. Some mobsters are only in crime because they don't know any other way of making money; given a legitimate way of getting rich, they'd be happy. Not Sammy. "I'm a crook. What am I doing selling jeans?" he told his friends. "Let's get the fuck out of this."

When Sammy and Debra had been married for a couple of years, Debra's father put a down payment for them on a house in suburban Staten Island. Their new home was a big step up from their Brooklyn apartment, and Sammy struggled to make the monthly payments. They would also need to find money to furnish the place, and landscape the garden—all the average preoccupations of an average suburban couple.

Gravano's solution, however, was not at all like your average suburban householder. His answer for how to pay the bills was to raid a drug dealer's house, beat him up, and rob him. After taking care of his mob masters, he took home $50,000, which he gave his wife. His biography recalls, "I told Deb, 'We're in good shape. I'm giving you a little money. Put it on the side, so you can pay the rent . . . I'm going to do some construction on the house and we'll buy some furniture and things.'"

When he became a member of Cosa Nostra in 1977, Gravano solemnly internalized the rules and edicts about how the organization comes before a man's family, his children, and his God. (One mobster quotes an initiation ceremony in which the aspirant is asked: "If your child lay dying, would you leave his bedside if Cosa Nostra called?") He was one of many aspiring mafiosi who embraced the idea that he belonged to something greater than his own life, and was eager for an opportunity to prove where his loyalties lay.

Such an opportunity would present itself just two years after his initiation, when Debra's younger brother Nick Scibetta got into trouble. He was a wild young man, and a cocaine addict. After he had caused fights in nightclubs and drawn unwelcome attention to the mob, he then made a major error by beating up the son of a Gambino family boss. Several times, Gravano, by his own account, had to step in to save his brother-in-law from serious trouble. Paul

Castellano finally ordered Nick killed, and insisted that Gravano's crew had to do it, although Gravano was to be left out of the job. Gravano had to choose between standing up to the boss of bosses or allowing Nick to die. He chose the latter. "The bottom line is that I let it happen," he says in *Underboss*. "I didn't know his body would be chopped up afterward."

Like other women who know what their husbands are capable of, Debra must have suspected that Gravano had a hand in her brother's murder. Although she didn't know the whole story at the time, she would subsequently learn the truth from his book. And yet she stuck by him.

Sammy's big financial breakthrough came at the end of the 1970s, when he secured a foothold in the construction unions. With his first taste of serious money, Sammy did the thing most city mobsters seem to do after they've acquired the Lexus and the Rolex: he bought a house with thirty acres of land and turned it into a stud farm for breeding and training trotting horses. This house, near Cream Ridge in New Jersey, became a rural haven for his family—by this time they had two children, Karen and Gerard. But it was a haven only in appearance: when there was trouble, he would send Debra and the children back to Staten Island and hole up at the farm with his mob associates. There was often trouble during these years of Gravano's intense power play. Debra had to go where she was told and try not to panic. Like other mob wives, she had bits of information about what her husband was up to, and had to piece the rest together.

Debra was not idle herself. According to Gravano's biography, she was also dabbling in real estate. That might explain how she was able to buy an office building that served as the headquarters for her husband's construction company. When they wanted a bigger house on Staten Island, she apparently bought that too. Gravano, with help from the construction unions, rebuilt the place: it started as a wooden frame house and he rebuilt it in brick and doubled its size, put in marble floors and a swimming pool in the back garden. At last, with a big house in the city and the farm in Jersey, Debra Gravano was beginning to enjoy the status that went with being a mobster's wife.

If at times she was made to feel like a treasured possession, there

Virginia Hill at the Kefauver Committee in 1951.

Antoinette Giancana modeling, against her father Sam Giancana's wishes, in 1952.

Victoria Gotti, daughter of crime boss John Gotti, novelist and gossip columnist.

Camille and Joey Colucci (second from left) at his sister Jackie's wedding, 1964. Joey was the first victim of Sammy Gravano.

Mob enforcer John Branco with wife Caroline.

WANTED BY THE FBI

RACKETEERING INFLUENCED AND CORRUPT ORGANIZATIONS -AIDING AND ABETTING; INTERSTATE TRANSPORTATION IN AID OF RACKETEERING; HOBBS ACT-COMMERCIAL INSTITUTIONS; FILING FALSE INCOME TAX RETURNS

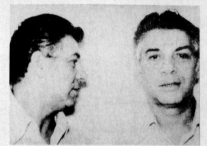

ALBERT CAESAR TOCCO

DESCRIPTION

Born, August 9, 1929; Chicago, Illinois; Height, 5'11"; Weight, 200 pounds; Build, stocky; Hair, black (greying); Eyes, brown; Complexion, medium; Race, white; Nationality, American; Scars and Marks, scar over right eye; Occupations, restaurant owner, garbage disposal business owner, vending machine business owner; Remarks, Tocco has been variously described as a "hit man," "enforcer," gambler and operator and/or owner of houses of prostitution. He is known to be a charmer of women however, has the propensity to be extremely close-mouthed and reclusive at times; Social Security Number Used, 355-14-3829.

CAUTION

TOCCO, A KNOWN MEMBER OF AN ORGANIZED CRIME FAMILY
INDICTED AND IS BEING SOUGHT IN CONNECTION WITH HIS INV
"STREET TAX" CONCERNING EXTENSIVE "CHOP SHOP" ACTIVIT
TITUTION ACTIVITIES AND THE CONTROL OF LAND USED FOR

Albert Tocco's FBI poster, issued shortly before his arrest in 1988.

FBI agents from left to right, Bob Pecoraro, Jack Bonino, and Wayne Zydron receive an award for capturing Albert Tocco.

Susan Berman poolside at The Flamingo, Las Vegas, where she grew up.

Gerardo Somoza

Betty Loren-Maltese on trial for racketeering in Federal Court, Chicago, 2002.

A/P Worldwide

Anthony Graziano after his arrest in the mid '80's.

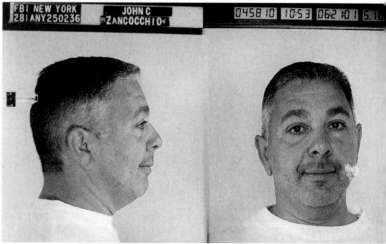

John Zancocchio after his arrest for loan sharking and tax fraud in 2001.

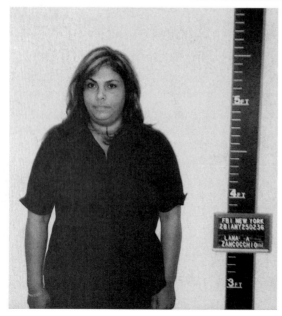

Lana Zancocchio after her arrest for tax fraud in 2001.

Brenda Colletti protesting outside the Philadelphia courthouse.

Sammy Gravano (center, right) leaving a party at the Ravenite club
to celebrate John Gotti's acquittal, 1990.

Debra Gravano (right) leaving court in Phoenix, Arizona after her son's sentencing, 2002.

was also plenty of unpleasantness that went with the job. In 1985, as Gravano would later testify, John Gotti and his crew, including Gravano, murdered Paul Castellano, boss of the Gambino family. Debra would have heard about the murder on the news, and then, according to his biography, her husband told her he had to leave for a while, "maybe for weeks, maybe months, years. I don't know how long." Castellano's murder marked a big step up for Gravano in the family; presumably, Debra knew that too, and what it would mean to her man.

By October 1990, investigators were building a racketeering case against Sammy Gravano and his boss, John Gotti, but before they made their move, Gravano went on the run. He describes, in *Underboss,* the night he told his wife that he would be leaving, and that he might be gone a long time. She did not ask him any questions, nor did she break down. This was part of the deal. Her job was to keep the family together; she would get no news, and there would be no one she could ask—she just had to think of something to tell the kids, and hope he would eventually come home.

The next time Debra saw her husband, two months later, he was in prison garb, in a visiting room at the Metropolitan Correction Center. Just days before, Gotti, as his biographer Jerry Capeci records, had summoned Gravano to a meeting at his headquarters at the Ravenite Social Club, where the FBI had intense surveillance in place, and inevitably they were raided. Things did not look good for the mobsters: the FBI had recorded thousands of hours of conversations in which Gotti implicated himself and Gravano in a number of serious crimes. While the men were in prison, Gravano noticed his boss's behavior becoming increasingly erratic and dictatorial. When he figured out that Gotti was planning to testify against him, Gravano decided to act first.

In November 1991, almost a year after his arrest, Gravano was moved to a secure unit. Subsequently, it became public knowledge that he was cooperating with the government and would give evidence against John Gotti at trial. His decision caused a sensation. Not only were his former mob associates shocked by his betrayal, but the press vilified him—the *New York Post's* front page announced "King Rat!" Apparently, some people like their mobsters to be proper outlaws: they should *never* help the authorities prosecute other criminals. Whatever Gotti had done in his thrilling career in Cosa Nostra—which included ordering at least five murders—in the public eye it could never be as bad as his underboss's act of treachery.

This warped morality was shared by Gravano's family. They had enjoyed the financial rewards and the status of an underboss's family. People paid them respect. His daughter, Karen, had relished being a mobster's daughter; like her brother, she made capital of her father's notoriety. She hung out with a gang of Mafia kids who drove expensive cars and swapped stories about their mob fathers.

When her father told her he was going to cooperate, Karen was devastated. Gravano described the moment in *Underboss*: "Debbie says, 'No!' She's shocked, she's scared, she's everything. My daughter is hysterical. Completely and totally. Her idol, her father, is about to join forces with the enemy. . . . She's crying. 'No, Dad, please!' and she runs right out of the visiting room."

The effect of her father's ruined reputation on Karen's life would be instant and total. From being given respect as Sammy the Bull's daughter, she would be outcast as the child of a rat. Mobsters are discouraged from cooperating with the law not just by an appeal to their sense of loyalty but by threats of extreme violence. For the families, however, the public shame can affect their whole lives. While an increasing number of mobsters cooperate to reduce their sentence, there are a few hard-line pockets of resistance, particularly among Italians of the old school, who view cooperation with the law as the lowest form of betrayal.

These hard-liners are often women. One young Italian woman stabbed her father in the stomach to prevent him from giving evidence against the Mafia. Such extremes are not unknown to the American mob. In the early 1990s, "Wild Bill" Cutolo, a capo in the Colombo family, was murdered. His son decided to avenge the murder by helping the FBI catch the culprits. In 2002, a notice appeared in the In Memoriam columns in the *New York Daily News*, which read: "My brother: I'm sorry your family took the easy way out. Especially the Pansy on his crusade. I promise to take care of him just as you would. Remember all your blood runs through my veins." The notice was placed by Cutolo's sister, Barbara DePalo. The threat was not directed at her brother's killers, but at his son.

As far as DePalo was concerned, her nephew, the so-called Pansy, had committed the ultimate crime in cooperating with the FBI. Her chilling words are a reminder of the old Sicilian maxim: *sangue chiama sangue*—blood cries out for blood. Like the women of southern Italy who keep blood feuds burning from generation to generation, DePalo swore to kill her own nephew and avenge a wrong greater than murder: betrayal of the old Mafia values.

In Sicily, the wives of mafiosi who collaborate with the authorities have publicly denounced their husbands, declaring the men dead in their hearts, pronouncing themselves widows. This performance is a bid to save their lives from retribution, but also to save their reputations from shame and dishonor. It was this course that Debra Gravano chose. In response to the news that her husband was going to cooperate, she decided not to go into witness protection with him. To demonstrate her severance from the mob's blackest traitor, in 1994 she divorced him. Perhaps she made her decision when she learned that her husband had killed her brother. Or maybe she wanted to punish him for destroying their lives by deciding to cooperate. Whatever the reason for the divorce, it wouldn't be long before Debra took Sammy back.

When Gravano's biography was published in 1997, it claimed that Debra had divorced her husband, sold the property she owned in New York, and moved away with their children. Sammy, it said, was living somewhere on his own. The reality was somewhat different. Sammy and Debra were living a mile away from each other and running a business together. Court records show that while Gravano was in jail in Arizona, Debra and the children had moved to Tempe, a suburb of Phoenix, presumably in order to be able to visit him. On his release after five short years, in December 1995, Gravano, then aged fifty-six, bought an apartment near Debra's home. Perhaps he planned to make it up to her and rebuild relations with his family. More likely, there was no one else he could turn to.

In the spring of 1997, Sammy left the witness protection program in order to be able to see his family without constraint. Resuming his old identity also meant that he was able to publicize the book, and, in an appropriately tasteless stunt, he was photographed signing baseball bats. By this time he'd had most of the tattoos removed from his upper body, and had undergone plastic surgery on his face, all in an effort to protect him from potential predators. The procedure did not disguise him, but it did improve his looks, straightening his nose and lifting his jowly jawline.

After he'd settled in Arizona, Gravano, who went by the name Jimmy Moran, could not stand to live like your average citizen. If he worried that his old mob associates would come after him, that was nothing compared to the horror of being a nobody. When he met people in his new neighborhood, he couldn't resist dropping hints about his identity. Debra, too, seemed reluctant to let go of their roots. She had lived the life of a mob wife for two decades, putting up with the hardships but also enjoying the highs: the sudden influx of easy money, the respect of the neighborhood, a certain flavor of risk and uncertainty. Debra was probably no better at resigning herself to anonymous small-town life than her husband. She bought a restaurant in Scottsdale for their son Gerard to run, which they called Uncle Sal's (Sammy was an Americanization of Gravano's real first name, Salvatore). Gravano and his wife set up a swimming-pool cleaning service and a construction company, which they called Marathon—the same name as his New York company. When a neighbor guessed his real identity, Gravano made no attempt to deny it.

Gravano was not the only one unable to resist flaunting his mob history: his son had a bull tattooed on his ample belly, and would threaten people: "You know who I am? I'm Sammy the Bull's son!" This was not the equivalent of having "Dad" lovingly tattooed on his skin: it was the mobster, not the father, that Gerard was celebrating.

The family did not improve their social circle in Tempe. Karen found a new boyfriend, David Seabrook, who had been convicted of attempted murder at fourteen and for jumping bail at sixteen. Gerard hung out with a rough bunch, some of whom had been linked to a violent gang back in their schooldays. Gravano and his wife employed some of these local lads.

Gravano and Debra were not making much money in the swimming-pool business—without Gravano's union clout, he wasn't getting the contracts—and it wasn't long before he returned to a life of crime. When Gerard, aged twenty-two, was arrested for sending a quantity of marijuana through the mail, instead of redirecting his son toward a legitimate living, Gravano went into business with him and his drug dealer friends. In 1999, the youth of Phoenix were enthusiastic users of ecstasy at weekend raves. The plan was to use Sammy the Bull's name and reputation to frighten off other drug dealers and monopolize the ecstasy market in Arizona. Gravano, who had acquired three guns despite being banned from owning firearms as a convicted felon, told one drug dealer: "I own Arizona. It's locked down. You can't sell pills without going through me."

Certainly, Gravano's reputation as a tough guy made an impression. Michael Papa, a young friend of Gerard's who ran the ecstasy ring, told a friend: "You know he killed his wife's brother . . . I said he's a fucking mess, you don't know what will happen with him, family or not, it doesn't matter to him. You double-cross him and you're fucked." Investigators estimated that Gravano's ecstasy ring was taking up to $1.2 million a month, and Gravano was taking fifty cents a pill. Gravano's son was not the only family member involved in the enterprise of supplying the youth of Arizona with their party drugs—his wife and daughter were part of the operation, too. Debra was the banker for the group: Gravano later admitted giving her $70,000 to keep in a safe in her house, which Michael Papa would collect to buy ecstasy. On another occasion, Gravano instructed Debra to give Papa $100,000 in cash to buy the drug. Karen routinely transported money between her father and mother for use in drug deals.

During his days in Cosa Nostra, Gravano used to talk about holding the organization dearer than his wife and family. He could have added that his wife and family were necessarily part of his criminal life: he could not function without their support, their silence, and loyalty. What's less obvious is why Debra chose to take an active role in her husband's criminal operation. Perhaps she saw a return of the man she knew, before he became a rat—the man who had won a spectacular deal with the government and was still prepared to risk everything to go back into crime; the man who was not afraid of anybody.

In the early months of 2000, the Gravano family was subjected to increasing surveillance, and records of conversations reveal a family fraught with discord and division, with the bullying figure of Sammy Gravano at the center. *Arizona Republic* reporter Dennis Wagner described how a bug in his office picked up Sammy telling stories, singing, throwing tantrums, cursing and yelling at family members and, occasionally, confiding in the family dog.

Wiretaps also caught Gravano discussing murder with his wife. Gravano was owed $25,000 by one of the dealers. According to wiretap summaries, Debra asked, "If he doesn't come up with it . . . are you going after him?" Gravano is recorded saying, "If he doesn't show up . . . then I'll take him out. It's too bad. . . . Boom. Boom. Boom. Boom. Boom."

Another long phone conversation between Gravano and his daughter revealed that their Mafia roots still clung to the family, no matter how far they had traveled. Karen called her father to complain about the behavior of Gerard's girlfriend, Mallory, who had apparently been out flirting with another man while Gerard was home with a broken leg. Still smarting from the humiliation of losing her friends when her father became the most famous rat in mob history, Karen was sensitive to any slight on the family's reputation. The dominant theme of the conversation was that by humiliating Gerard, Mallory was disrespecting the Gravano family name: "I can't believe this is happening to me, to us," Gravano said. "I don't know what to do. The respect Gerard is getting is through me."

Later on, according to government records, Gravano put a gun to his son's head and threatened to shoot him for bringing shame on the family. He also allegedly plotted to kill Mallory because she had boasted around town that she was dating "Sammy the Bull's son" and was bringing nothing but disrespect to the family.

As his drug operation expanded, Gravano started doing business with a New York ecstasy dealer, which brought him perilously close to his old stamping grounds. We now know that one of his former Gambino cronies, Huck Carbonaro, was planning to murder him. But once again Gravano was saved by the law: on February 24, 2000, he was arrested by a police SWAT team. His wife, son, and daughter were also arrested. Officers reported finding three guns at Salvatore Gravano's Tempe apartment and an "arsenal" at his wife's house.

Detectives from the Phoenix police department had identified Gravano as the brains behind the ecstasy operation, directing at least thirty-six people to transport and sell the drug. The family name worked very much against them by this stage. Debra, desperate to post bail for her husband, became a target for a con man obsessed with Gravano. The man told investigators that she had been looking for a hit man to eliminate witnesses, and wore a wire as he asked Debra if she wanted him to threaten anyone. She did not take the bait, repeating that she needed to raise the money to get her husband out of jail. Bail was set at $5 million, and Gravano remained in prison.

Almost a year after their arraignment in Arizona, as a result of their contacts with the New York drug gangs, Gravano and his son were indicted by a federal grand jury in New York for continuing a criminal enterprise. In the meantime, their partner in the ecstasy ring, Michael Papa, had begun to cooperate with the authorities. Knowing how damning Papa's testimony was likely to be, as well as the hours of surveillance tapes in possession of the prosecution, in June 2001, the Gravano family decided to plead.

Gravano pled guilty to possessing ecstasy for sale, operating a criminal syndicate, money laundering, and possession of firearms by a convicted felon. Gerard pled guilty to conspiracy to distribute ecstasy. Debra and Karen admitted to lesser crimes.

The government moved to seize all the family's assets—the Scottsdale restaurant, Debra's house, and Karen's apartment. Gravano, the most famous turncoat mobster in history, got a spectacular payback when Michael Papa took the stand at a presentence hearing in March 2002 and described Gravano's concern that one of the group would weaken and rat out the rest.

In the fall of 2002, Gravano was given twenty years in New York and nineteen years in Arizona, to run concurrently. At Gravano's sentencing in Brooklyn's federal courthouse, prosecutor Linda Lacewell argued that, in spite of being given a very lenient deal in exchange for his testimony, Gravano had not been able to resist returning to crime: "This was a crime of power and a crime of arrogance because he couldn't sit in Arizona and be a pool salesman. He wanted the leadership. He took these kids, capitalized on their bizarre worship of him as some kind of criminal celebrity. He wants to have his name out there, he wants people to know he's in charge. Why? Because he can't let go. He'd rather not be out on the street if he can't be in control."

In *Underboss*, Gravano makes great play of the fact that Gotti wanted his son to be in the Mafia with him, claiming that a decent father would want a better, legitimate life for his children. While declaring he never wanted his son to be in the mob, Gravano makes a prophetic statement: "If he winds up in the life, he's sure to end up either being whacked or going to jail himself." Gerard Gravano is currently serving nine years, and has requested a transfer to an Arizona facility, to be near his girlfriend and their baby son.

Gravano is serving his sentence at a high-security prison in Colorado known as Supermax. Debra and Karen got five years' probation. There was gleeful gossip at Gravano's sentencing about how the underboss's wife was now working on the checkout at a Tempe supermarket. No doubt Debra still makes the trip to visit her husband in jail. She and her husband are tied to each other by bonds stronger than anything life in the mob, or the criminal justice system, can throw at them. As Sammy himself described their relationship in *Underboss:* "We would be like wolves who mate, that stay with one another for good."

18

ON January 31, 2003, Betty Loren-Maltese, the former mayor of Cicero, Illinois, was driven through the gates of the federal penitentiary in Dublin, California, to begin an eight-year sentence for racketeering. Almost ten years after becoming mayor, Loren-Maltese, fifty-three, had been convicted of defrauding the town of Cicero of $12 million through a mob-backed scheme. Her coconspirators, all but one of whom were found guilty, included a former chief of police and a Mafia boss. As Loren-Maltese hurried inside the prison gates, her lawyer stopped to give a brief statement to the waiting press pack. It was a meager last supper for the media, who had feasted for years on the mayor's outrageous antics and her downfall.

Loren-Maltese had been installed as mayor in 1992 by her husband, Frank Maltese, who, as the town's assessor, was a crucial City Hall connection for the mob. Betty Loren-Maltese's swift and unopposed elevation had shocked no one familiar with the workings of Cicero politics. What surprised everybody, even those who thought they knew her, was how, once in office, Betty had grasped hold of power and used it to serve her own ambitions. She became one of the few people who decide when they don't need the Mafia anymore.

Betty had been introduced to the mob, like every other Mafia woman, by a man, but if the mob thought she would be intimidated, or charmed, into doing their bidding, they were dealing with the wrong woman. Operating in a man's world, both in politics and organized crime, Betty asserted her will through sheer force of character, displaying a capacity for dishonesty, vindictiveness, and greed equal to any boardroom executive in a suit and tie, and even greater ambitions.

Betty Loren was born in Baton Rouge, Louisiana, in 1950. When she was still a baby, her father's business, a bar and ice cream parlor, went bust, and he moved the family back to his native Chicago, where his Lithuanian parents still lived. The family settled in the western suburb of Cicero, where Betty's father worked as a janitor. Betty, whose yearbook photo shows a glum-looking teenager with a beehive hairdo, dropped out of high school, took a job as clerk, and got married at the age of eighteen. She would divorce just five years later, and little is known of her first husband.

When she was twenty, according to some accounts, Betty Loren was working as a cocktail waitress at Michael's Magic Touch, a mob-run topless bar and brothel. Cicero was a "wide open" town, one of the few in the United States where vice was allowed to flourish if the owners paid a "street tax" to the local mob bosses. Michael's Magic Touch was *the* place for risqué entertainment in the western suburbs, and the mob was a familiar presence in its darkened booths. Taking a job as a cocktail waitress in such a place didn't look like a promising step for a smart girl like Betty, but it turned out to be the most significant move of her young life. An IRS investigator who had the place under surveillance says it was at Michael's Magic Touch around 1970 that she met Frank Maltese, a jovial, kindly man twenty years her senior, who was friendly with the owner and took a shine to her. In spite of their age difference, and the fact that both were married, they started dating, and became a familiar item in the neighborhood restaurants and bars that Frank frequented. Loren–Maltese always said she met Frank at a charity bingo game she attended with her mother.

Frank Maltese, nicknamed "Baldy," was gregarious and well liked, a man of short stature and long lunches, his rotund figure was well known in the back rooms of local politics. Cicero was notorious for its association with America's most famous hoodlum, Al Capone, and Maltese's title of assessor was largely honorific in a town famous for its unelected officials. His more important, unofficial, role was to act as liaison between the mayor and the mob.

For over a decade, according to government records, Maltese had provided mob boss Ernest "Rocky" Infelise with a hotline to City Hall. The two men would occasionally meet over lunch, and by the mid-1970s, Betty was increasingly seen with them. By this time, Betty was no longer a cocktail waitress, and no longer married. She had earned herself a GED and published a community newspaper. She had also obtained a license to sell real estate—experience she would put to good use years later, when she had money to invest.

Betty smoked and gambled, and told funny stories like a man, but everything else about her was almost aggressively feminine. She had big hair and a big bosom. She wore outrageous false eyelashes, bright pink lipstick, and provocative clothing, favoring low-cut blouses and leopard print. Even though she sometimes put Frank down in front of others, his friends thought he had done all right for himself.

Frank's live-and-let-live attitude suited him perfectly for his role in the crime syndicate. People in Cicero liked him, and in addition to his job as assessor, he always made time for good works, like organizing baseball for kids. He knew the value of getting the people on your side. Although not a bad guy himself, he was just the man to oil the works for organized crime, the kind on whom the mob depends to work the system on their behalf.

"You had to know Frank," Betty has said. "Frank would help anybody, everybody; he was just that type of person."

In 1982 Frank moved in with Betty at her suburban red-brick bungalow on Austin Avenue in Cicero, and got a divorce from his wife. Having already helped Betty to a job at City Hall running the traffic violations department, he now got her promoted to assistant deputy liquor commissioner, working for Steve Bajovic, who was later convicted of skimming license fees.

The mob's presence in Cicero began in 1923, when Al Capone set up his headquarters there, moving his brand of intimidation and street-brawling political control to the western suburbs. If people lament the fact that Cicero's reputation is still linked to Al Capone, it is a legacy that very few have tried to shake off. The Mafia's rule, albeit behind the scenes, has been uninterrupted ever since.

Although Frank Maltese was never proposed for membership in

the Chicago crime syndicate, he wielded immense influence on the mob's behalf, but always behind the scenes, and always in the nicest possible way—just helping his friends. Frank enjoyed the razzmatazz that went with organized crime: the respect people paid him when he lunched at his favorite restaurants in the company of Rocky Infelise. He also dabbled in mob business; in the summer of 1986, drawing on his wide network of gambling friends, he became a bookmaker for Infelise. But while Frank was enjoying his new hobby, in the mid-1980s the IRS began an extensive investigation into Infelise's criminal activities, in particular his gambling and loan-sharking businesses.

In 1988, Betty and Frank, after having dated for seventeen years, finally got married. In spite of Frank's looming legal troubles, the wedding was a lavish affair; a stretch limo delivered the happy couple to the Carlyle Banquet Hall in Lombard, where they hosted a reception for hundreds of guests, including Rocky Infelise and two of his lieutenants. The bride, aged thirty-eight, marrying her second husband, wore a white meringue dress, with veil. The groom, aged fifty-seven, on his third wife (all three of them named Betty), crammed his portly figure into a starched shirt and tuxedo.

The guests danced and drank the night away. But the party was soon over: not long after Frank made an honest woman of Betty, federal investigators had a breakthrough. One of Frank's associates decided to become an informant for the government. The lifelong mobster Bill Jahoda had grown tired of the Mafia life and had been disturbed by recent mob murders. Jahoda's cooperation ultimately nailed Infelise and his crew.

On one occasion, Jahoda was sent into City Hall wearing a body wire, to talk to his old friend Frank Maltese about the betting operation. "Frank was a very rotund guy," says IRS Special Agent Tom Moriarty, Jahoda's handler. "Frank liked to eat. Frank usually ate lunch for about three hours. We sent Jahoda in three times and he was still at lunch. 'At lunch' in Cicero could mean anything—you could be 'at lunch' for a couple of years. Anyway, that day, Frank didn't come back to his office."

The mob's favorite lunch spot at that time was Schullo's restaurant in Cicero, where Infelise would meet his lieutenants, as well as Jahoda and Maltese, to discuss business. Occasionally, they would be joined by Betty. She had gotten to know Frank's friends pretty well. The austere, intimidating Infelise had a temperament completely different from Frank, but they all got along fine. According to one investigator, Betty learned a lot from Infelise.

In 1991, the FBI's investigation into Infelise and his street crew came to a head with the arrest of twenty people on charges of racketeering. Most of the accused, including Maltese, pled guilty shortly before going to trial. Infelise was tried and convicted of racketeering and sentenced to sixty-three years. Maltese got three years, but before he went to jail, he was diagnosed with cancer of the pancreas. His doctors told prosecutors that if they sent him to prison, he would die as soon as the door was locked behind him. In any event, Maltese died before he was due to start serving his sentence.

Before he got ill, according to an investigation by the IRS, Maltese had had time to arrange for the town's insurance business to be transferred from the long-standing provider and put in the hands of an outfit run by the mob. In November 1992, the administration of Cicero town employees' health insurance claims was contracted out to an unknown company, Specialty Risk Consultants, Inc. (SRC), which had been incorporated just a few weeks before and had no track record in claims processing. Although Mayor Klosak had objected to the move, Frank Maltese persuaded him to let the deal go ahead. SRC would be controlled, behind the scenes, by the man Infelise had named his successor, acting mob boss Michael Spano. Over the next five years, as prosecutors painstakingly demonstrated, SRC would siphon off $12 million of town funds, to be divided among Spano and his friends, including Betty Loren-Maltese.

A month after the SRC deal had been arranged, Mayor Klosak died suddenly of pneumonia. Frank Maltese, the popular political player who would have been ushered into the top job, was ineligible because of his mob-related conviction—besides his health was deteriorating. Klosak's death worried some of the mobsters who had enjoyed close relationships with City Hall, but if anyone was afraid that the next mayor might question their intimacy with the Cicero treasury, Spano reassured them that the position would go to someone who would take orders from him. Spano, as one of his associates later testified, was confident that Betty was a safe appointment because "she was Frank's wife, and Frank could control her."

Outsiders aware of Frank Maltese's position in Cicero government were nonetheless taken aback when it was suddenly announced that Betty Loren-Maltese had been named as the town's interim mayor. On hearing the news, Tom Moriarty remembers feeling shocked and dismayed. "I just kind of shook my head. I thought, this is Cicero, I guess it'll never change. It was just the chutzpah of these people: Mike Spano replaced Rocky Infelise, and Betty replaced Frank. In fact it was even more blatant. There wasn't even a smokescreen anymore: they made her the mayor."

The negotiations that allowed Betty Loren-Maltese to be installed as interim mayor of Cicero took all of seven minutes. In a meeting behind closed doors at City Hall on January 12, 1993, her husband, Frank Maltese, and other board members engineered her appointment. One man closely following this shift in Cicero's political elite was IRS Special Agent Bill Paulin. He recalls: "We knew that Betty was not going to be a reformer. Anybody that is appointed from within like that is not a reformer, it's going to be business as usual. When Betty became mayor, Frank was still the power behind the throne until he died."

Betty's personal style, at least, was refreshing: the bouffant wig, mahogany eye shadow and false eyelashes ensured instant recognition by the man or woman in the street, and she launched herself into her new job with tremendous vigor. In spite of her husband's well-known connection to the mob, Loren-Maltese represented herself as a force for change. She had her own political ambitions, and would pursue them with energy and imagination.

Within the first few months of taking office, Betty appointed a youth commission with the objective of improving sports and play facilities. She also provided services for seniors: bus rides, outings, and snow clearance. She privatized garbage collection and sent eent چ

teams of workers out to clean up abandoned lots and buildings. These initiatives were largely cosmetic, but she knew her constituency: such improvements attracted favorable notice, especially among the older population, who had never received so much attention. In return, Cicero's senior citizens offered Loren-Maltese their unswerving loyalty.

She also launched a publicity offensive to improve Cicero's image. In an effort to eclipse the looming shadow of Al Capone, she claimed Ernest Hemingway as Cicero's most famous son—even though he was born in nearby Oak Park. Outside Town Hall, there is a sign bearing the names of Loren-Maltese and Ernest Hemingway. Her name is on top in big, bold letters: in Cicero, as one local reporter pointed out, Nobel Prize winners get the small print.

Loren-Maltese is big on signs; it's all part of her cult of personality. Drive around Cicero and you will see her name everywhere, often in gold lettering: "Another blighted building removed on behalf of Betty Loren-Maltese." "A safe place for kids to play, brought to you by Betty Loren-Maltese."

Signs weren't all she used to burnish the town's image. When she took office, she gave a press conference, and told reporters that Cicero didn't deserve its reputation. "Every community has a problem but apparently we get the notoriety because everybody knows the name Cicero," she said. "Everyone assumes that there's hit men with machine guns on the street."

For the wife of a senior town employee convicted of racketeering, such pronouncements were fabulously brassy. But such bold revisionism set the style of Loren-Maltese's leadership. If the people of Cicero detected any cynicism, it was nothing less than what history had taught them to expect.

After a few months of interim rule, Betty sought election in the spring of 1993, and hired a former reporter with the *Chicago Sun-Times* and now stand-up comedian named Ray Hanania as her publicist. At first, Betty did not feel confident about doing interviews on TV or radio, but Hanania persuaded her that her style would be popular with ordinary voters: he was convinced she could appeal to the middle class and housewives as one of the people—Bungalow Belt Betty. After a few years in office she became a practiced self-publicist, and would never be caught without a sound bite.

Hanania worked with Loren-Maltese on the local Republican paper, the *Cicero Observer*. She apparently dictated what she wanted in the paper—an indignant reporter counted seven photos of Betty Loren-Maltese in one sixteen-page edition. Like so much else that went on in her jurisdiction, Loren-Maltese insisted on being involved in every detail.

Betty's house in Cicero was a fairly modest suburban brick bungalow. In 1991, she and Frank had raised their property profile, buying a weekend retreat beside the picturesque Lake of the Four Seasons in Indiana, a cedar-sided ranch home with a boat dock. Friends from the town staff helped with the renovations. Betty, who can't swim, was often to be found fishing for bluegills from the pier. In August 1993, she threw a party for Frank at the Indiana house, and three hundred of his political pals turned up to celebrate his career.

A few months after her interim appointment, Loren-Maltese was elected mayor for a full term. One of her closest advisers would be Ed Vrdolyak, a wealthy lawyer and political wheeler-dealer who had served as a Chicago alderman for twenty years.

On October 19, 1993, Frank died, at the age of sixty-three. At the funeral, Vrdolyak, who had visited Frank almost every day during his illness, stood at Betty's side. The men Maltese had served were in jail, but others had emerged, and as the priest intoned the burial rites, they lost no time in cementing their relationship with his widow. Frank was no longer there to whisper in her ear, but Betty found plenty of others willing to offer support and advice. According to IRS sources, Michael Spano, a dapper, diminutive figure with slicked-back brown hair, conveyed Rocky Infelise's condolences from prison. Frank's old friend Emil Schullo, Cicero's chief of police, whose family had a long association with the mob, came to pay his respects. Schullo spoke to Betty. "We will take care of all your needs," he said. She didn't ask who "we" were.

When the funeral rites were over, Vrdolyak took Loren-Maltese's arm and together they led the procession to the waiting limousines. With all these men paying court, all of them wanting something from her, perhaps this was the moment she understood how much power she could have now that Frank was gone.

19

IF the mob had put Betty into the top job in the belief that she could be controlled, their illusion did not last long. Betty had ambitions of her own, and assumed a position of power as though it had always been her plan.

"This was her opportunity," says Bill Paulin, who observed with interest the ascent of Loren-Maltese. "Now she didn't have to walk in Frank's shadow, she became Frank. She wanted the respect and the love that was granted to Frank, she felt that was hers."

Ray Hanania's intuition had been correct: the big hair and low-cut tops went down well with the Bungalow Belt. They also caught the attention of the media. In one magazine photo shoot, Betty was caught leaning provocatively on her desk, looking less like a mayor than a madam. As her brassy appearance suggested, Betty Loren-Maltese was not a person of half measures. She was a woman who let her feelings be known, who inspired intense loyalty, and equally intense enmity. She herself has said: "People either love me or they hate me." The problem with Betty is that people usually start off doing the former, and end up doing the latter.

A political cult of personality grew up around her. She demanded—and got—absolute loyalty. Even her enemies agree that when you're in favor with Betty, there's nothing she won't do for you—but you are expected to give as much in return.

Betty tried to instill a collegiate atmosphere in City Hall, insisting that her staff were her friends. People were encouraged to drop by her office, which was a cluttered, girly affair, decorated with soft toys and a collection of porcelain clowns. Loren-Maltese's desk was crowded with plants, flowers, photographs, and awards, and the room was thick with cigarette smoke from her two-pack-a-day habit. A couple of times a week she would have lunch in her office with a coterie of ladies, women she had worked with throughout her years at City Hall. They would sit in the conference room adjoining her office, and two police officers in a patrol car would be sent fifteen miles into Chicago to buy Lithuanian dumplings.

One of the first things Betty did was to make Emil Schullo her chief of staff, creating a new role for him as public safety director. Gang violence had become a major problem among the town's rapidly growing Hispanic population, and together they launched a crusade to drive the street gangs out of Cicero. The measures they proposed included banning gang members from the town, even from visiting their families, which drew criticism from civil rights organizations. Loren-Maltese also vowed to crack down on graffiti, and sent offenders out to do community service wearing pink aprons—a move probably more effective as a publicity stunt than as a cleanup initiative.

Another of Betty's extraordinary feats was to name the public safety building after her late husband, a convicted felon. As she unveiled Frank Maltese's name emblazoned in gold letters on the building's ugly brick façade, a film crew from CBS's investigative program *60 Minutes II* attempted to film the inauguration, but were thrown off the premises.

Another of Betty's key friends and supporters during her first year in office was identified by prosecutors as mob boss Michael Spano. The two spoke frequently on the telephone. On one occasion, agents conducting surveillance on Spano followed his car driving a circuitous route through the backstreets of old neighborhoods, taking detours down blind alleys and doubling back. Eventually Spano's car arrived outside Betty Loren-Maltese's house, just a couple of miles from his starting point.

On Thursday nights, recalls agent Paulin, the mob boss and the mayor would often go gambling together. Spano would pick her up in his Cadillac, sometimes accompanied by her mother, Kitty, and they would drive to the riverboat casinos in Aurora, Illinois. Their favorite spot was the Hollywood Casino, where they would often stay until three or four in the morning. Spano liked craps, while Betty went for the slots.

Although these outings became more frequent as time went on, Betty's working relationship with Spano had in fact begun the moment she took her seat behind the mayor's desk. Spano already had his hands in the town's coffers through his company, SRC, before she'd even arrived. At one point early in the relationship, Betty tried to assert herself with Spano. When the town fell $724,000 behind in health insurance claims from its employees, Loren-Maltese wrote a complaining memo and threatened to replace the firm. Spano reportedly reassured SRC's manager that he would "handle the problem with Betty"—which, apparently, he did. Whether he threatened to oust her from the mayor's office or indicated how much money she stood to gain, she never raised the matter again.

In February 1993, SRC went from handling just the municipal health claims to controlling all of Cicero's insurance, including everything from police cars to local carnivals. For a while, the scheme worked beautifully. Anyone who might have policed the town's insurance business was brought in on the scam. When the money started pouring in, everybody got a new car: investigators noted that Spano bought himself the mobster's classic black Cadillac with gold piping and gold hubcaps.

Those who questioned the town's financial dealings quickly learned their mistake. Early on, town employee Robert Balsitis had expressed alarm about SRC's handling of the town's insurance to Frank Maltese. Balsitis was soon reprimanded by mob boss Michael Spano, who told him to do as he was told. Unaware of Schullo's relationship with Spano, the hapless Balsitis later confided to the police chief that he believed the mob had taken over the town's insurance business. He was promptly summoned to the mayor's office, where Loren-Maltese grilled him about whether he had confided his suspicions to anyone else. He refused to answer her questions, and shortly afterward was moved to another department. He was later fired.

Meanwhile, SRC was draining town funds, charging more than the previous firm's fee to handle insurance claims. For every claim processed, the company tacked on a 20 percent charge, and the extra funds came straight out of the treasury. By mid-1993, the town's insurance costs had increased from $60,000 to $95,000 a week.

As the town's spending got totally out of hand, the assistant controller, Gene Berkes, received memos from SRC's manager informing him of the rising cost of the town's insurance. Berkes brought up the matter with Loren-Maltese, insisting at City Hall meetings month after month that the company handling the insurance was corrupt, and that if it wasn't replaced, it would bankrupt the town. Loren-Maltese listened silently. After a while, Berkes was no longer invited to meetings. Then he, too, was fired.

The beneficiaries of the Cicero insurance fraud had ambitious plans. Together, the group bought a golf course on an island in the Menominee River in Wisconsin's Northwoods, which they planned to turn into a casino resort. Spano's business partner John LaGiglio, who ran SRC and laundered the proceeds, had been instructed to acquire a suitable property, and had bought and restored the Four Seasons golf course, a picturesque spot where the hotel and casino were eventually to be built. Loren-Maltese had invested $100,000 in the scheme, and Spano had flown other prospective investors to the site. But when the development ran into a series of expensive setbacks, more investment was badly needed.

Early one morning in the autumn of 1994, John LaGiglio picked up Greg Ross, a former IRS agent who was now working as SRC's accountant, and the two men drove to Cicero to collect Betty Loren-Maltese and Michael Spano. Ross later became a government witness, and described the day trip. The four set off in LaGiglio's spacious conversion van on the six-hour drive to the golf course, to observe LaGiglio's progress and, he hoped, kick in more funds.

Ross later remembered that as they were barrelling along the expressway at seventy miles an hour, Spano suddenly decided he wanted to drive. Instead of telling LaGiglio to pull over, he grabbed the steering wheel while they were still traveling at speed, and elbowed LaGiglio out of the way while he climbed into the driver's seat. It was the sort of macho caper one might expect from a risk-loving Mafia boss, trying to assert his control.

Once the group arrived at the golf course, LaGiglio, a short man with a thick gray beard, showed them around. As they inspected the clubhouse, which had been decorated under the supervision of LaGiglio's wife, Bonnie, the four tried to picture the place as a luxury casino. Betty was particularly excited when they went up to the second floor, where she found power points set along the walls eighteen inches apart. These would supply electricity for her beloved slot machines. Whether it was the slot machines or something else, Betty was sufficiently impressed with the place to invest another $200,000 before the summer was over.

On the way back to Chicago, the group made a detour to look at Mike Spano's holiday home on the scenic Wolf River in Wisconsin. When Spano bought the place, it was a dilapidated family cottage, but with $300,000 of Cicero town funds, he had succeeded in transforming it into a palatial two-story riverside house with a marina. Large windows overlooked a broad stretch of river frontage, with a dock for Spano's motorboat and jet skis, and inside were generous, luxuriously appointed rooms with vaulted ceilings. Spano was not a man to hide his wealth: he enjoyed the finer things in life, and liked to share them. A less imposing figure than the old boss Rocky Infelise, Spano needed to show his status in other ways, with the trappings of wealth and power. As Agent Bill Paulin commented wryly: "What's the sense of stealing money if you can't show it off?"

Despite their shared success, the cozy relationship between Mayor Betty and the mob did not last. Her desire for control, both in public and private life, demanded a level of personal commitment and loyalty from those around her comparable to a mob boss and his acolytes. Circumstances would soon strain those loyalties to the breaking point.

In her early years in office, Betty hated to be alone. Since Betty's work was her life, she always expected her colleagues to be her friends, and insisted they accompany her to official events, charity dos, and fund-raisers. Often she invited Emil Schullo, her police chief, who would drive her to functions himself. When she promoted Schullo, she had his office moved next to hers, so that he could pop in to see her any time he liked. They were seen together so frequently that rumors began to swirl around City Hall that they were having an affair.

People now say that Betty was in love with Emil, and that her unrequited feelings for him caused the first major disaster of her career. As a woman operating successfully in a man's world, perhaps she was undone by trying to bend a man's affections to her will. Unfortunately, at that time Emil was dating another woman, whom he later married. Allegedly embarrassed by Betty's attentions, when required to act as her escort, he would often take someone else along with them as chaperone, or else drop her off to play golf or go fishing and pick her up later in the day. Betty's flirtatious behavior grew more public, and more excruciating. On one occasion, a former colleague remembers, when Emil was on crutches with an injured foot, she playfully yanked his shorts down.

Just as Betty insisted her colleagues should be her friends, according to one insider she did not like her male staffers to have girlfriends: she thought it diminished their loyalty to her. When Emil moved into his future wife's apartment, Betty reacted to the move not just as a woman scorned, but as a boss betrayed. In her fury, she had Emil removed from his new position. His next-door office was cleared, and his stuff sent back down to the police department. One former town employee says she went around the department asking, "Are you friends with me or Emil?"

Loren-Maltese's account of the quarrel is different; she claims she discovered a plot to oust her. According to her, a conversation took place at her husband's funeral between Ray Hanania, Schullo, and others in which they schemed to cast her aside and take over the town. "They had a plan and they were going to take their time," she later told a reporter. The plan was allegedly to run another candidate against her in the 1997 election. "They undid themselves, but they took me with them. These people professed to be my friends. But they were not my friends. These people were the ones my husband trusted."

Whatever the origin of the schism in the Republican ranks, the feud had devastating consequences. Betty's people were divided. Those who sided with Emil formed a rival group within the party.

In a move she felt was heretical, the "graveside plotters" put together an alternative list of candidates for the next election. The group launched their own newspaper, the *Cicero Life*, to counter Betty's *Observer*. The two camps waged war in their newspapers, slandering each other and making accusations and counteraccusations.

Betty was always liable to turn against those who wouldn't do her bidding. Now, with a full-scale war declared, things turned really ugly. "To her the job was personal," Hanania told the *Chicago Tribune*. "She became vindictive, striking out at people who had been loyal to her for years."

Former friends instantly became her enemies; quite often there wasn't even a fight, the offenders were simply "out." Soon after their falling-out, Loren-Maltese started making preemptive strikes against the businesses to whom Schullo had given municipal contracts. Unfortunately, most of these were also Michael Spano's contacts, and the fallout spread.

When Spano first realized that Betty had an emotional investment in Emil, according to agent Paulin, he foresaw the situation getting nasty. He became well acquainted with her during their Thursday-night outings, and Spano could see that if she wasn't happy, their lucrative arrangement with City Hall could fall apart. He had told Emil to sort things out with her. Unfortunately, Emil had not sorted things out. He had merely moved in with his girlfriend.

Spano had issues with Loren-Maltese that went beyond her unprofessional feelings for Schullo. The mob boss later complained, in a conversation secretly recorded by a government informant, that she had gotten "greedy." "None of this . . . would be a problem, if she would just stay the way she was, the way we were. It would be no problem. But she got fucking greedy and she got pissed at Emil."

The "way we were," romantic as it sounds, refers to the sweet deal that Spano and his friends had with City Hall. While things were going well, and the money was flowing, perhaps inevitably, the friends began to fight about how much was due to each of them. There was tension because LaGiglio's golf course venture was becoming a money pit, and no one was seeing the returns they expected (Loren-Maltese was one of the few who ever made money on her investment). A combination of greed and mismanagement began to shake their loyalties. There was also a prodigious battle of egos brewing between Loren–Maltese and Michael Spano.

When Betty was put into City Hall to do the mob's bidding, they had no idea how ambitious she was for herself. Her secretary later testified that Betty had total control over the town board, and town board decisions were always unanimous.

"Betty had become the player that Frank was," observes Bill Paulin. "And ultimately in the end, more so. Frank Maltese was happy being the level that he was at—but she had aspirations. That's the difference between those two. Frank had achieved low-level mobdom. She wanted high-level mobdom."

While Loren–Maltese's cultlike followers did her bidding in City Hall, she began to believe the hype. "She's in an environment where everyone is playing to her," Paulin went on. "Everybody except for Spano. Spano's the mob boss, but everyone else is kissing her ass. With this treatment for years on end, you get self-inflated, you end up thinking you're bigger than you are. And that's what happened to her.

"She's getting grander, she's getting bigger." Paulin sounds ominous as he considers her frame of mind. "Maybe she's thinking, *I don't need Spano.*"

20

WHILE a power struggle was developing between Loren-Maltese and Spano, federal agents were scrutinizing their financial dealings. And as their personal vendettas got out of control, they got careless. Paulin remembers: "I'm sitting back here with my investigation, watching these people display evidence and exposés in these little Cicero papers. They're throwing hand grenades back and forth, she's attacking and they're responding in kind. These are some very disturbing times for the politics of Cicero."

In the mid-1990s, the FBI started investigating town representatives they suspected of corruption. "We started developing cases but at first we couldn't attach anything directly to Betty Loren-Maltese," says FBI agent Thomas Bourgeois. "We had been looking into health and housing, collection of parking fines, these were all problem areas. I called Cicero a 'government based on kleptocracy': anything they could steal, they would. If anyone saw shady business going on, they just turned away. Betty oversaw this mess."

As the FBI's organized crime unit looked into links between City Hall and the mob, they finally discovered who was behind SRC. By the end of 1996, the IRS started issuing subpoenas for financial records, and the individuals involved in SRC quickly tried to distance themselves from it. Loren-Maltese publicly accused the mob of pillaging the town's coffers and held press conferences in which she vowed to get to the bottom of the scam that had been robbing Cicero blind.

Loren-Maltese's public performance had a dual purpose. If she had not enjoyed quite such a high profile, she might have been in some danger. Following her offensive against violent Hispanic gangs, Loren-Maltese claimed she had been threatened, and demanded a twenty-four-hour security guard. Her critics said these bodyguards were never really needed, but they nevertheless lent her an air of importance. Whether the threat from gangs was real or imagined, after her split with the mob, she was probably glad of her bodyguards—she retained them, paid for by the town of Cicero, for several years. At times she used her security detail for dramatic effect: on one occasion she came out of her house to meet a reporter and photographer, accompanied by two armed police officers. The press has not always been kind to Betty, but this response seemed exaggerated.

Once the problems with SRC became public, Betty turned on her old friends, claiming that her husband's last words to her were a warning to watch out for the mob. Her enemies responded in kind: "She would cut your legs off," Emil Schullo's brother told the *Tribune*. "She's a vicious, vindictive person."

After her bitter falling-out with Spano and Schullo, Loren-Maltese went all out to prove that she could win an election without the support of her former friends. Her election tactics are legendary: people noticed that the only signs in people's gardens were hers—one resident claimed her supporters ripped up the original signs and planted hers in their stead. Those who refused to contribute to her political fund were liable to receive a visit from the feared "code enforcement" department, who could fine you for failing to mend a broken window. Part of Betty's success was that she fostered support among the rapidly growing Hispanic population, and built a new power base among people who would not normally vote.

Loren-Maltese was returned to office with a huge majority in 1997. This reelection would mark the beginning of a frenzied phase of Betty's rule, another chapter in the soap opera in which she made more enemies than friends. And all the while, in the background, federal agents were stepping up their scrutiny of her financial affairs.

For someone under federal investigation, Loren-Maltese then

made an extraordinary decision. Either believing that she would be acquitted of any wrongdoing or simply hoping the SRC mess would go away, she adopted a baby. The deal was brokered by one of her loyal employees named Vince Iacino, whose friends Richie and Dawn Golen were about to have their third child. The pregnancy was unplanned and the couple worried that they didn't have the financial means to raise another child. When Vince suggested that the childless forty-six-year-old mayor could adopt the baby, Betty leapt at the chance, and the arrangements for adoption were quickly put in place. Dawn now says she had reservations about giving up her baby, but alleges Iacino threatened her that if she backed out, "things could be made to happen." Iacino and Loren-Maltese both deny this. Loren-Maltese's lawyer said the baby was given up freely.

On the day of the handover, when the baby girl was just three days old, Betty turned up at the hospital with her lawyer and three security guards in suits and dark glasses. A shaky video of the occasion shows the hospital ward, with nurses squeezing past the guards, and Betty in a tight-fitting russet suit and high heels, struggling to dress the howling newborn. The tiny baby is eventually delivered into the back of Betty's huge black Lincoln Town Car, and driven away with her new mother, and bodyguards.

Back at City Hall, having fired Emil Schullo, Loren-Maltese was in need of another chief of police. Violence among Hispanic gangs was on the rise, and the mayor was under intense pressure to do something about it. After a long search, her choice was David Niebur, a police chief of legendary toughness from Joplin, Missouri.

Niebur had worked in Illinois and was familiar with Cicero's reputation for graft. Loren-Maltese assured him that she wanted to clean up Cicero's famously corrupt and sleaze-ridden police department, and he found the challenge irresistible. "I knew Cicero's reputation very well," he told me. "That was the mystique that drew me to the job. I thought if you could clean up Cicero, you could do anything. They'd be waiting in line to hire you after that."

In December 1997, Niebur accepted the job—a move that would turn out to be the biggest mistake of his life. He realizes now that there were warning signs. For one thing, in his interview,

Loren-Maltese asked him inappropriate questions about his private life. Then, when he got back to his office in Missouri, an FBI agent was waiting to talk to him. At this stage nobody apart from himself, Loren-Maltese, and the town attorney knew he had been hired for the Cicero job. It turned out that the FBI had tapped Loren-Maltese's phone lines. The agent told Niebur that the FBI had been investigating Cicero for some time, and requested his help.

Once he took up his position, Niebur's first task was to handle the gang problem. "It was my observation," he says, "that she thought I would be so busy fighting crime that I would not see the peripheral issues."

The "peripheral issues" were acts of brazen corruption within the police force, unchallenged and unhindered at any level. One of the major scams that Niebur discovered was institutionalized car theft. Brand-new vehicles were being purchased for the police department. These top-of-the-line vehicles, including SUVs and Cadillacs, would then vanish from the inventory. With the help of the FBI, Niebur discovered the cars had been given to mobsters as gifts.

An even more widespread scam involved the towing of vehicles. Niebur learned that cars were being towed off the street on the pretext of parking violations, and then being sold as unclaimed. Worse, Niebur learned that the documents that certified the cars hadn't been claimed bore a forgery of his own signature. The police department was never even notified that the vehicles had been towed. Niebur found that the car theft had escalated to where it was completely out of control: at one point, two hundred cars were being towed every night, ostensibly because they were obstructing street sweepers. Residents whose cars were too old and battered to sell had to pay up to $800 in cash to get them back. When Niebur investigated the company that had the exclusive, and lucrative, contract to tow cars in Cicero, he discovered that in the space of two years it had contributed more than $30,000 to the political campaign of Betty Loren-Maltese.

Most of these corrupt practices predated Loren-Maltese, who had inherited a police department devoid of any sense of civic duty, or even legality. But Niebur is convinced Betty Loren-Maltese was implicated in these goings-on. "I believe Betty was condoning these scams, otherwise they wouldn't have lasted. Within a week I learned that nothing went on in the police department without Betty knowing. Everyone in local government was hired by Betty, and all of them were required to do political work for her. She had a system of informants: the minute anything happened, they ran to Betty."

Loren-Maltese's grip on her staff was secured by her use of spies and gossips. In spite of her professed ethos that they were all friends working together, there was a climate of fear in Cicero Town Hall, and colleagues were encouraged to inform on one another.

Niebur realized he had been hired under false pretences. "I had been convinced she was in earnest, that she wanted to rid the department of corruption. In fact, she wanted to be rid of people who went against her. She had political vendettas against police officers. The same people were fingered for disciplinary action again and again. No one dared speak publicly against her."

If she was not sincere in wanting the police force cleaned up, Loren-Maltese certainly made capital of her new appointee. Niebur lent an air of professionalism to her turbid police department. Just as she had with his predecessor, she required her new police chief to accompany her to functions: she wanted to show off the tough cop she had hired. And he, realizing the absurdity of his position, went along and played the part.

Loren-Maltese's vendetta against officers who were not politically aligned continued. Following an investigation of officers who lived outside the residence zone, around twenty were fired. These, according to Niebur, were officers who refused to do her electioneering work: they were required to canvas door to door *in uniform,* and anyone who refused to do so was fired. Others who opposed her election were reassigned. John J. Flood, president of the Combined Counties Police Association, commented: "It is clear that she is out of control."

There were other aspects of Betty's political work that rang alarm bells for Niebur. Her major fund-raiser was an annual golf outing, and Town Hall employees were expected to sell tickets. Small businesses that did not fork out $500 for a ticket would find the dreaded code enforcers on their doorsteps the following day, issuing fines. Some would be closed down altogether.

Niebur also had troubling evidence of infiltration of the police by organized crime. He had suggested to Loren-Maltese that she should ban the illegal joker-poker slot machines found in every diner, tavern, and launderette, which were widely known to be owned by the mob. She insisted they should stay. Later, he informed her that his men were going to seize the machines. By the time his teams got to work, most of the machines were gone—someone had been tipped off. The machines they did manage to seize were locked up in a police room, with the money still inside, and taped up with an invisible seal that would show if they'd been tampered with. The next day, all the machines had been unlocked and emptied. The door to the police room had been opened with a key, and the owner of the machines, a crime syndicate member, had been given all the time he needed to unlock and empty his cash boxes.

Niebur lasted four miserable, grinding months in the job. His work in Cicero ended when he handed over his records of the car-towing scam to the FBI. As soon as Betty discovered her police chief had been assisting the FBI's investigation, he was out.

"After we turned the towing records over to the FBI, I never had another conversation with her. I was completely frozen out," Niebur recalls. "A week before she fired me, she had a birthday party, a seven-course meal for two hundred people at an Italian restaurant. Until then there had not been one event at which I had not sat next to Betty at the top table. The first week I was hired, she had invited me and my wife to sit with her and the governor, George Ryan [who later came under investigation]. At this birthday party, my wife and I were put way in the back, and she was very cold to us.

"Betty could be very warm and very nice," Niebur adds. "She always wanted to pay for everything, always had large amounts of cash. If she liked you, there was nothing she wouldn't do for you. But if she took against you, there was nothing she wouldn't do to get back at you."

Niebur discovered he had been let go when he was at home on the evening of April 24, 1998, being debriefed by FBI agents. Two of Betty's people arrived at his house with a letter from her, saying he was suspended, and that his links with Cicero were at an end. They took his car and his uniform. She had him fired on the pretext of insubordination, with a series of trumped-up charges that were later thrown out at a tribunal. The charges were dismissed, and Niebur sued for wrongful dismissal. In March 2001, he was awarded $1 million in damages, but he still didn't get his job back. He hasn't worked since. No one, he points out, likes a whistle-blower.

"Betty is Betty," sighs Niebur, the super-tough cop she destroyed.

It is a measure of Betty's personal charisma and charm that people she has let go—usually on outrageous pretexts—can be persuaded to come back and work for her again.

One such person was Phillip Bue, who was hired by David Niebur as his deputy. Like Niebur, Phil Bue rose to the challenge of cleaning up Cicero. He believed it was his chance to make a difference.

Bue was put in charge of operations, which included billing and supplies—two areas mired in corruption. Although people always appeared willing to help, he remembers, once behind closed doors they would obstruct his orders. Bue doesn't doubt that the main obstruction was Betty, and yet he is still willing to concede that she was surrounded by villains and badly advised. "Betty was Cicero. Betty was the city council. Betty ruled, and Betty's rule was law. I point to the people around Betty. Had she had good lieutenants around her, she would have done a good job."

Even though she was firing police officers who violated residency requirements, she insisted that Bue should not have to move his family in order to conform. It was typical of Loren-Maltese's rule by personal favor. Bue was genuinely impressed that Loren-Maltese had successfully cleared out the sex industry in Cicero, shutting down the brothels and strip joints that used to litter the area (it was an initiative that went down well with residents). But even he was shocked by her behavior when she discovered that he and Niebur had handed the car-towing records to the FBI.

"It was like fire coming down from on high. Lawyers came running with writs saying Stop This and Cease That, then our charges came down . . . it was like fire from an angry god. I left that day. I said, I'm getting out of here, I don't know what's coming next.

"That evening she gave a press conference, in which she and her lawyer, Rick Rayle, produced a laundry list of trumped-up charges. They were malicious, damaging allegations—and really totally unnecessary. If she had called me and said, This isn't working out . . . I would have gone quietly. I didn't need to be dragged through the mud, and my family scared to death. It was incredibly uncalled for. But it was an attempt to cover up the fact that we were cooperating with the state on their investigation."

Even more telling was Loren-Maltese's behavior when, after his very public firing, Phil Bue was ordered to come back to work. "One of Betty's assistants called me to her office. There was Betty at the door, smiling, saying Welcome back. She said, 'Are you and your wife mad at me?' I said, 'Mad at you? Mad at you? The word is livid, Betty. None of this had to happen.' She looked down, like a little girl, and carried on with her business."

Even though Betty effectively ruined his life, Bue still manages to forgive her. He refuses to take it personally. "I like Betty very much," he says. "I thought she was very charming. She was very open with me, she was very cordial to me. I'm not a Betty hater, though she's caused a lot of heartaches in my life. I saw her as very humorous in a tongue-in-cheek, ribbing sort of way. Not the usual type of politician. She was pretty straightforward with me.

"Betty was very angry that we betrayed her. Loyalty is everything to her. There are many ways to betray Betty, it seems, since most of her closest friends seem to have fallen out with her."

Even those who have not yet fallen out with Betty seem to be afraid of her. Very few people were prepared to be interviewed, let alone quoted, on the subject of Betty Loren-Maltese. The word most often used about her is "vindictive": she has threatened writs against anyone who challenges her, and those who have entered into legal conflict with Loren-Maltese know she does not give up easily.

In April 2001, Loren-Maltese, who had beaten her old friend and new foe Emil Schullo to the Republican nomination, won a landslide election against Democratic challenger Joseph Mario Moreno. Federal monitors were called in to oversee the vote after a grubby campaign in which Moreno was accused by Loren-Maltese's people of being a drunk driver, a wife beater, and a deadbeat dad. When Moreno protested, the accusations were withdrawn—but she won anyway.

But while Loren-Maltese enjoyed her third term in office, federal investigators were putting the final touches on their case against her and the other beneficiaries of the SRC insurance heist. The U.S. Attorney's Office prepared charges against ten people involved in $12 million dollars of false insurance claims, all paid for with Cicero town funds. Named in the indictment were government officials and Mafia associates: Mayor Betty Loren-Maltese, former police chief Emil Schullo, and former town treasurer Joseph DeChicio, along with mob boss Michael Spano and his son Michael Jr., Spano's lawyer, Charles Schneider, and his business partner, John LaGiglio, as well as LaGiglio's wife, Bonnie. Also indicted were the brains behind SRC, accountant Greg Ross, and insurance expert Frank Taylor.

Early in the morning on Friday, June 15, federal agents arrived at Betty Loren-Maltese's lakeside home in Indiana. They were met by her armed guards, members of the Cicero police department, who were ordered to drop their weapons. She was served with a warrant for her arrest, and then the agents waited politely outside while she put on her face. She would need it to confront the media throng that awaited her inside the revolving doors of the federal courthouse.

The same day, the head of the Chicago FBI gave a press conference, and announced: "The Cicero candy store is closed."

21

THE first day of the trial of Mayor Betty Loren-Maltese, mobster Michael Spano, and their six codefendants was an event anticipated with glee by the Chicago media. This would be the first time government officials and mob bosses had ever been seen together at the defense table in federal court. The trial opened on May 30, 2002, almost a year after the arrests, which had given reporters and columnists plenty of time to gear up their coverage for the Betty show. The camera tripods were massed in the federal building's echoing marble hall. Although the defendants accused of racketeering, fraud, money laundering, and income tax violations included an ex–chief of police and a bottle-blonde mob wife, as well as the mob boss and his son, Betty was the one the people had come to see.

She did not disappoint: although dressed down for court in a modest dark green trouser suit with a small, understated stars-and-stripes pin, her hair was big, her lashes were long, and her lipstick was Bazooka pink. She arrived at the courthouse every day escorted by two security guards, and was always accompanied by at least one loyal supporter, sometimes two or three, handpicked from her still-devoted following in City Hall.

The first day in court presented a tough test for Loren-Maltese: under the searching eyes of the media, she was forced to sit in a serpent's nest of her worst enemies. These men had been her friends, and they had betrayed her. She had not spoken to Spano, or Schullo, or any of them, for years, since their bitter falling out, and she didn't intend to start now. If they did exchange a few words, it was, as Betty put it, "Nothing you could print." Her lawyers had strived to have her case tried separately but had been turned down. So here she was, stuck in a federal courtroom in Chicago—not Cicero, where she could have expected a regular turnout of loyal supporters—surrounded by people she could not look in the eye. Every time she raised her head from doodling in her notepad, she was confronted by the sight of Emil, overweight and slightly scruffy, sitting directly opposite her. Her proximity to a man who had caused her so much pain and embarrassment made her squirm.

At the end of the first day, Loren-Maltese's lawyer, the genial Terence Gillespie, had a discreet word with the judge in chambers. Explaining that there was some history between the players on trial, Gillespie asked for a change to the seating arrangement. Judge Grady, who was intent on keeping this unwieldy and politically explosive pool of defendants under control, agreed. The following day, another massive table was hauled in, and the defendants and their lawyers split into two groups, one behind the other. Loren-Maltese and her attorneys sat at the front table, with Schullo and his lawyer off to her right. This way, when she looked up from her notes, the worst sight that would assail her would be the prosecution team at their table in the center of the courtroom, led by the youthful-looking, spiky-haired Assistant U.S. Attorney Mitch Mars.

The opening bout was nasty and undignified, as each defendant laid the blame on the others. Loren-Maltese's attorney maintained throughout the trial that his client was out of her depth as town president, and that she was perhaps not entirely on top of things (this insulting reference to his client's intellect was spoken blushingly, almost apologetically). It was a view of Mayor Betty that must have surprised anybody who had worked for her.

Before the opening skirmish, defense counsel and prosecutors alike were expressly forbidden to mention organized crime. Judge Grady had ruled that any talk of organized crime would muddy the waters. To the great disappointment of both the media and the prosecution (not to mention the jury), the evidence was largely based on the paper trail tracked by IRS accountants: instead of mob scandals, the court was shown invoices and phone bills. And as the trial dragged on for more than thirteen weeks, deprived of the merest mention of Al Capone, reporters complained bitterly about its dullness.

By popular consent, the high point was the appearance on the stand of Lila Torello, the seventy-year-old widow of the notorious mob enforcer Turk Torello, also known as "the Butcher." Torello had run a trucking company, later run by Michael Spano and John LaGiglio, that served as the mob's base of operations in Cicero. Lila, whose late husband rather improbably used to call her Doodle, cut an elegant figure in court, wearing high heels and a gold shawl. Under questioning, she revealed that she had lent $460,000 to Spano and LaGiglio—which dispelled any doubts about what sort of inheritance Turk must have left her when he died at only forty-eight. She still lives in the fancy stone-clad Cicero house, with an imposing front porch and wrought-iron work on the windows and doors, that she had shared with her husband. Spano had invested her money in the Wisconsin golf course—although, unlike Betty, she had not seen any return on her loan. She had, however, obtained a promissory note from Spano, pledging to repay her at ten percent. "I never lent any money to anyone at less than 10 percent," she testified under a grant of immunity, displaying all the pride and dignity one might expect of a rich mob widow.

Listening to her testimony, Spano merely smiled.

During breaks in the proceedings, Loren-Maltese and her pals would hot-foot it down twelve floors in the elevator and stand outside the revolving doors smoking cigarettes. This became the place for her informal press briefings, where reporters could approach her for a few words. In spite of the strain, Betty would usually manage a witty or self-deprecating remark.

As the trial drew to a close, prosecutors put the finishing touches on their portrayal of Loren-Maltese as the controlling figure behind the fraud scheme. The jury was told that wire transfers of money rose sharply soon after her appointment as town president in early 1993. They were told that Loren-Maltese saw all the paperwork, and "knew what was going on." Votes on most town issues were unanimous, prosecutor Matt Schneider said: "You don't dissent when Betty Loren-Maltese is running the town board. She was totally in control of government and politics."

In spite of her attorney's instructions not to talk to the media, toward the end of the trial, the irrepressible Betty could contain herself no longer. She suddenly popped up on a local radio talk show, and did a couple of quick interviews with the papers, spouting the rebuttals that she might have made had she been asked to take the stand. Speaking to the *Chicago Tribune*, Loren-Maltese said she never knew Spano or LaGiglio to be criminals. "I knew them as my husband's friends," she said, adding that Spano "befriended" her after her husband's death, and that they would gamble at the riverboats twice a month. She maintained she was an innocent party to this friendship: "Knowing someone and being involved in illegal activity is two different things."

"I won't be convicted of guilt by association," she told a crowd of reporters and TV cameras in the lobby of the courthouse.

On August 23, after a marathon eleven days of deliberations, the jury found Loren-Maltese and five of her codefendants, including Michael Spano Sr., guilty of racketeering and conspiracy. Bonnie LaGiglio was convicted only of tax fraud. Only former town treasurer Joseph DeChicio was acquitted. As the verdicts were read, Loren-Maltese looked down. After nearly ten years, she would be stripped of her position as mayor. Her attorneys attempted to escort her out of the courthouse without making a statement, but the hoard of reporters and photographers jostling for a look at the fallen woman were too much, even for battle-hardened Betty. She retreated into the building, and was later whisked out of a rear entrance. For once, crowed the papers, Betty has nothing to say.

Soon afterward, however, Betty was crying foul to the local press, and portraying herself as a victim, landed in trouble by her late husband. She told a reporter she had gone to her office to clear her desk and yelled at Frank's picture: "What the hell did you get me into?"

"I've not been at the cemetery to see Frank since I was arrested," she said. "I feel like he betrayed me, too. No matter how good he seemed to me and all the good things he did for me, he used me."

Several other people have also described Betty as a victim, saying that her husband set her up in an impossible position with the mob breathing down her neck, and that she couldn't avoid doing business with them. "The rule behind the scenes has always been organized

crime, since the days of Al Capone," says local historian Richard
Lindberg. "Betty was put up by Henry Klosak and Frank Maltese.
She was in a sense a victim of the whole situation. Betty inherited a
link with organized crime."

However, Lindberg acknowledges that if Betty had a certain
complicity with her mob bosses at the start, she soon found her own
way of doing business. "She went along with the system. She was
controlled but she knew what was going on. When she was handed
power, she enjoyed it and knew what to do with it. She knew how
to hang on to it."

Those who describe Betty as a victim very likely take that view
because she was a woman, and as such, assumed she was unable to
stand up to the mob. No one called Frank Maltese a victim. There
are those who believe she genuinely wanted to make a change in
Cicero. One of those friends, who she later fired and vilified, now
says: "Back then I really believed she wanted to do the right thing.
She was a nice person. I felt she was a good person surrounded with
bad people, who gave her bad advice."

Loren-Maltese called the verdict "unjust" and "unfair," while her
attorney insisted there was no evidence that she had received the
monies alleged by the prosecution, and announced her intention to
appeal. (At the time of writing, her appeal is still pending.) But the
government had not finished with Betty. In November, she was tried
on her own for tax fraud. Prosecutors tried to show that she deliberately failed to declare the $350,000 of ill-gotten gains she invested in
the Wisconsin golf course and spent on her sporty Cadillac Allante.

Betty declared the government was trying to destroy her. After the
tax case ended in a mistrial, the government was less interested in destroying Betty than in getting its money back, and sought restitution
of $10 million from Loren-Maltese and her codefendants. The Wis-
consin golf course was already in government hands, but the feds were
eyeing other properties, including Spano's summer residence, and a
house in Las Vegas belonging to Loren-Maltese.

The discovery of this luxurious home in Vegas, which Loren-
Maltese had bought for $460,000 in 2000, had caused an outcry in
the Chicago press: while Loren-Maltese was using residency requirements as a pretext to fire police officers who would not do her po-

litical work, she had herself been living part of the week in Nevada. She moved her elderly mother, Kitty, and her adopted daughter, Ashleigh Rose, now five years old, into the house in an upscale gated community, and spent three days of every week there.

The hacienda-style house, with terra-cotta roof tiles, has four bedrooms, a three-car garage and a swimming pool. Loren-Maltese claimed that she had sold her Indiana vacation home to buy it because she wanted to move her family to a safe place after receiving threats. Some demurred that Sin City was not necessarily the place you would pick if you were looking for a stable, safe home for your mother and child. But Betty's motives for buying a place in Vegas soon became clear. Although her nights out gambling on the riverboats with Mike Spano had come to an end, her love affair with the slot machines was far from over. While trying to get a handle on her finances, the government obtained records of Betty's gambling habits during the trial period. What they found was staggering. Loren-Maltese had wagered $18.8 million at casinos in Indiana, Illinois, and Nevada over three years, and spent more than sixteen hundred hours gambling in 2000 and 2001. Papers filed by the prosecution in early January 2003 showed she had wagered more than $12.1 million at the Flamingo Casino in Las Vegas over two years. A detailed breakdown of the hours spent at each casino showed Betty's gambling habit intensifying as the trial wore on. The Friday before the verdict was due, Betty was at the Trump Casino in Gary, Indiana, from midnight till after 4 A.M. By nine o'clock that night, she was back at the slots, and stayed until after three in the morning.

"She gambled in the early morning, late morning, early afternoon, late afternoon, early evening, late evening; pick any hour of the day . . . ," said prosecutor Mitch Mars. The prosecution's impressive charts of Betty's casino attendance note that on Christmas Day 2001 Betty visited the Rampart Casino in Las Vegas, where she remained at the slot machines till dawn.

Special Agent Paulin observes: "Her gambling got to ridiculous levels right after the indictment, and during the trial it was like a person on a binge."

This snapshot of a gambling addict was a bizarre new twist in the saga of Betty Loren-Maltese, but it would not be the last. The prosecution had sought the details of Betty's slot-machine slavery to counter her attempt to portray herself as a good mother. Her attorneys were seeking a reduction of her sentence on the grounds that she was a single mother and needed to be at home to take care of her child. The prosecution declared that the extent of her gambling "suggests that Loren-Maltese's quality time commitment to her daughter has been substantially limited by Loren-Maltese's quality time commitment to casino gambling." Loren-Maltese's lawyer denied this: "None of the time that she was gambling took away from the time that she should have or could have been spending with her daughter."

The next round of the skirmish over Betty's sentencing got even nastier. Ashleigh Rose's biological mother, Dawn, now remarried and using her new husband's name Weleba, saw a news report on TV in which Loren-Maltese's lawyers claimed that, if Loren-Maltese went to jail, Ashleigh could become a ward of the state. Weleba said that rather than see her daughter sent to a foster home, she would take her back. Adoption laws rule out this sort of to-and-fro parenting, but that did not prevent an ugly episode in which Weleba told news reporters she had been pressured into giving up her baby, and that Loren-Maltese had adopted the child "for political gain." Others accused Loren-Maltese of adopting the child knowing that she was likely to go to prison, and believing that, when the time came, being a single parent would gain her a lighter sentence. Weleba's offer received no response, and the child continues to be cared for by Loren-Maltese's octogenarian mother.

When it came to sentencing Loren-Maltese, Judge Grady was severe. He chastised her for abusing the trust invested in her position, and made no allowance for the fact that she is a single mother, even raising a question about the wisdom of her decision to adopt. "I have no reason to doubt the expression of love that she has made in this court," Grady said. He did, however, "have substantial reservation of the timing of the adoption in relation to her notice of the fact that she was a pretty good candidate for a criminal prosecution."

A candlelight vigil had been held by her supporters outside Loren-Maltese's Cicero home before the sentencing, and the judge received dozens of letters from loyal supporters, full of praise for Betty. But the letters produced the opposite effect than the one intended. Judge Grady accused her of "wholesale betrayal of the naïve faith of a whole town of trusting people."

Grady also cut down the defense's assertion that Betty Loren-Maltese was an innocent dupe of the insurance scam's real perpetrators: "What Mrs. Maltese did was to permit the looting of some $12 million from the treasury of the Town of Cicero. She did it single-handedly. . . . She didn't need to tell any underling to do anything. She did it all herself. Why? Because she was the boss. She was the unchallenged boss. She ran that town in a way that was tight and admitting of no contradiction, no opposition, no objection. . . . If anybody did try to object or raise an objection, she fired them."

Grady declared Loren-Maltese's contact with Spano and LaGiglio "highly incriminating." Summing up, Grady said: "I have searched as thoroughly as I can for some trace of a mitigating circumstance, and I am unable to find one, not a single one."

Betty Loren-Maltese was sentenced to eight years in prison. Her share of the theft was determined to be $3.25 million, which she was ordered to repay. Since she had refused to provide any information as to her income or assets, Judge Grady acknowledged that the government was going to have a hard time collecting. "It's going to be like pulling teeth collecting the first penny of the forfeiture."

Knowing, by now, that the likely response of Loren-Maltese to such distressing news would be to head for the nearest casino and stay there till morning, the government requested that she be banned from gambling. In the end, Grady simplified matters by bringing forward the start of her imprisonment.

So it was that, on January 31, 2003, Betty Loren-Maltese was picked up from Oakland Airport by her friend and lawyer, Rick Rayle, and delivered in a rented SUV to the minimum-security women's unit at the federal penitentiary at Dublin, California. Dublin had already enjoyed a certain amount of notoriety as the place of confinement for Hollywood madam Heidi Fleiss and kidnapped-heiress-turned-bank-robber Patty Hearst. Inmates reportedly address Betty as "Mayor." Her daughter, Ashleigh Rose, seeing her flat-haired adoptive mother for perhaps the first time ever, asked her, "What happened to your head?"

Loren-Maltese maintains she had no involvement with the mafia, and was guilty by association only. "Because I was Town President," she told a reporter, "[they said] I had to know, which is not fair."

Meanwhile, back at the IRS offices in downtown Chicago, Special Agent Bill Paulin says we haven't heard the last of Betty. If anything, says Paulin, she may emerge stronger than her foe, Mike Spano. "She became more ruthless, definitely more aggressive. It's only odd in that she's a female, and that's what's unique about her, that she's been able to survive and get to a level that really goes beyond the usual. She's become very much like Rocky Infelise: after all, she learned from him."

Paulin does not see Betty Loren-Maltese as a servant of the mob, nor does he agree that she was "used" by her husband and his friends or, as some have claimed, was a victim of circumstance. "As far as I'm concerned she is in the mob. Everybody has a role. Her role was to be the political arm of organized crime. One can't exist without the other: it was a very responsible high position."

Though Betty has lost her job at City Hall and even jokes about having to work, along with her eighty-year-old mother, as a waitress, Paulin does not believe she is finished. "She's not out of it. You're really never out of organized crime. [The Chicago mob] may still view her as an asset. If she maintains a semblance of power, they may still keep her around."

22

AS the mistress of a mob boss, Dorothy Suffel felt she had found a place in the glamorous world of organized crime. She had trained as a lawyer but had always been fascinated by mob figures, who were treated like celebrities in her neighborhood of Middle Village, Queens. Although her parents were perfectly respectable, law-abiding people—her father was a professor, her mother worked in a law firm—like most people she knew, they had friends who were connected in some way. That's the way it was in her neighborhood. When it came to it, Dorothy's decision to cross the line from the legitimate world to the Mafia was a small step. Like many other genuinely law-abiding people, she was impressed by the respect that mobsters commanded, the aura of excitement around them. Although she was not a natural felon, and breaking the law, even in small ways, made her terribly anxious, she was drawn to the glamour and excitement of their lives—or what looked like excitement from the outside. Blinded by admiration, she allowed herself to be involved in criminal activities that she would live to regret.

When she first met the Mafia boss who would wreak havoc in her life, Dorothy was twenty-eight. Having been with the same man since her teens, she now found her marriage had run into difficulties; she was not sure which way her life was going and was very vulnerable. She entered the precarious role of the boss's *goombada* under the illusion that it would give her some status in his world. A

Mafia mistress enjoys the confidence of her man, often to a greater extent than his wife does; if she can be useful to him, he is liable to involve her in his work. Dorothy liked the idea that she could have a role as an associate and do business for the mob. But if she believed that being a mistress she would enjoy a degree of freedom and autonomy, she would learn the hard way that a *goombada*, just like everyone else, is under the boss's control.

After getting involved with the Mafia, Dorothy lost her moral compass; she lost all sense of who she was. The aspiring lawyer would transgress the rules of both civil society and the Mafia and, ultimately, she would find she no longer had a place in either world.

Dorothy Suffel, tall and slim, with long legs and long blonde hair, graduated from beauty school when she was twenty and went to work at a hair salon in Queens. Her clients included wiseguys who had been involved with the Pizza Connection, an international heroin trafficking ring. In 1988, aged twenty-one, she married Anthony Tamboni, her boyfriend of several years, and they moved into an apartment on Hanover Square in Manhattan. A few months after their marriage, Dorothy embarked on a career in law. Having been encouraged by her mother to get legal training, she earned a law degree from St. John's, as well and some credits toward a master's. Throughout her twenties, however, she remained undecided about her vocation and shuttled back and forth between hair salons in Queens and law offices in Manhattan.

After a few years she and Anthony, an electrician, were doing well enough to buy a second apartment down the hall, for Dorothy to use as an office. But if the couple were prospering financially, their relationship was not going so well. Dorothy would later reveal, although she did not give any details, that in the summer of 1994 they started having problems from which they would never really recover. The couple's relationship was still under strain in December of that year. Both very sociable people, they would go to parties and get drunk, and then have terrible fights. One of those parties would prove fatal to their marriage, and change Dorothy's life forever.

On December 16, 1994, Dorothy and her husband went to a

Christmas party given by a family friend named John Lombardi—
John and Dorothy's fathers had been best friends for years. One of
the people who noticed Dorothy that night was Andrew Russo, a
powerful figure in the Colombo crime family. She knew Russo as
John's uncle. Their families were old friends from Queens, and her
parents knew Russo's sister. Dorothy also knew he was in the Mafia:
Russo's arrest in the 1980s had been much talked about in the
neighborhood, including at the salon where Dorothy had worked.

It did not escape Dorothy's notice that Russo was treated with
respect by the other party guests. People around him behaved as
though he were a movie star. Dorothy and her husband had been arguing a lot, and after a few drinks, she craved some male attention.
His sister introduced her to Andrew. At sixty-one, he was much
older than Dorothy. He had thinning gray hair and a deeply lined
face, but, as they spent a few minutes chatting and flirting, she found
him charismatic.

"I've heard a lot about you," she said. "I heard you represented
yourself in court."

Russo laughed. Dorothy had him confused with his cousin, former Colombo boss Carmine "the Snake" Persico, who had defended himself in a murder conspiracy case. "You're thinking of
someone else," he said. "My sister says you're a lawyer. You do any
criminal law?"

"No," she replied. Her bits of freelance work hardly qualified her
to be called a practicing lawyer, but it always sounded good. "At the
moment I just do some entertainment law."

They talked for a few more minutes, then someone else came up
to pay their respects to Russo, and Dorothy slipped away. But Andrew caught up with her later: a bunch of people were going on to
Elaine's, so why didn't she and her husband come along?

A few days later, Dorothy saw her friend John, who told her that
she had made quite an impression at his party. "Andrew was very
struck with you," he said. "In fact, he told me he thinks you're the
best thing since sliced bread."

John told Dorothy she should be honored by his uncle's attention. And she had to admit that, in spite of everything—their age

difference, the fact that they were both married, and that he was a convicted felon—she was. She and her husband went out with Russo and his wife, Ruthie, a couple of times after the Christmas party. Because he was her parents' age, and because she wanted to show respect, they called Russo "Uncle Andrew."

Every time John invited her to a party with Uncle Andrew and his crowd, he impressed on her what a privilege it was. At one party, Dorothy and Andrew downed several martinis and flirted outrageously with each other. The following day, she got a phone call. It was Uncle Andrew, inviting her out to see the farm at Crane Neck on Long Island where he was staying. Whether or not she gave a fleeting thought to her foundering marriage at that moment, Dorothy accepted. At around midday she drove out to Long Island but got lost on the way. He came out to meet her, and they had lunch at a nearby Italian restaurant, where they again had several martinis each.

After lunch they walked unsteadily to their cars and drove over to Crane Neck, passing several impressive mansions along the way. Once inside the farm's electronic security gate, Dorothy was given a tour. The place belonged to Russo's friend Dennis Hickey, who had made his money in garbage and was proud of it. He had built himself a fine retreat, with a gazebo on the water, a statue of a bull, and ornaments made from garbage cans decorating the yard. A helicopter landing pad featuring Hickey's initials was also marked out with garbage cans. Russo was the mob muscle for Hickey's garbage business, and had the run of the place. The house was well protected, with video cameras and infrared sensors in the driveway to warn of any unexpected company. Safe inside their electronic haven, Dorothy and Uncle Andrew, relaxed and laughing after their boozy lunch, had sex in the afternoon.

The following day, she returned to Crane Neck, and this time found the farm on her own. Russo was waiting. He was living at Hickey's place while his wife stayed at home, which made it easy for Dorothy to see him alone. He told her there was a lot of heat on him: the cops were always snooping around; it was easier to stay somewhere else. Besides, since he had come out of prison the previous August, he had found it difficult to adjust to being with his wife again.

His marriage was not the only thing troubling Andrew Russo at the time. His son, Jojo, along with his nephew, had been convicted of conspiracy to murder and racketeering, and was serving a life sentence.

The Colombo family had been in turmoil since the 1980s, when they were hit with the full force of the RICO law: in 1987 the boss, Carmine Persico, and his underboss were both given one-hundred-year sentences. Persico had made capo Vic Orena the acting boss until his son got out of jail, but in 1991 Orena made his own bid for leadership and the family split into factions. The two crews waged an all-out war, firing at each other from cars and lying in ambush, engaging in frenzied shoot-outs in the city. By the end of the war, the faction loyal to Persico was victorious, but the cost was high: twelve people were dead, including two innocent bystanders, and many more were wounded. In 1992, Orena was convicted of racketeering and murder. During the Colombo war Andrew Russo had been in jail, serving eight years for labor racketeering. After his release, he was given the title of acting boss.

One of Dorothy's first dates with Andrew was a trip to federal court, where Jojo Russo's lawyer was petitioning for a retrial. It was perhaps not the most romantic outing, but such legal battles were a fact of mob life, and Dorothy desperately wanted to be part of it. In court, Dorothy saw Jojo waving from the defense table. Since Andrew's parole conditions prevented him from associating with other organized crime members, he couldn't visit his son in prison, and he asked Dorothy to go instead. He told her it was because Jojo would be lonely, but he had other motives. With her legal credentials, Dorothy could visit a prisoner without questions being asked—and she could always claim client confidentiality. She was the perfect person to deliver messages back and forth for them.

Dorothy had never been inside a prison before, and the first time she went to the Metropolitan Correctional Center (MCC) in downtown Manhattan to visit Jojo, wearing stretch trousers and boots, she was turned away for being inappropriately dressed. Mortified, she rushed home to change, thinking she had made a complete fool of herself, and that the other attorneys would know that she wasn't a proper lawyer. After her first visit, she started going up to the MCC every Wednesday morning, arriving as close to eight o'clock as she could manage (she was frequently late) and staying till noon, chatting to Jojo and delivering messages from his father. Each time she went, Andrew would give her a bundle of trial transcripts to carry in her briefcase, so it would look as though she and Jojo were working on his case.

Dorothy soon found she enjoyed making herself useful. After talking to Jojo, she would stick around to visit with his codefendants in the MCC. Jojo sent her to observe other trials taking place in Brooklyn federal court involving members of the Colombo crime family. She was glad to do it: it made her feel part of the scene. Russo and his crew used a code—everyone had a nickname, such as Faces or Dick Tracy—and she would write them down carefully in a notebook to avoid making mistakes. Nervous about getting something wrong, she knew that asking questions would only cause trouble. In time she became far more anxious about getting in trouble with her mob friends than about breaking the law.

For a while, she felt she'd become Russo's regular girlfriend. He took her to restaurants, to nightclubs, and to see *Phantom of the Opera*. And they constantly went to parties—however dire their legal troubles might be, Russo and his friends loved to party. On one occasion Dorothy took her husband to a party at Crane Neck. The guests included singer Laine Kazan and actor James Caan. Dorothy's husband had brought his camcorder along. As he swept the lens across the room, taking in the glittering crowd, James Caan playing the piano, he focused on his wife, slow-dancing with Uncle Andrew.

Before the end of January, Dorothy had been let into another secret chamber in Russo's mysterious life. One night he received a phone call while they were at the house in Crane Neck. After he got off the phone, Russo told Dorothy they were going for a drive together. They followed the Long Island Expressway several miles farther out on the island until they finally reached a horse farm, also owned by garbage magnate Dennis Hickey. Once inside the house, Andrew introduced Dorothy to a woman whom he called Teresa—but she corrected him, "No, I'm Lauri, my name is Lauri."

It turned out that Teresa Castranova, a.k.a. Lauri, was hiding out at the farm to avoid a subpoena. During Jojo Russo's trial, she had recognized one of the jurors as an old school friend, and after the guilty verdict, Russo had sent a private detective over to the juror's house to try to elicit information that might help in his appeal. The woman had gone straight to the judge, and Teresa had been summoned to give an account of her actions before a grand jury. Rather than face the subpoena, she decided to go into hiding.

If Dorothy had been paying attention, she might have glimpsed her own future in how Teresa Castranova was being forced to live. She might have realized that having an affair with a mob boss was not something you could do and then stop doing, that although you weren't a wife, or even a number-one girlfriend, the relationship would take over your life. But Dorothy was not attending to danger signs. She was loving the Mafia life. She had even started to talk like her new friends, casually dropping words like "heat" into conversation. To reinforce the almost ritualistic fantasy world she had entered, none of her new friends used their own names. Teresa was Lauri, or Frankie, or the Brat. Russo was Big Guy, or simply "our friend." Jojo, who always had great plans to open casinos and buy yachts, was known as Gatsby. Teresa called Dorothy "Oz," as in *The Wizard of Oz*, while Andrew referred to her as "the lawyer." Having her own nickname gave Dorothy the feeling of being part of the gang. After they started sleeping together, Andrew told her she had better stop calling him "uncle": he liked to call them "the gangster and the lawyer."

Despite these quaint monikers, the Oz-like unreality into which she had descended would, in a short time, start to unravel. Unlike her cinematic namesake, however, for Dorothy the warning signs of darker challenges that lay ahead would not be spelled out plainly, in cursive skywriting. Indeed, Dorothy would have to become more intimate with the Russos and their circle, and more closely bound to their needs, before she could begin to see just how dangerous they were.

23

DOROTHY and Teresa began to spend a good deal of time together; whatever days they didn't see each other, they spoke on
the phone. Their friendship began with an exchange of confi-
dences: over lunch one day, Teresa revealed that she was Jojo Russo's
girlfriend. Teresa had gone every day to watch his trial and offer her
support, but she had not been able to visit him in the MCC because
of the risk that someone would spot her.

As they made their way through a bottle of wine, Teresa said, "I
know about you and Andrew."

Dorothy was surprised, because Andrew had told her not to tell
anyone about them, but she was pleased that Teresa knew. It helped
to have someone to talk to.

Meanwhile, Dorothy was proving more and more useful to Russo.
Her trips to the farm to keep Teresa company were a service to Jojo,
who was aware of the sacrifice Teresa was making, stranded out in the
country, separated from her son who was living with her mother during the week. Teresa talked a lot about Jojo's trial: she was obsessed
with the possibility that his conviction would be overturned. She
went over and over the facts of the case, returning to her theme that
Jojo was innocent and had been wrongfully convicted. In Dorothy,
she found a sympathetic listener.

Dorothy was now spending all her time with her new friends.
After she had been seeing Russo for just two months, he remarked
that it felt as though they had known each other for two years. He

started giving her advice on how to dress: since she was posing as his lawyer, he said she should try to look a little less flashy. Dorothy had always liked dressing up; she wore chunky jewelry, high-heeled shoes, and very short skirts. She used to binge shop for clothes, running up huge credit card bills during shopping sprees on Fifth Avenue, fitting herself out like a Mafia princess. Ironically, here was a mobster telling her she was overdressed.

Dorothy's husband was losing patience. Since the night he'd caught her on camera in the arms of Andrew Russo, he could never seem to get her on the phone. One night, while she was out having dinner with Russo and Dennis Hickey's wife, her pager beeped continuously. It was her husband. When she finally called him, he said, "If you don't come home now, don't bother coming home at all."

"Fine," she said, and hung up. That night she stayed with Russo at Crane Neck. Her marriage was over, but she had a new man and a whole new life.

Her new life began to look a bit of a mess when, the following night, she had to sleep on the floor of the apartment she and her husband had bought to use as an office. She stayed up at the farm with Teresa for a couple of nights, but then that became a problem: Andrew told her that she and Teresa were seeing too much of each other and could be arousing suspicion. Sometimes she slept in her office, but it was far from ideal—it was just a few doors down the corridor from the place she had shared with her husband. Often Dorothy stayed at her mother's house in Queens.

In the meantime, she was doing a lot of legwork for the Russo family. She found them property lawyers for conveyancing various properties they had acquired in New York and Florida, she obtained money orders and paid bills and mortgages. When Russo talked about opening a nightclub, she even offered to get a liquor license—she had always wanted to run a bar or a restaurant, and she thought this might be her chance. Perhaps she could see herself running a mob joint, where she'd be surrounded by tough guys who would laugh and joke with her. She desperately wanted to be part of their world and gain their approval. She would have done almost anything, and they encouraged her: for them, a woman with legal training and no previous convictions was very useful.

Dorothy soon discovered, however, that life with the Russos was fraught with difficulties and unseen dangers. The more she helped them, the more worried she became about making a mistake. Her anxiety was heightened by a friend of Jojo's, who warned her that she was being manipulated. "They're going to put you in the middle," he told her. "They're going to tell you to tell somebody something and if they don't like the message, they'll blame it on you, they'll say you got it wrong."

Inevitably, Dorothy got caught up between Jojo and Teresa. When Jojo first went to jail, Teresa had written him anonymous letters with fake return addresses. Even so, she worried that these might be traced. Now that Dorothy was on the scene, Teresa could give the letters to her. She also made sandwiches for Jojo, which Dorothy was to hide in her briefcase (it was against prison regulations to bring in food). So Dorothy's briefcase, along with legal documents and illegal sandwiches, contained love letters from a fugitive from justice, letters with SWAK—"sealed with a kiss"—scrawled on the back.

During Dorothy's visits, Jojo would read the letters, then tear them up and give them back to her. Teresa had told her friend not to throw the ripped-up letters in the trash, in case someone was following her and could retrieve the pieces. She was told to flush the pieces down the toilet. These instructions only added to Dorothy's nervousness. It hadn't occurred to her that she might be followed. If something went wrong everyone would know it was *her fault*. She became so paranoid she started keeping the letters in her legal folders. When a folder was full, she would store it and start a new one. After a few months, she had piles of incriminating papers in her possession that she didn't know how to dispose of.

Without meaning to, she accumulated information about her new friends in organized crime, in itself a dangerous thing. One night she was having dinner with a friend in Manhattan when Andrew paged her.

"Hey, what're you doing?" he asked. He sounded a little drunk.

"Having dinner with a friend," she told him. "What about you?"

"You're not going to believe this," he said.

"What?"

"They're making me boss."

Dorothy was taken aback. After she had been warned so many times against talking openly about business, here was Andrew telling her *on the phone* that he was being made boss of the Colombo crime family. He had had a few beers to celebrate and was obviously dying to tell someone.

Obviously Russo thought he had total control over Dorothy. Her role as messenger and go-between had become semiofficial—if she made a payment or did some other business, she would be given a few hundred dollars. At Easter, Russo gave her a "gift" of $2,500. In addition, Dorothy's legal qualifications, such as they were, meant that all her dealings with the family were covered by lawyer-client confidentiality, and she could never be forced to testify. For the moment, this protected her as well as everyone else.

During this time, Teresa started watching Dorothy closely. She had occupied Dorothy's role before the subpoena came down, and she was beginning to feel jealous. While Andrew was in prison, Teresa had written to him and visited him, bringing news of Jojo's trial. She had been studying to be a paralegal so she could help Jojo with his legal affairs; she had been the trusted confidante in the heart of the family. After Jojo's conviction, she had gone so far as to try out various disguises, including a long curly brown wig, to see if she could get into the MCC without being recognized. Now she was stuck out at the farm, and here was this blonde, going to see her man every other day.

There was one family ritual Dorothy was left out of. Every week, Teresa cooked a big Sunday lunch for Dennis Hickey, his wife, and Andrew up at the farm. Dennis and his wife were close friends of Andrew's wife, and although they saw Dorothy often enough at restaurants, she was not welcome at these intimate Sunday meals. Sundays were lonely times for Dorothy, newly separated. They were family days, it sometimes seemed, for everyone but her.

On one of these Sundays, as it turned out, Dorothy was glad she had left the farm early. While Teresa was preparing Sunday lunch, Andrew's probation officer turned up at the house unexpectedly. Teresa fled upstairs at the sound of the car and hid under the bed, while Andrew gave the probation officer a brisk tour of the outbuildings. All the while, Teresa's little son, who was visiting the farm as he did most weekends, ran around shouting, "Where's mommy?"

Eventually, the constant mood of impending danger within Dorothy's new circle began to do its damage. Everyone watched his own back while trying to manipulate the others. Andrew Russo did not want allegiances between other members of his crew and friends to grow too strong, and he felt threatened by the bond between Dorothy and Teresa. Both women had become malleable because of their infatuation with the crime family and, sure enough, they turned on each other.

April 29 was Teresa's birthday, and the women went out to a disco to celebrate. Dorothy was out of sorts. She had been with Russo for four months and he was still no nearer to making any kind of commitment to her: he said he wanted to carry on seeing her, but he refused to stop seeing his other girlfriends—"I have obligations to other people," he told her. Teresa said she thought he was treating Dorothy very badly, and told her to forget about him and find herself another man. Dorothy wasn't much in the mood for flirting, but there was a man at the disco who was paying her a lot of attention. She got pretty drunk, and after a couple of dances, with Teresa's encouragement, she went outside with him. They got into his car and he kissed her. They made out in the car for a long time. Dorothy was so drunk she didn't have an idea of the time. After a couple of hours, Teresa had to come looking for her. The dancing had ended and the bar was closed. They went back inside, and Dorothy staggered to the bathroom, where she threw up. After this unpromising beginning, the following week Dorothy saw the man for a date.

At the end of May, Dorothy took a vacation in Italy for a few days. She was beginning to realize she would never be Russo's only girlfriend, that he would never leave his wife; she would only ever be his *goombada,* and she wanted more. She and her husband, Anthony, had seen each other a few times since the night he told her not to come home, and when she came back from Italy, she moved back in with him. But they could not work it out, and after two weeks of fighting, she left again.

Meanwhile, some new poison was infecting her mob friends. Teresa had been to visit Jojo in jail while she was away—the grand jury investigation had concluded, so she was no longer under threat of a subpoena. Dorothy and Teresa were at Jojo's house, visiting his wife Lucretia, when everything blew up. When the two women left the house and got into their car, Teresa started yelling at Dorothy, accusing her of flirting with her man. Jojo had told her that Dorothy had been coming on to him during their long hours in the prison visiting room. Meanwhile, Teresa had left her handbag behind by accident, and while the women were having a screaming fight in the car, Lucretia was looking through the bag, where she found a letter and read all about Teresa's affair with Jojo. By the time they got back to the farm, Jojo's wife was on the phone, yelling and crying, and demanding the truth about Teresa's relationship with her husband.

Soon after that horrible night, Russo and Dorothy were driving home from a party in Manhattan when Russo told her he couldn't see her anymore. "Teresa told me everything," he said. "Don't we have enough problems without you dating an FBI agent?"

Dorothy was shocked. After encouraging her to date the guy she met at the disco, Teresa had decided—or pretended—that the man was an agent, and had gone straight to Russo. She had played right along with Russo's tactic of fostering jealousies between those closest to him. Dorothy phoned Teresa and asked her: "Why did you do that? You knew they would try to turn us against each other, you told me that."

"I had to do it," said Teresa. "I'm sorry, but I had to do it, I love him and I'm not going to let him get hurt."

Whatever Teresa's motives—whether she was protecting Jojo, Andrew, or just herself—the women's friendship was over. After that telephone call, they never spoke again. Dorothy had a letter from Teresa in her bag to take up to Jojo, but she never gave it to him. When she eventually found it, she left it on a pile of papers in her room.

As complicated as Dorothy's life had become, much worse was to follow. As she tried to extricate herself from the Russo family, she discovered the extent to which the Mafia exerts power over its people. Dorothy found she was no longer in control of her life.

WHEN Dorothy visited Jojo Russo's codefendants at the MCC, she would occasionally discuss their cases and review their efforts to get their convictions overturned. One of these prisoners was Larry Fiorenza, known as Larry Tattoos. An associate in the Colombo family with a previous conviction for armed robbery, he had been a hit man during the Colombo war, in one of the crews loyal to Russo's cousin, Carmine Persico. He was a good-looking guy, bulked up on steroids, with prison muscles, but he was a sick man: a longtime drug user, Larry had been diagnosed with AIDS and had developed hepatitis and cirrhosis of the liver.

During one of her meetings with the five codefendants, Dorothy became convinced that Larry was flirting with her. One day, as he was going back to the cells, Larry asked if she could call him down alone next time.

All things considered, Larry Fiorenza could hardly have presented a less appealing package, but Dorothy fell for him. With Russo, Dorothy was never the only woman; she would always be just another *goombada*, eating Sunday lunch on her own. Now she had met a man who needed her, who had no one else. She felt sorry for Larry, and she thought she could save him.

There were difficulties from the start: Jojo Russo suddenly turned possessive. Because Jojo was a capo and senior to him, Larry had to ask him for permission to see Dorothy alone. Jojo refused. "What about my father?" he demanded. Dorothy explained it was over between them. After Andrew had accused her of dating an FBI agent,

Dorothy had only seen him a few more times; even though she had asked him not to, he continued seeing other women. By midsummer, their six-month affair was over.

As far as Jojo was concerned, that was not the point. Dorothy could not leave the boss and start an affair with an associate—it was a question of respect. Jojo could not let this flagrant insult to his father stand. He told Dorothy she had to choose between Larry and him.

"You were my lawyer," he complained. "You can't start seeing him."

"I was not your lawyer," Dorothy reminded him. "You have a lawyer. I'm running around for you people, and I'm getting exposed to all sorts of trouble. I'm not getting any recognition for what I do."

"You've got a bad attitude, you know that?" said Jojo. "I am the boss. You do things my way. It's either me or him."

After giving it some thought, Dorothy decided to respect his orders. She told Larry she had to stop visiting him for a while. She didn't want to upset anybody.

"Whatever you think," he told her. "Look, I don't have anything to offer you, I'm stuck here in jail, and if you want to walk away, you want to back away from me, I'll understand. But these people took enough from me already. I ain't backing down."

If Dorothy didn't want to stir up trouble for herself, she particularly didn't want to cause problems for Larry, so for a few weeks, she stopped visiting. It seems typical of Dorothy that she had found her way into another intractable situation, and then tried to wriggle out without anyone getting angry with her. By starting a relationship with Larry, she had publicly disrespected Andrew Russo, but she refused to see it that way. Convinced that she had only ever acted out of a selfless wish to please, Dorothy was angry that the Russos should try to stop her from dating another man. After everything she had done for that family, she felt defiant: what had they ever done for her? Later, she would testify about her fears, and a series of warnings she received. On one occasion, she saw Jojo's lawyer in court, and asked him why Jojo was so upset about her relationship with Larry. He replied that her behavior could start another war within the family. Since the first war had left a dozen people dead, it was a heavy responsibility to lay at her door.

Jojo's lawyer was not the only one to give Dorothy a stern warning. In January 1996, her old family friend John Lombardi, at whose fateful Christmas party she had met Andrew Russo, invited her out for a meal to celebrate the New Year. Over dinner, John asked whether she had seen Jojo lately. She was noncommittal. He asked her if she was seeing anybody, and she told him, after a pause, that she was seeing Larry.

"I thought you were told not to see that guy," he said.

"Well, I don't think that's fair," she replied. "I did a lot to help your family, I never asked for anything, I was helping them and this is how they treat me?"

"You could do a million nice things for my family," John replied, "you do one wrong thing, that's it."

Not long after this conversation, Dorothy complained to Andrew Russo's friend Al Viterelli that everyone was upset with her about this relationship, and she thought they were being ridiculous.

"It's a rank thing," he told her, "it's an ego thing. You broke a rule."

That Dorothy had gone behind Andrew and Jojo's backs to continue an affair with a man inferior to both men in rank was unforgivable. She later discovered that this was not the only thing troubling her former lover. Dorothy knew far too much about the Russo family business to be getting emotionally involved with a guy who was likely to be stuck serving a life sentence. Viterelli was the first one to warn Dorothy that she was now perceived as a liability, a prime candidate for cooperation.

"Everybody thinks that you're going to sing and fly."

With that warning in her ears, Dorothy was now extremely wary. Larry had also been warned: one of his codefendants told him he had broken a rule, now he had to stop seeing Dorothy and apologize. Larry did neither. By now they were united in defiance of the bosses, which brought them closer together. Dorothy continued to see him at the MCC in one of the glass-fronted booths designed for lawyer-client meetings. She would bring him food, vitamins, and condoms: if a sympathetic guard was on duty, they would be left alone to have sex in the visitor's room. He once asked her to bring him a bottle of wine, but she refused, telling him it was bad for his liver. Already she had an opportunity to save Larry Fiorenza from himself.

When her divorce from Anthony came through in February 1996, Dorothy was surprised to get a call from Andrew Russo. He said he was calling to congratulate her. "You're free now," he said, perhaps thinking she might come and celebrate with him.

"Yes, well, I'm marrying Larry," she said hastily.

"What do you want to do that for?" said her former lover soothingly. "Why don't you get your sneakers and come out to the farm? We could walk around the track."

Listening to Andrew's friendly tone as he laid on the charm, Dorothy managed to resist.

In April 1996, Dorothy married Larry Fiorenza at the MCC—a union of two needy people who saw some chance for salvation in each other. She wanted to be needed, to be the center of someone's life. Since Larry was stuck in jail, she could feel secure in the knowledge that he was thinking only about her. He was getting food, sex, and legal advice, and with Dorothy's help, maybe even a pass out of jail. The Russo family's opposition gave their union a romantic glow.

Dorothy had been doing occasional legal work, but most of it was no win, no fee, and she never earned enough to live on. Now that her payments from Russo had stopped, she was short of money and ran up huge credit card bills. In one eight-month period, Dorothy incurred debts of $20,000. She had five credit cards, as well as charge accounts with several stores, including Bloomingdale's and Victoria's Secret. She and her mother would buy themselves nice clothes, including full-length fake fur coats. Dorothy's spending went beyond retail therapy: as her life began to spin out of control, her shopping habit became an escape.

Having been little more than a messenger girl for Andrew and his son, Dorothy now started working in earnest for Larry Fiorenza. She filed a motion for a new trial. Although she had no experience in criminal law, and her legal work was a shambles, she dreamed that by winning a new trial, Larry would be set free and they could start a new life together.

Like so many women in Dorothy's position, her love for Larry Fiorenza had transformed him in her mind from a violent criminal into a victim. Although he had been convicted of armed robbery, she excused him on the grounds that he had been a drug addict at the time. During the Colombo war, he had taken part in more than a dozen murder attempts, but she argued that he was always an unwilling member of the hit squad. Whatever explanation he offered her for his crimes, however unlikely, she clung to it as though her life depended on it.

Women who fall in love with criminals tend to decide, because they love them, that they're not criminals at all. Often their overwhelming desire is to save the man, and this involves redeeming his past. It's a generous act of love, in a way, but it often ends up revealing more about the woman than about the man she loves. She may feel she should not, or cannot, love him if he has committed those terrible acts, so she decides that he hasn't.

Susan Berman, writing about her father, encountered the same dilemma. She wondered what it revealed about her nature if she could still admire her father once she knew the details of crimes he had committed. She found that, by putting a glamorous outlaw gloss on his actions, by making them acts of courage rather than violence, she could carry on loving him. Of course a daughter is different from a lover: she does not choose to have a murderer as a father, and cannot, even if she moves to the other side of the country and changes her name, escape the relationship. Dorothy Fiorenza sought out bad men to redeem them. She willingly accepted her husband's version of his role in the mob, as a dissenter who tried to turn his crew members away from acts of violence.

If she expected sympathy from other women, Dorothy was mistaken. A female lawyer for one of Larry's codefendants laughed in her face. "You were Andrew Russo's goombada and you marry Larry Fiorenza? Are you crazy?"

Dorothy tried to explain that she wasn't the only woman Andrew was seeing at the time, that it wasn't serious.

"Well, I wouldn't have put up with it either, but you know how they are."

While protesting that everyone was overreacting, Dorothy also knew exactly the sort of characters she was dealing with. Larry did too. He told his wife it was only a matter of time before the Russos would take their revenge. Andrew Russo was back in prison by this time—he had been arrested in September 1996 for labor racketeering after an investigation into his business dealings with Dennis Hickey, and was denied bail. This might mean the Russos would bide their time, but they would be sure to exact revenge on Larry in the end. Dorothy and Larry focused all their energy on winning a retrial, in the hope that he would get out of jail before the Russos got to him.

But in February 1997, Larry was out of luck. Jojo and two of his associates won a retrial, but Larry Fiorenza did not. It was a major blow. Dorothy wrote to the judge, as Larry's wife and legal counsel, asking him to reconsider his decision. The judge responded by removing her from the case, on the grounds that her emotional involvement disqualified her as his lawyer.

Dorothy and Larry's options were running out. They started to consider cooperating with the authorities. If Jojo got out of prison, they would both be in danger; if they cooperated, they could leave the area and start again somewhere safe. But Dorothy's attempt to seek advice was met with a startled response. She went to see an old friend, a lawyer and colleague of her mother's. He could see no advantage in throwing her lot in with Larry Fiorenza and then being cast adrift in the witness protection program. "What do you want to do that for?" he said. "Your husband's sick, you'd have to go and live in the boondocks, give up your nice life as a lawyer—you'd be crazy, don't do it."

This was not what she wanted to hear. In spite of the warnings she had received, Dorothy went ahead and called the U.S. Attorney's Office. As she later said: "The trust was going to have to start with somebody."

Trust is a concept alien to the Mafia environment, where it is habitual to expect potential danger from all quarters, *especially* close friends. Dorothy Fiorenza was a different breed. Having grown up in a legitimate family, she maintained a sense of fair play. She felt the Russo family had abused her and she had a right to protect herself. Turning to the law and cooperating with the authorities did not cause her any moral difficulties. She was only helping Larry; she was certainly not expecting to have to testify herself.

In May 1997, she met with two FBI agents and told them Larry

Fiorenza wanted to cooperate, assuming they would be interested only in what Larry had to tell them. But when her husband spoke to prosecutors, he told them how she had helped the Russos cover up jury tampering. Dorothy was shocked to learn that she could now be prosecuted for a crime. As usual, Dorothy had never really considered the implications of what she was doing. Larry, on the other hand, had it all worked out. He had made absolutely sure that his wife would stay in this with him.

In 1997, Larry was given a liver biopsy and was told he had between five and ten years to live. In April 1998, at his sentencing for murder conspiracy, it became clear that, however many years he would survive, he would spend the rest of his life in jail. At this point, cooperation was the couple's only chance.

In August 1998, Dorothy was summoned before the grand jury to answer questions about jury tampering. She faced a possible ten-year jail sentence for her part in helping Teresa Castranova hide from a subpoena. She pled guilty as part of her cooperation deal, and was instantly disbarred.

In September, she was moved to a secret location and told to dye her hair to disguise her appearance. Fiorenza was put in isolation. The list of government witnesses against Hickey and Russo in the jury tampering case was about to be unsealed, and the authorities did not want either of them to be in circulation. Dorothy could no longer visit her husband, and was allowed to phone only once a week. When called upon, she would meet with agents to go over points of information, identify people from photographs, and provide other corroborating information. Terrified at the prospect of testifying against the Russos, she suffered from anxiety and insomnia.

Midway through the jury tampering trial of Andrew Russo and Dennis Hickey, Dorothy Fiorenza, exhausted and strained, took the witness stand on January 12, 1999. Hour upon hour, under the stare of her former lover, she had to replay the most unedifying chapter of her life.

For someone with legal experience, Dorothy did not do well in the witness box. Her emotional involvement with the defendants, her nervousness at being in the presence of her former lover and friends, made her, at times, almost incoherent. She stuttered and misremembered on so many occasions that the defense frequently accused her of lying. Assistant U.S. Attorney Daniel Dorsky, the prosecutor who had gone over the evidence with Dorothy on several occasions, had a difficult job: her manner made her sound deceitful even when she was telling the truth.

When one of the defense attorneys asked her if she knew she was committing a crime by pretending to be Jojo Russo's lawyer, she replied: "I should have, but I wasn't thinking about it." It was the sort of answer that gave rise to a bruising attack, as the lawyers trumpeted that the witness was incapable of distinguishing between fiction and reality. Voices were frequently raised as Dorsky tried to defend his witness against the braying triumphalism of defense attorneys who dismissed her as a fantasist.

If the defense lawyers were brutal, the judge was occasionally contemptuous. At the end of her testimony, Dorothy recounted one of the threats her former lover had made. Russo had been talking about his brother-in-law, who had become a cooperating witness. "He said," she recounted haltingly, "that if he ever—if he ever found him he would . . . He told me if he ever found him he would nail his balls to the wall, pour kerosene around his body and light a match."

As she recalled Andrew Russo's menacing words, after three days of grueling interrogation under his unwavering gaze, Dorothy finally burst into tears. But she would find no sympathy in court. By this time, Dorothy had tried everyone's patience.

"You can stop the whining," snapped the judge. "It's irritating."

On February 1, 1999, Andrew Russo and Dennis Hickey were found guilty of jury tampering. Andrew, aged sixty-five, was given four years eight months, which was added to his ten-year sentence for racketeering and parole violation. "I'll be seventy-eight, if I live that long," he responded bitterly in court. In the meantime, Jojo Russo's conviction for conspiracy to commit murder had been reinstated by the court of appeal.

Before the verdict was reached, Dorothy Fiorenza, aged thirty-two, had left her home and family and disappeared into witness protection, where she would soon be joined by her terminally ill, forty-year-old husband. Her marriage to Larry Fiorenza, not entirely surprisingly, did not last outside the artificial neon glare of the prison visiting room. A couple of years later she made a secret trip back to New York to try to get her law license reinstated. Given her repeated assistance to known felons in breaking the law, her request would be a very long shot at best. The grounds for her appeal against disbarment, she said, were that when she met the mob boss and became one of his mistresses, and when she subsequently destroyed her marriage, broke the law, and married a convicted murderer with a terminal illness, she had been suffering from manic depression. This, then, was Dorothy's explanation for the disastrous actions that had ruined her life: she had not been herself.

Dorothy's lawyer admitted that attempting to have her law license reinstated was more a matter of personal pride and dignity than an indication that she would be practicing law again. Nonetheless, her application was denied.

In many ways, Dorothy was a victim of the glamorous image of the mob. She thought that being a *goombada* would release her from the dependence and drudgery of marriage, and that she could assume a role in the boss's entourage without relinquishing control of her own life. She learned that, once involved with the Mafia, no one is in control of their own destiny. What is more—and this applies to a *goombada* as much as a hit man, or anyone else—there is no easy way out. The way Dorothy chose to escape the mob, by testifying against her former lover and going into the witness protection program, meant that she had to abandon her former life. In the end, the only way to save herself was to effectively extinguish her identity.

25

WHATEVER else anyone says about Betty Tocco, everyone agrees she is very attractive. People compare her to Demi Moore or Michelle Pfeiffer. They describe her mane of black hair and extraordinary eyes. When she took the stand to testify against her husband, mob boss Albert Tocco, she caused a sensation, and gave a packed courtroom unprecedented insight into a Mafia marriage. There was much speculation about the motive for her betrayal. Many observers believed she did it for her husband's money. She maintained it was because she did not want to watch her son grow up to become a member of the mob. Whatever the truth, testifying against her husband was the one way she could make sure he would go to prison for a long, long time.

After her husband's trial, Betty vanished. She became someone else, living a long way from anyone who ever knew her. The witness protection program requires participants to take a new name and to sever all contact with family and friends. Conditions in the program are so stringent that almost no one goes into it unless it's a matter of life and death. For a convicted mobster, giving up his friends to avoid life in prison is a fair trade-off. For a woman who has been seduced by the Mafia life, it may be her only way out.

Nobody likes a snitch, and defense lawyers are customarily harsh on turncoats, flinging salacious allegations and personal details around the courtroom in an attempt to undermine the witness's credibility. In the case of wives and girlfriends, the questioning amounts to character assassination; the vilification heaped on the few women who have testified against the mob, in court and in the press, makes uncomfortable reading. After they have been stripped of their dignity by the courtroom ordeal, these women are finally divested of their identity, and disappear.

Because Betty Tocco is still in the witness protection program, I was unable to talk to her directly, but I did read the transcripts of her evidence. I also managed to contact Bob Pecoraro, the FBI agent who worked with her and got to know her better than anyone during her cooperation. Over the two days I spent talking to Special Agent Pecoraro, who is now retired from the FBI, he told me of Betty's great courage and sacrifice. He had never spoken of these events, and their recollection still caused him emotional distress.

She was born Betty Orbeck in Oak Lawn, Illinois, a leafy suburb of Chicago, the daughter of hardworking Greek parents. As an aimless teenager, she married young, but the relationship didn't last. By her twenties, she was a single mother of a four-year-old girl, surviving on food stamps and welfare. To make ends meet, she modeled lingerie and swimwear at restaurants which served businessmen's lunches. The job was not what she had imagined for herself. Knowing she could do something better with her life, when she was introduced to a charismatic, wealthy older man, she believed she had found her ticket.

On July 5, 1974, Betty was posing in provocative lingerie at Lorenzetti's, a large Italian restaurant in Chicago Heights favored by the local mob, when she was called over to a table where three Italian men were having lunch. They chatted her up for a few minutes, devouring her with their eyes. Later, one of the men asked her for her phone number. He said it was for his friend; she smiled politely and said no.

The next time she was working at Lorenzetti's, the owner of the restaurant came bustling over to her and told her one of his friends wanted to meet her. She couldn't very well turn down her employer and, by this time, she had become a little intrigued by this Italian guy who seemed so interested in her.

When she had finished her shift and got dressed, she and another girl were ushered over to the men's table. Lorenzetti said: "Betty, I want you to meet a friend of mine, a dentist, Al Tocco." Betty and the other model sat down with the dentist and his friend, and smiled and listened. He was charming, and she noticed he dressed well. The way he played up the dentist role, she realized it must be some kind of in-joke.

She was modeling at a restaurant called the Brown Onion when she next saw Tocco. This time, she went out to dinner with him. By now, she had figured out that he was not a dentist. She was fascinated by him and by the way people behaved around him. He was a real man, a dominant type, and although he was intimidating, she liked his assertiveness, and she was flattered by his attentions. He was older than she, in his mid-forties, and had classic Italian looks: piercing dark eyes and a mane of black hair flecked with gray at the temples. He wasn't a big man, but he had an unmistakable power and she saw its effect on others just as she felt it herself.

On his FBI Most Wanted poster, fifteen years later, Albert Tocco was described as "a charmer of women"—an aspect of his character considered so dangerous it required a public warning. No doubt the young Betty Orbeck would have concurred.

Betty and Albert started dating, and he would take her to dinner at the best restaurants in the area, where everybody knew and respected him. He seemed infatuated with her, which she found irresistible. She took him to meet her parents, who thought he was wonderful. After a few months, she moved in with him.

Betty was in love. Albert Tocco was rich, and there she was, living in his condo in Glenwood, near Chicago Heights. It was a comfortable place with smoked-glass French windows leading onto the balcony, a real bachelor pad. Tocco always wanted her to look good, and he bought her clothes and jewels. Her life with Albert was something new and exciting, and she never wanted for money.

The only problem at that relatively peaceful stage of their relationship was that she couldn't get pregnant. Although they both had children from previous marriages, his son and daughter were grown, and they badly wanted a child together. Betty went to a fertility clinic for tests. When she did conceive, she had a miscarriage.

Meanwhile, Betty became acquainted with Tocco's circle of

friends in Chicago Heights. He seemed to know so many people that they seldom ate a meal together without one or more of his pals joining them for a chat. He even knew the mayor and the chief of police, who often ate at the same restaurants and would always stop for a word with Al. Betty began to realize the extent of Tocco's influence.

What Betty would ultimately learn was that Albert "Caesar" Tocco was a leading figure in organized crime in Chicago Heights. In the 1970s, this sprawling town south of Chicago was a blue-collar community that, like nearby Cicero, Illinois, was controlled by the Mafia from the top down. Crime flourished with the complicity of City Hall and a handful of local cops who took their payoffs with good grace.

Tocco's rise to power dated back to the 1950s when the mob boss in Chicago Heights gave him a start in vice and protection rackets. In the mid-1970s, Tocco served as underboss to labor racketeer Alfred Pilotto; he was also Pilotto's bodyguard and chauffeur. Betty and Albert often had dinner with Pilotto and his wife, Diva, and the two couples vacationed together in Florida.

One of the mob's most lucrative sources of income around that time were chop shops, auto salvage yards where stolen cars were disassembled and their parts sold. In 1977, as many as thirty people were murdered in what became known as the chop-shop wars in the Chicago area. As different mob factions fought for control of the car theft and salvage business, Tocco relentlessly expanded his operations. One chop-shop operator who also collected street tax for the West Side mob was reportedly cut up and fed to pigs on a farm in Indiana.

In addition to his chop-shop racket, Tocco had his own successful prostitution and gambling operations and collected street tax from other businesses operating illegally in Chicago Heights. Once a month, one of his collectors would appear at the various gambling dens, salvage yards, brothels, or after-hours taverns to collect a payment of $500. Everyone was afraid of Albert Tocco, and everybody paid. Those who didn't were given a warning by one of Tocco's band of hoodlums. One man had a car he was very proud of, which he kept in a garage at his parents' house. Tocco's men doused the garage in gasoline and set fire to it.

Anyone who refused to pay learned the hard way how ruthless Tocco could be. One of his collectors approached a jukebox salesman, Dino Valente, who told him: "Go to hell. It's a free country." Betty used to see Valente now and again when he came into Tocco's restaurant, Merlin's, to collect his earnings from the jukebox. One night, Betty had been having dinner with Albert at Merlin's and was just getting her coat on when Valente came in to make his collection. As she was leaving, Betty saw Valente and Albert together.

The next morning, Tocco told Betty that Valente was dead. She knew that Valente had been with Tocco shortly before he died, but Tocco told her not to tell anyone when or where she had last seen the man. He also sent her to Valente's funeral as his representative—he refused to go with her, so she had to go through the excruciating ritual alone. Soon after that, Tocco went into the jukebox business and took over Valente's routes.

By the end of the 1970s, Tocco was making millions from his extortion rackets. Widespread knowledge of the numerous murders associated with the chop-shop wars, as well as Tocco's reputation, ensured prompt payment. A U.S. attorney described Tocco's illegal activities as "lucrative, largely immune from the scrutiny of the authorities, and wildly successful."

Tocco's boss, Pilotto, had built himself a brick mansion overlooking a rolling golf course on the edge of town, its front entrance framed by a grand portico with tall white pillars. Albert Tocco was not a man for such ostentation, but he needed a house more suited to his station in life. He and Betty had outgrown the condo. Betty's daughter Gina was nine years old, and becoming very willful. Gina and Tocco argued a lot—he called her manipulative, and often told her he had her number, saying: "You can't trick the trickster." Betty and Albert agreed it would be good for everyone to have more space.

In 1979, the couple found a ranch house on 207th Street in Olympia Fields, a residential area on the edge of town where the houses were set back from the road amidst big gardens. Once they owned the place, Tocco had it completely remodeled. They built a large screened porch at the back, and a master bedroom with an en suite bathroom on one side. The drive swept up to a three-car garage and a front door with fancy ironwork and colored glass. The construction was done by a company belonging to one of Tocco's friends, the police commissioner, and when the work took longer than anticipated, the costs overran. When Betty complained that they were paying over the estimate, Tocco told her that since he was paying cash under the counter, he wasn't going to kick up a fuss.

The lounge had floor-to-ceiling windows, but to deter curious onlookers, they were mirrored with a bronze tint. The interior was done up in Mediterranean style, with arched doorways and tiled floors, deep leather sofas and shag pile carpets, glass tables and gold lamps. There were large wardrobes for her designer clothes and fur coats and his large collection of sports jackets, monogrammed shirts and matching shoes. In the kitchen hung an embroidered pennant on a gold rope emblazoned with Tocco's nickname, "Caesar." Gina had her own room, and there was a nursery, in case they should ever need it.

By the time the renovations were finished, they had made a dream home. Not that Tocco was home very often. One of his oldest friends, Billy Dauber, had been released from prison in early 1977. Tocco had looked forward to Billy's homecoming and talked to Betty about him a lot, reminiscing about their younger days—the businesses they had run together, the scrapes they had gotten into, committing crimes together. Tocco had driven down to Kentucky to pick Billy up on the day he was released, and Betty met him and his wife, Charlotte, a few days later, at dinner. They saw each other regularly; sometimes Billy and Charlotte would invite them to their apartment. Albert was often out with his male friends and associates, and Billy saw him for lunch or dinner most days.

Billy, who wore a hat with a feather in it, was a bit of a wild man. He lacked Tocco's authoritative, cool approach to business. Although Tocco was fond of him, he kept a close eye on him. Billy had been out of prison for three years, running a chop shop and collecting for his old friend, when Betty started hearing complaints about his behavior. She would hear Tocco on the phone, mentioning that Billy's temper was uncontrollable, his tactics were outrageous, and that he was becoming a liability. Worse still, he was holding back some of Tocco's money. As Tocco's displeasure grew, he added a terrible accusation: there were rumors that Billy was informing for the FBI.

One night, as the two couples dined together, as they had so often in the past, the atmosphere was unusually strained. Betty overheard Billy telling Albert that he knew he was out of favor, and Albert responding angrily: "That's ridiculous, how can you say that?"

When Tocco left the table to go to the men's room, Billy turned to Betty and told her he knew he was going to get killed, and that Tocco was going to do it. Shocked, Betty said: "You two have been friends for so long. How could you ever think something like that?"

"I know it," Billy said miserably. "I know how things go. Albert's the only one who could do it."

Betty never mentioned this conversation to Tocco, but soon afterward he told her things were getting a little heated around Chicago Heights, and that for her safety, they should travel in separate cars. After that, whenever they went out for dinner, they would take two cars, drive different routes, and meet in the parking lot.

One morning in July of 1980, Betty was sitting at the kitchen table with Tocco's elderly mother, who was living with them at the time. The women were drinking coffee and listening to the news on the radio. One of the lead items concerned a shooting in Will County, south of Chicago Heights, described as a gangland murder. Two people, a man and his wife, Billy and Charlotte Dauber, had been ambushed and shot to death in their car. The car had been run off the road and the bodies pumped full of bullets.

The women said nothing. Betty tried to light a cigarette but it stuck to her dry lips. Tocco came home later in the day and asked Betty if she had heard about Billy. She said she'd heard it on the news. When his mother was out of the room, Betty asked Tocco why he had been murdered. "He was a snitch," Tocco said. "He was stepping on too many people's toes."

"But what about Charlotte?"

"Charlotte was in the wrong place at the wrong time."

Betty was profoundly disturbed by Charlotte's death. If these people could kill one of their own and murder his wife because she happened to be there, who would protect her, if the time came?

She and Tocco had a fight about the Daubers' funeral. Betty wanted to go, but Tocco forbade her. When she protested, he shut her up and told her to stay out of it.

Not long after Billy and Charlotte were murdered, Betty discovered she was pregnant.

26

MICHAEL Tocco was born in March 1981, a big healthy boy with a mop of black hair. Albert doted on his son, and sometimes slept with the baby lying on his chest. Still, he was seldom home. Albert loved to gamble, and he often went to a local club called The Pit to shoot craps or play barboot. (His lawyer would later say that the loves of Albert Tocco's life were "gambling, his eighty-eight-year-old mother, and his eight-year-old son.") Tocco frequently met his male friends for dinner, leaving Betty at home alone with the baby—he was out so often with his associates, Betty began referring to them sarcastically as his "girlfriends." She rarely saw anyone other than close family members. Unlike Albert, she did not have a wide circle of friends, and she almost never socialized with other mob wives, most of whom she couldn't stand.

Albert's friends would visit the house on 207th Street, and although she used to leave the men to talk in private, Betty sometimes caught sight of money changing hands. Albert's chief collector, a tall southerner named Clarence Crockett, would often stop by. On one occasion Betty poked her head in to offer the men coffee and saw Albert stuffing a thick envelope in his jacket pocket. She never minded leaving the men to talk business—she didn't really like any of his friends, and she had begun to despise the way they all scurried around to do his bidding and to spy on each other. They all had typical Mafia nicknames, but she had her own names for them: in addition to the girlfriends, she called them the Brownies, and Squinty Eyes. When Albert's friends called on the phone, even though Betty recognized their voices, they would talk in code, introducing themselves as "the man from the East" or some such mysterious moniker.

Albert had a number of business concerns, and he was a powerful figure in Chicago Heights; a lot of people called on him for favors. He played godfather to many who needed his influence with local government—and who rewarded him richly for his services. One such person was Herbert Panice, who wanted to open a late-night strip club and approached Tocco for help in obtaining a liquor license. Tocco arranged a meeting between Panice and the mayor, at which the mayor complained that Chicago Heights really didn't need yet another sex club, whereupon Panice lost his temper and stormed out. Nonetheless, a few weeks later, Panice had his license. Shortly afterward, Tocco appeared at Panice's club, saying, "We're partners now," and held up four fingers, to indicate that he was expecting a monthly tribute of $4,000. Panice paid up without a murmur—even when Tocco increased the payment to $5,000. Like Albert's many other friends who had received favors, Panice would come over to the house on Christmas and Thanksgiving, bearing gifts for the family.

In 1981, Al Pilotto was indicted in a labor union bribery case. His mob associates were anxious about information the aging boss might give the authorities and apparently decided not to run any risk. Before the trial, while playing golf, Pilotto was shot four times by unseen assailants, but survived. He was later convicted of union violations and went to prison, but in any case, he was finished. Tocco, already the unofficial boss of Chicago Heights, moved seamlessly into his place.

Tocco sold the jukebox business and bought a small cafe called the Over EZ, an unobtrusive little place in an unremarkable suburban strip mall. But he had no intention of going into the restaurant business—the Over EZ was a front for his sports betting operation. His men would hang out there most of the day, and gamblers would come and place their bets, or drop off the money they owed. Tocco made no attempt to pretend the cafe was a profitable business: they only ever served coffee, and if anyone ordered something to eat, they'd bring it in from a restaurant across the road. Tocco himself would turn up at some point in the day, always looking dapper in one of his many colorful sports jackets, and sit at a table in the rear, holding court among his inner circle. His close friends hung on his every word; no one else dared approach him.

Although he could be congenial, Albert was never trusting, and he was constantly testing those around him. An undercover agent who hung out in the Over EZ observing the gambling operation recalls that Albert might buy you breakfast one day, then the next day he'd look you in the eye and tell you he didn't trust you. Violence was never far beneath the surface. One of his collectors later described Tocco as "very vicious."

In 1983, Tocco sold the Over EZ and went into the garbage business by taking over Skyline Disposal, a refuse collection company with a substantial fleet. Betty was put on the payroll, and occasionally ran errands. Shortly after taking over the garbage business, through his contacts in the city council, Tocco doubled his fee from the city for collecting refuse.

Betty, who just a few years earlier had been on welfare, now belonged to a rich man who showered her with gifts. He bought her two cars, a Mercedes 450SL with gold wheels and her initials inscribed on the dashboard, and a beautiful yellow convertible Cadillac Eldorado with pale leather interior. She loved jewelry, particularly big earrings to offset her thick black hair and manicured nails. She also loved buying clothes, and spent thousands of Albert's dollars at a fancy boutique in Chicago Heights called Today's Lady (it wasn't exactly Saks but it was the best the Heights had to offer). Federal agents who caught sight of Betty at that time observed that she looked every bit the classic mob wife.

Wanting to give her and the kids a vacation home, Albert bought a condo in Daytona Beach, Florida, and she and Michael and Gina would fly down there for a holiday a couple of times a year. Sometimes Albert would go with them, but as soon as they landed he would be off meeting his own friends and conducting business. Sometimes Betty, and certainly Gina, preferred it that way. Albert could be very silent and uncommunicative at times, and when he was in a foul mood they stayed out of his way.

Albert grew increasingly jealous of his beautiful girlfriend. Whenever they attended a family occasion, a party, or a wedding, Albert would never allow her to mix with other guests. If a man asked her to dance, Albert would see the guy off with a muttered threat. Betty was never allowed to move from her seat or talk to anybody. Although by nature a funny and warm person, she felt she could only shine and be herself when she was out without him. Only then did she relax and have a laugh.

Albert cared a lot for his son—he bought the lot next door to their house and built him a swing and a tree house—but he did not always manage to separate business from family life. When he was five, Michael started kindergarten nearby, and his class took regular field trips to see their fathers' places of work. Betty arranged a visit to the Skyline garbage company, and another parent invited them to a local garage. When he came home, Michael proudly showed his father a souvenir cup from the garage. Albert grabbed the cup and threw it on the floor, growling: "That guy don't pay."

Another point of contention between Betty and Albert was Albert's older son George, who had been in trouble with drugs. When he was nineteen, Albert bought a sandwich bar and made George the manager to give him some kind of legitimate income, but the venture wasn't a success, and the father and son often got into arguments. When Albert wanted George to move in with them, Betty was against it. In the meantime, Albert had divorced his previous wife, Penny. (George died in a motorcycle accident in December 2003, aged 47. He was drunk at the time.)

In 1984, after a long IRS investigation, Albert was named in a RICO indictment for running a gambling operation. Just days before he went to trial, and a full ten years after their first meeting, in a small ceremony attended by close members of the family, Albert and Betty were married. It is possible that he wanted to ensure she would not be called as a witness against him, since a wife could not be forced to testify against her husband. In fact, as IRS agent Tom Moriarty remembers, they did not plan to call her, since they were aware that whatever else Mr. and Mrs. Tocco talked about over the breakfast table, they did not discuss his business.

Tocco's trial lasted six weeks; the prosecution called over eighty witnesses, including gamblers and undercover agents who had posed as gamblers. Betty was not in court. The case had attracted a good deal of press coverage: since Tocco had come to the public's attention as a suspect in the murder of Billy Dauber, his fame as a crime boss had spread far and wide. Betty's looks and flamboyant appearance would have attracted even more unwelcome attention—besides, it was not as though Albert needed moral support. If he had been convicted, he could have received ten years. In the end, the jury acquitted him alone of all the defendants. Having escaped a jail sentence, with his position in the Heights apparently unassailable, the groom went home to his bride.

If Betty had been following the press coverage of her new husband's trial, she would have learned a great deal about his reputation as a ruthless crime boss. But before long, she was to learn something about him that no gambling investigation could uncover—something so dreadful that years would pass before she spoke about it.

27

O NE evening in the summer of 1986, Albert seemed anxious as
he got dressed to go out to dinner. As he straightened his tie at
the dressing-room mirror, he called to Betty that he was meeting Chickie and Nicky and would probably be home a little late. As
he kissed her good-bye, he said he would call her later. She reminded him they had people coming for lunch the next day, but he
didn't reply as he got into his Lincoln and sped away.

Albert often had dinner with his mobster friends Nicholas
Guzzino, Albert Roviaro, and Dominick Palermo, known as Nicky,
Chickie, and Toots. Betty was accustomed to her nights home alone
and, apart from the boredom of another night on her own, thought
little of it. Only her husband's apparent edginess seemed out of the
ordinary.

By around two in the morning, when he hadn't come home and
hadn't called, she started to worry. She got in her car and went
down to the garbage company. It was a gloomy, dark building with
a low roof. The trucks stood in a line at the back of the lot, reeking
in the warm night air. Then Betty saw Albert's car. It was parked in
its usual place. She stared at it, trying to make out whether it was
loaded down. If Albert had been killed, his body could have been
left in the trunk. She walked to the back of the car and, after a pause,
opened the trunk. It was empty.

Betty had keys to the building, so she went into Albert's office.
When she turned on the light, she saw the clothes that Albert had
been wearing to go out to dinner, neatly arranged on a hanger. His

wallet, keys, and lighter were on the desk. Betty realized something was wrong—very wrong—and Albert might not be the one
in danger.

What follows was revealed in testimony, in two trials, by Betty
Tocco and FBI agent Bob Pecoraro.

Betty drove home and got into bed. She had just closed her eyes
when the phone rang. She leapt for the receiver, and caught sight of
the time: 4 A.M. It was Albert on the line, furious, almost hysterical.
Several moments passed before she could understand what he was
saying. "Get your fucking ass in the car and get down here! I need
you to pick me up," he yelled. He was breathless and raging, screaming obscenities, but she managed to get the gist: he was at a pay
phone out in the country somewhere in Indiana, about fifty miles
from home, on his own, on foot. She scribbled the directions down,
pulled on a pair of trousers and a shirt, and ran out to the car. As she
drove her Eldorado through the gray light of dawn, she wondered
what the hell had happened out there. How come he was on his
own? Had his friends tried to kill him?

When she found him, about an hour later, he was standing by
the side of the road, wearing blue overalls from his garbage company. As he got in the car, she noticed he was covered in dirt and
scratches. His boots were caked with mud, and his hands were
grimy. He was raging and cursing. She had never seen him in such
a state. He was beside himself, shouting—not at her, but almost to
himself: "I've just spent the night hiding in the fucking woods,
goddammit, we've just buried the Spilotro brothers and those
motherfuckers, Chickie and Nicky, they must have heard somebody coming—they ran off. I don't know where the fuck they
went, it was pitch black out there. They had walkie-talkies, and I
didn't have one. Those fuckers left me out there—I couldn't find
a fucking thing in the dark, I spent the whole night in the woods,
till I finally found the pay phone. Who the hell could I call? Can
I trust those guys? It's all that asshole Toots's fault. They just left
me out there. And somebody's going to find my prints on that
fucking shovel."

She listened, aghast, and drove. The only words he actually addressed to her were, "Take me to Chickie's place." As morning broke, she pulled up at Chickie's house, and Albert got out of the car and knocked at the door. Chickie's wife came to the door in her dressing gown, and said he wasn't there. Albert got back in the car and, without asking him what had happened, Betty drove them over to the garbage company, where they went into the office. Albert made several phone calls, trying to track down Chickie and Nicky while she sat and waited, studying her fingernails. She knew the Spilotro brothers, everybody did, and she knew Tony was a pain in the ass, but murdered? By her husband?

Finally they drove home, and he took a long shower as she started wearily preparing the food for their Father's Day party. The barbeque would have to be lit in the backyard, and the meat prepared for the grill. There were salads to make and desserts to be finished. Gina and Michael were hanging around the kitchen, being more trouble than help. They were expecting Albert's mother and sister with her family, but extra people always seemed to materialize on these family occasions—there could be as many as thirty people turning up. She just had time to get dressed and fix her face before the guests started arriving. As she dashed into the bedroom to find something to wear, she saw Albert fast asleep in bed. She left him there and went to answer the door to the first arrivals.

All day, as Betty handed around chicken wings and plates of Italian sausage, people were asking, "Where's Albert?" She was so embarrassed that her husband should leave her to cope with a family occasion, on Father's Day, no less. What was she supposed to tell them? "Oh, he's sleeping, he spent the night burying the Spilotros. . . ."

Tony "the Ant" Spilotro was a Chicago mobster who had risen quickly through the ranks of Cosa Nostra. He became the chief enforcer for the Chicago mob in Las Vegas in the 1980s, protecting their interests in the Stardust Casino and skimming millions from the counting room. Spilotro tortured and killed with relish; like his mentor, "Mad Sam" DeStefano, he made violence an art form—on one occasion he squeezed a man's head in a vise until his eyes popped out of their sockets.

Spilotro (later immortalized by Joe Pesci in the film *Casino*), left to his own devices in Las Vegas, got completely out of control and disobeyed the mob's rules of criminal practice—robbing tourists and committing murders in the city. All this brought tremendous heat on the mob, not only in Vegas, but also in Chicago—some of Spilotro's men were persuaded to cooperate with the authorities, and their information led to the arrest of major figures in the Chicago mob. The bosses decided that Spilotro had to go.

The manner of his undoing indicates how far Spilotro had enraged his mob superiors. He and his brother, Michael, were savagely beaten, stripped to their underpants, and driven out to a field in the middle of nowhere. There they were buried in a shallow grave by Albert Tocco and his crew.

About a week later, the farmer who owned the field was out spraying his crop with pesticide when he noticed that his corn had been flattened in places and saw signs that something had been dragged across the ground. Suspecting poachers, he called his gamekeeper, who arrived with a shovel. The men saw an area where the ground had been disturbed, and the gamekeeper started digging, expecting to find the carcass of a deer. Instead, he found a body—two bodies.

By the time the police arrived, the site had been trampled over, and cigarette ends littered the area. The crime scene had been so thoroughly disturbed, little evidence could be gathered. The bodies were exhumed. After a week of decomposing in the warm ground, the police could tell they had been horribly battered. However, the autopsy report showed that they had not died from the beating—they had suffocated. Tony Spilotro and his brother had been buried alive.

No one has ever been prosecuted for the murder of the Spilotro brothers. Although most mob informers had a theory, no one ever confessed, and it was never determined whether the same crew beat and then buried them. One informant later claimed that Albert Tocco had boasted of "having fun" with Tony Spilotro when he beat him up, but this has never been substantiated.

If Albert emerged unscathed from the Spilotro episode, it caused irreparable damage to his marriage. Betty was shocked and frightened by what she had seen and heard. For the first time she was implicated in a crime, and although she realized Albert had not meant to tell her what happened, she had heard too much. And then there had been the grueling Father's Day party, when she had had to put a bright face on for a family occasion, and all people wanted to know was where Albert was. It was so humiliating. What must they have thought?

More than anything, she felt, he had shown so little considera-tion for her—it was almost as though she didn't exist. Screaming abuse when he phoned her at four in the morning, cursing all the way home when she had driven so far, and talking about the crime as though she couldn't hear. What had she become?

As she slipped further into the role of the good Mafia wife, Betty was expected to run errands for her husband without ever asking why. She never questioned him about his business, but he would talk on the phone right in front of her; when they went to a restaurant, people would join them at their table and talk about business. She'd be preparing dinner at home and he'd be talking to one of his friends in a way that made it sound like they were going to kill someone. She found it funny that they would be plotting a murder right in front of her and she would be standing there, making tomato sauce, pretend-ing not to hear. It struck her as an absurd situation, but it also began to anger her. They were behaving as though she didn't exist.

His criminal life, which she had mostly ignored, began to frighten her. Every time a murder was reported in the papers, Albert's name was mentioned as a suspect. And on more than one occasion—such as the time the jukebox owner was killed—she knew Albert had been with the victim just before he died.

As Albert and Betty's fights intensified, they began to talk about divorce, but he always let her know he had power over her. If she said she wanted to leave, he would say, "Well, you go, you get the hell out of here, but you leave the kid here. You're not taking this kid with you. If you divorce me you'll never see him again." And she believed him. Often, when Michael would hear his parents fighting, he would come out of his room crying and beg his father to leave his mother alone.

Michael in fact saw little of his father during these years. Occa-sionally Albert, in an expansive mood, would tell the boy to jump in the car, and they would drive over to Toys "Я" Us. "Buy whatever you want, Michael," his father would say. And Michael would set off down the aisles, picking out boxes and bikes, games and toys, and they would toil back to the car together, carrying his packages. But once they had unloaded the stuff at home, Albert would be off again in the car and wouldn't reappear before bedtime. Michael would later say that instead of all these new toys, he would much rather have had his father around once in a while to play with him.

Albert frequently missed family occasions. He would forget the children's birthdays and their important school dates. Betty, whose own loving parents would never have missed a graduation or an anniversary, got sick of explaining to the children why their father wasn't there. Michael was also getting bullied at school. On the playground he was taunted by the other kids, who chanted: "Your dad's in the mob." Mortified and tearful, Michael would shout back, "It's not my father, it's my uncle."

Meanwhile, things were not going well for Albert on the business front. Three of his former collectors were arrested and pled guilty to car theft, and decided to cooperate with the authorities. In November 1987 Tocco received a subpoena to appear before a grand jury. Realizing that he was under investigation, he knew it was only a matter of time before the noose closed around him. The following year he sold the garbage company and started withdrawing cash from his bank accounts. By September 1988 he was withdrawing amounts of $9,000 from his bank several times a week—just below the $10,000 limit that would require him to notify the IRS. He then left $250,000 with an old friend, restaurateur Carlo Lorenzetti, telling him to give it to Betty when she needed it. On September 17, after a meeting with his lawyer, he packed a suitcase and left home.

As winter descended on Illinois, Betty waited. She knew her husband was under investigation. She didn't know where Albert had gone, and she didn't think he would be coming back.

BOB Pecoraro was a street agent from New York with a single-minded dedication to catching criminals: apart from three daughters on whom he doted, nothing mattered to him so much as developing cases against organized crime. Pecoraro had arrived in Chicago in December 1978 at the end of a particularly murderous year in the chop-shop wars, when Chicago Heights was littered with bodies. These were challenging times for law enforcement, and the case on the Chicago Heights mob had been stagnant for some time.

Pecoraro was ambitious; he badly wanted to get Albert Tocco, but his office burdened him with so many cases that there was never time to dedicate the resources he needed to investigate the boss of Chicago Heights. By 1987, disillusioned and frustrated, he asked for a transfer.

"I had worked a number of chop-shop investigations, I had informants, I knew Tocco was behind those murders," says Pecoraro, now retired and living in sunnier climes a long way from Chicago. "I told my supervisor, I want to get Albert Tocco and I can't do that if I have fifty or sixty cases. I'm going back to headquarters where I can work organized crime. He said, 'You think you can get Albert Tocco? What do you need?' I said, 'You give me two good guys, let us work any hours we want, let us have cars, don't bother us, check in six months, see where we are, and if we haven't got anything, can it. He said, 'You got it.'"

Pecoraro's pursuit of organized crime consumed his whole life.

"I got divorced because of my job at the FBI. I was never home. I'd get into the office early, do a full day's work, then my fellow agent Jack Bonino would come in, and we'd go down to the Heights. I gave Bonino the name Captain Midnight because he's a real sociable type; he could stay up drinking with these mob guys all night. We were down there till one or two in the morning. We ate where they ate and drank where they drank. They knew who we were and they knew what we wanted. If they wanted to talk to us they knew where to find us."

Pecoraro's slight, energetic figure and piercing dark brown eyes were well known in mob hangouts all over the Heights. Soon Albert Tocco was seeing him everywhere—even sitting at his favorite table at Lorenzetti's. Pecoraro admits he found Tocco's presence forbidding. "The first time I ever spoke to him I was delivering a subpoena. He was actually scary, the way he looked at me, and the way he talked to me," he recalls. "He didn't say anything threatening, but his look and his coldness actually sent chills down me."

Tocco's demeanor did not put Pecoraro off his mission. "Actually it made me want to do more."

Through Pecoraro's team, and some mobsters who were already in jail, the FBI nurtured a number of informants, and the investigation into Tocco's criminal empire started to gather momentum. By mid-October 1988, prosecutors were preparing an indictment against Tocco and his chief collector, Clarence Crockett. But before he had time to serve a warrant, Pecoraro began to suspect the boss had given him the slip. He spent every day in the Heights, hanging out at Tocco's favorite places and meeting with his informants, but he was nowhere to be seen. When his case agent finally told him to put a twenty-four-hour watch on Tocco's house, Pecoraro refused. It's too late, he said. He isn't there.

Nevertheless, when he had the arrest warrant in his hand, he and three other agents took it over to the house on 207th Street. It was late afternoon and beginning to get dark when they knocked on the door. Betty Tocco opened it.

"Mrs. Tocco?" said Pecoraro.

"Yes."

"We're with the FBI, we have a warrant for the arrest of your husband."

"He's not here."

"Well, can you tell me where he is?"

"I don't know. But he's not here."

"Do you mind if we come in and look around?"

"No, I don't, but just you."

At that moment Pecoraro knew he wouldn't find Albert Tocco at home, but he went in for a cursory search—just to be sure there were no hidden doors or secret rooms, and to give him time to chat with the wife. She seemed civil enough, and after a while he asked if the other agents could come in, since it was getting pretty cold outside. She let them in and they stood in the hallway near the front door. There were more questions about Albert Tocco's whereabouts, and one of the agents, cold and cross, got impatient—he had heard so many mobsters' wives say they didn't know anything about their husbands, what they did, or where they were, he snapped: "Of course you know where he is. Why don't you just tell us?"

At this Pecoraro stepped in to scold the agent. He was trying to be agreeable, and this fellow was ruining any chance of creating a good rapport with the fugitive's wife. He gave Mrs. Tocco his card and thanked her politely, and the agents left.

About an hour later, Pecoraro's phone rang. It was Mrs. Tocco. She said she wanted to talk to him, and suggested they meet for a cup of coffee. Pecoraro was amazed. He always tried to be friendly to potential informers, and always left his number, but the last thing he expected was for Albert Tocco's wife to call. When he put the phone down and told the other agents, they were equally surprised, and immediately suspicious. They warned Pecoraro not to meet her, that it must be a trap. Maybe she had told her husband about the visit and he'd be waiting for Pecoraro in the parking lot. She's married to this guy, they said, it must be a setup.

Of course they knew Pecoraro would go. He could never resist a potential informant, and the wife of the boss was too good to miss. But his colleagues were still wary, and when, after a series of phone calls and changes of plan, he finally sat down to wait for Mrs. Tocco in a local restaurant, about a third of the tables were taken up with FBI agents, while another half dozen kept watch in the parking lot.

Betty Tocco came into the restaurant alone and sat down opposite Agent Pecoraro. They reintroduced themselves and chatted for a while. She told him a bit about her life with Albert. She was tired of having a husband who was never home, she said, and who always missed the children's important events. He had even missed her daughter Gina's wedding. She told him Michael was getting bullied at school. She was sick and tired of the life, she said, and now Albert had taken off again, she didn't know where he was, and she didn't know what was going to happen. Now she had FBI agents turning up at the door, and she was sick of it.

Betty said she wanted to put a stop to the situation she and the children were in. She was particularly worried about Michael, and wanted to be sure he didn't grow up in the mob and end up like his father. Finally, she said she wanted to help the FBI with their investigation.

As they talked, gradually the other agents left their tables and went home, satisfied that their colleague was under no immediate threat.

"I'm curious," Pecoraro said to her at length. "Why did you call me?"

"Because you were nice," she said. "Nicer than that other agent. Albert's been telling me for years what fuckers you guys were. But you weren't. You were a gentleman."

By the end of their meal, Pecoraro was convinced that Betty Tocco could be trusted. He believed she was sincere in wanting to be an informant, and that she understood what it would mean. They had an instant rapport, for as well as being attractive, she was a likeable woman, very warm and personable.

Pecoraro went home that night knowing he had made a major breakthrough.

The next time he met with Betty Tocco, he took Jack Bonino with him. The two agents made a comical double act: Pecoraro short, talkative, and bouncy, Bonino tall and laid-back, with a big mustache that gave him a slightly whacky air, like an eccentric colonel. On that day, and for all their many subsequent meetings, the pair would meet

Betty in a parking lot at one of the many restaurants or shopping malls in the area. She would park the yellow Eldorado and get in the back of Pecoraro's black Dodge Charger or Bonino's Ford Fairlane, and they would drive somewhere for coffee, or, if it was going to be a long session, to a motel room. The agents would bring up points of information they had gleaned from other sources, and Betty would tell them what she knew. Bonino, who had been a little skeptical of Betty at the start, gradually began to have faith in her motives.

The case agent, Wayne Zydron, was a different matter. The FBI once secretly recorded a conversation between two mobsters in which Pecoraro was described as "the Italian orangutan, always jumping about and pointing his finger." In the same conversation, Zydron was referred to as "Chisel Face" because he seldom smiled. After that, Pecoraro always called his dour Polish friend Chisel—although his friends say he is a brilliant agent, they admit Zydron is not a "people person." Zydron refused to believe that Betty Tocco was telling the truth. "Don't be so naïve," he said to Pecoraro on one occasion, in front of other agents. "She's been with this guy for fifteen years and she's known you two months. What makes you think she's going to tell you the truth? Grow up."

Bob Pecoraro takes his job personally. He was wounded and humiliated by Zydron's lack of faith in his breakthrough informant, and determined to prove him wrong. The next time he saw Betty he asked her if she would mind coming into the office and talking to his case agent, because he knew that if he could only meet her, he would see how sincere she was, and understand that she was telling the truth.

If Betty was offended at being asked to prove herself in this manner, she didn't let it show, and she submitted to being sneaked into the FBI building through a side entrance and escorted up the back stairs. She walked through the bureau—under the curious eyes of several agents, who peeked around filing cabinets as she made her entrance—and took a seat in Zydron's office. There she sat with Pecoraro, Bonino, and Zydron, drinking coffee from foam cups, and answering questions about people and places in the Heights. After she left, Zydron reluctantly admitted he thought she was probably telling the truth.

During the many months of her cooperation, the four or five agents on the case became Betty's closest friends. In between interviews on points of fact concerning the investigation, they did a fair bit of sitting around, smoking cigarettes, and drinking coffee. During these down times, once or twice they chatted about her marriage. Pecoraro recalls: "I asked her, Why did you marry the guy, did you ever love him? She said, 'Well, I think maybe I did. . . .' She told me, 'He's a good husband and a good father because he provides. But that's where it ends.'"

29

L ATE one evening toward the end of November 1988, Betty
Tocco's phone rang. A voice she didn't recognize, with a foreign
accent she couldn't place, told her to go to a pay phone outside
the Rib Cage restaurant and wait for a call. It was not a request, and
the person on the other end of the line was hardly polite.

Suspecting the call had something to do with her husband, she
immediately dialed agent Pecoraro's number. He would know what
she should do. Pecoraro was some miles away from the Heights, so
he couldn't go with her, but he was extremely interested to hear that
this might be Tocco getting in touch. He said if Betty wasn't afraid,
she should take the call and see what he wanted—and maybe take
someone with her, just in case.

Betty drove a couple of miles over to the Rib Cage and waited by
the phone. At exactly 10:30 P.M., as she had been told, it rang. It was
not Tocco, but the same gruff foreign-sounding voice, and it was no
more polite than before. He told her to get Michael a passport: his father wanted to see him. That was all. She should expect another call
in the next few days to make sure she had done as she was told.

Over the course of three or four of these anonymous calls, Betty
was instructed to prepare Michael to go and meet his father. She was
to give $9,000 in cash to Tocco's cousin, Marlene Delisio, who would
buy the plane tickets. Betty was to fly to Florida with Michael just before Christmas, where Marlene would meet them and take Michael
with her. The man's tone never varied. He was at best gruff, at worst
downright rude, even though he used a code so that she would know

he was calling on behalf of her husband. She asked no questions. There was never any suggestion during these conversations that she might refuse. Nor was she invited to bring Michael herself.

After each call, she passed on the information to the FBI agents. Pecoraro and Bonino were on tenterhooks. The proposed trip represented a real chance for them to track down the fugitive Albert Tocco and bring him back to face trial—probably their only chance. But how could they persuade Betty to send her seven-year-old son thousands of miles away without her?

The agents constructed a plan: they would follow Michael and Marlene, and Michael would lead them to Albert. They would have him tailed twenty-four hours a day by local police and FBI agents, until Michael was safely back on a plane home. Only then would they arrest Albert. Since they didn't know exactly where Albert was—their best information was that he was in Greece, but they weren't sure—they couldn't guarantee the plan would work, but they promised Betty they would do their utmost to bring the boy home safely.

"I remember Betty saying, 'You're asking a lot,'" Pecoraro recalls. "We said this might be the only chance we have. . . . We gave our word that we would do our best to bring the boy home safe. In the end she felt she had no choice. If she didn't send him she would have to pay the consequences for not doing it. She was caught. Betty was looking right in the eye of the tiger."

After several long conversations, Betty agreed to go along with the plan. She had a strong suspicion that Tocco was not intending to return to the United States, and that if he wanted to see his son badly enough, he was capable of having him kidnapped. If that happened, she knew she might never see her son again. She also didn't particularly trust Marlene—whom she privately suspected of having an affair with Tocco—but if letting Michael go meant that Tocco would be arrested and brought back to America, and this whole bitter episode of her life brought to a conclusion, it was worth it. Anything was better than the uncertainty of being left like this, not knowing what was coming next.

On December 23, Betty flew down to Florida with Michael and met up with Marlene. FBI agents George Houston and Neil

O'Malley followed Marlene and Michael to New York, and boarded the same plane headed for Greece. Meanwhile, Bob Pecoraro and Jack Bonino flew direct to Athens. They spent a frantic twenty-four hours negotiating with the Greek police over permission to arrest Albert Tocco, since Greece had no extradition treaty with the United States at that time. The Greeks made no promises, but assigned a small detail to keep Tocco under surveillance.

On the morning of December 26, Bob Pecoraro waited in the Athens airport, disguised in a flat cap and aviator glasses, which made him look just like a Sicilian man of honor. He stood in a corner of the arrivals hall, trying to look unobtrusive, drinking coffee and smoking cigarettes with a handful of young undercover Greek police with long hair and leather jackets. Suddenly Albert Tocco walked into the airport. He was tanned and looked relaxed. With him was a Greek man whose face was familiar to the local police, and who they could see was carrying a gun. This man had been a suspect in the shooting of a Greek policeman, which worked in Pecoraro's favor: the Greek police needed no more convincing that Tocco must be a bad guy.

Michael and Marlene got off the plane, and father and son, who hadn't seen each other for three months, had a warm reunion. They hugged and left the airport holding hands and smiling, knowing nothing about the FBI agents on their tail.

For a week, Michael stayed with his father and Marlene at the Holiday Inn in Athens, visiting parks and other sights under the watchful eye of Agents O'Malley and Houston and their Greek counterparts. Agents Pecoraro and Bonino spent their days at police headquarters meeting with chiefs of staff and politicians, drinking tiny cups of strong sweet coffee, negotiating how they could get Tocco out of the country without violating Greek law.

After a week, much to the agents' relief, Michael and Marlene left the country as arranged, on their way back to the States. Pecoraro and Bonino were summoned by the national chief of police, who told them: "We will arrest Mr. Tocco tonight, and we are going to expel him from the country. We want you to get tickets on this TWA flight, we're going to put him on that flight, and we want you on the plane. Now, does he know any of you personally?"

He did.

"We don't want him to see you. You don't have any authority to do anything while that plane's in Greek territory. But you can do what you want when the wheels are in the air."

Pecoraro readily agreed. That night, he and Bonino boarded the plane and sat behind a curtain in first class, where Tocco would not see them. Agents O'Malley and Houston sat toward the rear. Just before takeoff, a cavalcade of police vehicles drove across the runway and pulled up beside the plane. Albert Tocco, struggling and shouting, was carried out of a police van and manhandled up the stairs into the aircraft. Once inside, he continued to shout and struggle, yelling that he was being kidnapped. He lashed out with his legs, trying to kick out a window, screaming that there was a bomb on board. As the other passengers murmured nervously, a stewardess tried to restore calm, assuring the passengers there was no bomb.

As the commotion continued, the captain emerged and spoke to Bonino and Pecoraro. "You want us to do something?" asked Pecoraro, barely able to contain himself.

"Don't be stupid, he's not supposed to see us," hissed Bonino. To the pilot, he said, "Just get this plane off the ground as soon as you can, and make sure he isn't given any sharp eating implements."

As the plane left the runway, Tocco, who had managed to delay takeoff for forty minutes, realized he was trapped, and subsided into his seat. He even turned and apologized to the passengers behind him, explaining that he was being taken against his will. Agent O'Malley, posing as a normal passenger, engaged him in conversation for much of the flight to Rome. There, Tocco refused to get off the plane. Pecoraro and Bonino had been first off, and were waiting to grab him as he stepped out, but he didn't appear. Finally, when all the other passengers had left the plane, O'Malley and Houston stood up, showed him their ID and escorted him into the airport, where a battalion of Italian carabinieri was waiting.

" 'The Italians gave him hell,' Pecoraro remembers. 'Oh, the big American mafioso. Not so big anymore, huh? *Un poco mafioso.*' "

On the next stage of the journey, from Rome to New York, the agents took turns sitting next to Tocco. Now it was his turn to give them hell. He had promised not to throw any more tantrums, so they didn't put plastic cuffs on him, but he was irrepressible, talked constantly about his case, and generally teased and tormented them for most of the six-hour flight (later, in court, he continued to tease them, claiming that the agents were drinking heavily on the flight, one agent alone consuming "forty or fifty miniatures plus a bottle of wine"). He protested that during his last trial, his position in the mob had been exaggerated: "They tried to make out I was this big mobster, the IRS called me 'Caesar,' like they're trying to portray me as some big Italian ruler. I never used the name Caesar in my life." (At this stage Tocco little imagined that the agents had access to his house and everything in it, including his shirts, monogrammed with the initials ACT, and the embroidered pennant in the kitchen emblazoned with the name Caesar.)

While on the plane, he also told the agents something that froze them. He said he had told his son that the FBI wanted him to cooperate and become a "stool pigeon." He told the agents: "I would rather watch my son burn to death than be a snitch."

In New York the party had to change planes again, and this time there was an ugly tussle with the New York FBI, who arrived in force at the terminal announcing, "We're taking your prisoner." There were angry calls to FBI bosses. Tocco, who by this stage had calmed down considerably, opted to remain with the Chicago agents and make the final stage of his journey into custody with them.

Finally, after an exhausting trip, Tocco and his four-strong FBI guard arrived at Chicago's O'Hare Airport, to be met by the agents' supervisor and a baying throng of press and photographers. Tocco had been featured on *America's Most Wanted* just a few days before, and the notorious fugitive was a huge story. Tocco pulled a yellow anorak hood up tight over his head and put on his glasses, which is how he appeared in the next day's papers—looking more like an aging angler than a mob boss.

The following day, Agents Pecoraro and Bonino met Betty Tocco in the parking lot of a shopping mall. She picked her way over the dirty snow and climbed into the backseat of their car. Betty was smiling and happy. As they drove a few miles to a parking lot behind a fast food restaurant, she thanked them for making sure Michael got home safely; she had had an extremely tense week and was hugely relieved that the whole episode had concluded successfully. She complimented the agents on their work.

Then she said she had something to tell them—something so terrible she hadn't dared talk about it before. She stammered and looked down, fiddling with the rings on her fingers. "I've been keeping something back," she said at length, "and I feel bad about it. You brought Michael back to me, and now I guess I owe it to you to tell you everything."

The agents twisted around to face her in the backseat and listened in stunned silence as she recounted the events of the night Tocco and his associates buried the still-breathing Spilotro brothers in a shallow grave.

The agents were speechless. The Spilotro murders had caused a sensation, and every law enforcement agency in the Chicago area, not to mention Las Vegas, had come up with theories about the killing—but no one had been fingered. Tony Spilotro had upset so many people that there were a lot of likely candidates, but no hard evidence. Here at last was a vital piece of the jigsaw.

Pecoraro had no doubt Betty was telling the truth, but he needed to corroborate her story. He asked her if she would be able to retrace her journey and drive them out to the roadside phone box in Indiana where she had picked up her husband that June night. She agreed. That was when she dropped her bombshell.

"I want to testify."

The agents looked at each other, wide-eyed.

"You do?" Pecoraro said at length. "Are you sure? Do you know what this means?"

"I've decided," said Betty. "I have to do it. You guys have worked so hard, and done so much . . . I want to testify against Albert."

It was an extraordinary moment: a sign that the agents had done everything right by their informant. They had gained her trust to the extent that she was prepared to reveal herself as their witness in court, before her husband. In their case against Albert Tocco, it was a decisive breakthrough: his own wife was prepared to endorse everything she had told them, in a court of law. It would be the first time a Mafia wife had ever voluntarily given evidence against her husband in court.

"Initially she had wanted to cooperate to help us find him," says

Pecoraro. "As we dealt with her over the months, she became more and more convinced that we were the good guys. The more she worked with us, the more faith she had that she was doing the right thing. She was impressed by the hours we put in, and the way we took care of Michael. In return, she wanted to do her best to be truthful and honest and to see out what she started.

"I had never raised the question of whether she would testify. Secretly you always want a live witness, but I knew what would lie in store for her."

By agreeing to testify, Betty would be exposing herself to risk of retaliation. Everybody knew the extent of her husband's violent rage. If she took the stand, Betty would have to disappear into the witness protection program, taking Michael with her. She would never see her home or her family again. But she had made up her mind. If she was going to help the FBI agents with this investigation, then testifying was the next step, and she was determined to take it.

Apart from being a positive way of helping the agents, for Betty, this move represented something she'd been after for years: a way out.

"Most of the guys I've been involved with in witness protection, we were doing them a favor more or less," says Pecoraro, who has been instrumental in putting twenty-two former mobsters in the program. "We were getting them out of a beef with the law. Betty did this all on her own. She wasn't a hardened criminal, and she was leaving a good life. She wanted out of that life. She wanted to divorce him, but she was frightened to death to do that, of what he might do. She said that even if she divorced him, he might kill her or he'd make her life miserable. Added to which, he had threatened her all the time about taking Michael away from her. He wasn't going to allow her to ever leave him—if she tried, he would get Michael. He was the one with all the money and all the contacts, and if it came to court, he could describe her as a whore and an unfit mother . . . She knew he could do it."

Over the next eight months, Betty spoke to her husband on the phone, and visited him in the Metropolitan Correctional Center in Chicago, without giving him any indication that she had joined forces with his enemies against him. The agents never asked her to wear a wire, since this would have put her at risk, but after each visit, she would call Pecoraro and report her conversations with Albert. During this time, Tocco did not help his cause: he was abusive and dictatorial. He would call her collect from prison, cursing and screaming, then demand that she run errands for him. She used to play bocce in a local league with friends and relations in the yard at Lorenzetti's restaurant. When he found out, he called her up, screaming and yelling: "I don't want you fucking going there, I don't want you going out with those people, you fucking whore . . . don't you go down there, you understand me?"

Then he'd call up a couple of days later, telling her to go down to Lorenzetti's and deliver a message to one of his friends. "How do you like that?" she told the agents. "First he called me names and forbade me to go down there. Now he wants me to go and see Nicky. Last thing I want to do is go see that Squinty Eyes."

In many conversations recorded, as a matter of course, by the prison authorities, the couple's increasingly rancorous relationship erupted into furious fighting. In one of these, later played in court, Tocco accused Betty of leading the FBI to him by phoning the hotel in Athens where he was staying with Marlene and Michael. Betty, in turn, was furious that Marlene had failed to call to let her know they had arrived safely; she also claimed that plenty of other people knew where Tocco was. The snarling tone of the conversation gives a pretty good insight into why Betty had an investment in seeing that he would never get out of jail.

Betty: "You're not interested in what happens to us."

Albert: "That's the first . . . well, why do you think I'm back here for, you jag-off?"

Betty: "That's, well . . ."

Albert: "What'd you think I'd come back here for?"

Betty: ". . . fucking jag-off . . ."

Albert: "What do you think I came back here for? 'Cause I was fuckin' worried . . ."

Betty: "I asked you?"

Albert: ". . . about you."

Betty: "I asked you why? Why did you do it this way?"

Albert: "Yeah, because of you."

Betty: "Bullshit. It's because you didn't have your fuckin' brownies reporting to you."

Albert: "No, 'cause you . . ."

Betty: ". . . fuckin' . . ."

Albert: ". . . called fuckin' Greece like a fuckin' jag-off, that's why."

Betty: "Oh, you're so full of fuckin' shit. You had made the arrangements, you wanted him to come there, I told that motherfuckin' bitch. As soon as I got an application for his fuckin' damn thing to get the hell out of here, that put the fuckin' trail on it. Everybody in the fuckin' Heights knew you were in Greece."

Albert: "Yeah."

Betty: "I was the only one who didn't know exactly where you were. Now call me the fuckin' jag-off."

Albert: "Yeah, you are. You are."

Betty: "No, you are."

Albert: "Fuckin' jag-off."

Betty: "You are."

Albert: "You are. There's somethin' wrong with you, baby."

Betty: "No, there's nothin'. Yeah, you know what's wrong with me? You."

In spite of their mutual rage and contempt, Tocco continued to expect his wife to run errands for him. One of these errands was to give his associates an order to carry out a hit. Tocco had turned against his friend Herb Panice when he learned he was cooperating with the authorities. He instructed Betty to go to a party given by a local businessman, where she would see his friends Toots and Nicky. She was to give them a message: "Albert wanted me to tell you it would be awfully nice if Mr. Panice would drop dead of a heart attack."

Betty carried out her orders, but both men made excuses. They were aware of continued investigations into their activities, and didn't want to draw any more heat. When Betty relayed their response, Tocco fumed with impotent rage.

During the months that followed, Betty received several instructions about getting money for Tocco's legal fees, and for his codefendant, Clarence Crockett—she would collect cash from Al Pilotto's wife. She also described finding bags of gold coins inside the storm door of the house. These had been dropped off, as arranged, by a person who was keeping some of Tocco's money for him; she was to convert them into checks at a dealer's. (Tocco's defense lawyers later accused her of fabricating this "gold fairy.")

Besides running errands for her husband, Betty was spending increasing amounts of time with the FBI agents. After she agreed to testify, she was interviewed for hours at a stretch by the U.S. attorneys. These interviews would take place in hotel rooms over a day or two, during which other agents would entertain Betty's son, Michael, play games with him in another room, or take him out to eat. He loved being with his new FBI buddies. "We had a ball with him," Pecoraro remembers. "He was a nice kid. A very smart kid."

During this period, Bob Pecoraro had a chance to talk things over with the boy. "I asked him if he was mad at us for arresting his dad," he recalls. "He understood everything that was happening, and he didn't resent us. That's a remarkable thing. This kid never held any grudges."

Michael was big for his age, and heavily built. He had chubby cheeks, and his mother's jet-black hair. He was an intelligent boy, and was doing well in school, in spite of everything. It was clear that the agents offered him a new role model in life, and he was delighted to find they had time for him, and that he could have fun with them. Michael and his mother had a playful and affectionate relationship; she teased him about the quantities of ketchup with which he always doused his food, and he would kid her back. For an Italian boss's son, who had so often been taken to the toy shop and told, "whatever you want," Michael was surprisingly unspoiled, and unlike most boys of his age in similar situations, apparently unimpressed by the behavior and attitudes of his mobster father.

One night, when Michael and his mother were lying in their hotel beds, talking things over after she had been in an all-day meeting, Michael said that when he grew up, he wanted to be an FBI agent. Betty was profoundly touched, and told the agents at breakfast the following morning what Michael had said. Her son's faith gave her proof, if she needed it, that she was doing the right thing. My God, she remembered thinking, if his father ever heard him say that, he'd go crazy. There was some deeper satisfaction in the thought. It meant she had won the boy's heart from his father.

During one of her meetings with the FBI, Betty broke down in tears. "We asked her what was wrong," Pecoraro recalls. "She told us after she met Tocco, she found out he ran houses of ill-repute, he had one down in the South Heights area. What she told us, because she knew he would bring it up in court, was that he forcibly put her to work in one of those places. He made her work there for three months. This was something that she was so embarrassed about that she didn't tell until right before the trial. She was crying . . . she told me it was horrible."

Why did she do it? I ask. Why would he do that to a woman he wanted for himself? Pecoraro shakes his head.

"If women like dominance and domineering men, that's exactly what we're describing. He puts her in a whorehouse, in a lockdown whorehouse and she can't leave, and then takes her out of there and marries her . . . she couldn't leave. Sometimes you have to think about how she got in that situation, I mean, I don't agree with modeling lingerie in the first place. So he forces her to work in a lockdown whorehouse, then she marries him. How do you explain something like that?"

As the trial drew near, Betty had to change her name. It was just one of the security measures that she adopted, but it was probably the most psychologically challenging. It was the only time during her cooperation that she ever appeared to waver.

Bob Pecoraro explained that she would need a new name in case anybody tried to find her. He told her to pick a name, and let him know what it was. She said she couldn't think of one. He encouraged her to go home and try to think of a name, so then they could get the formalities sorted out for the next stage of her life.

"The next day we met again, and she said, 'I can't think, I want you to pick a name for me.' I said, 'You want me to pick a name for you? Are you serious?' She said, 'Yes, I want you to do it.' That night I went home, thought about a couple of names, and the next day I said, 'Here's three names I thought of. Do you like any one of these?' She said, 'I like this one.' So I said, 'Then that's who you are.'"

Bob Pecoraro had never chosen a name for any of the other people he put in witness protection, and he took it as a sign of how
much Betty trusted and depended on him. It seems symbolic that he
had set her on her new path in the law-abiding world and shown her,
in a sense, who she was, and now she asked him to put his stamp on
her new identity.

Even with her new sense of self, it would take all the courage she
could muster to face what awaited her in the courtroom.

30

TWO weeks before the trial was due to start, a van drew up outside Betty Tocco's house on 207th Street. It was mid-October, almost exactly a year after FBI agents had first knocked at that door. Now those same agents were coming into the house to pack up and move Mrs. Tocco out. This was the beginning of the final part of the process. Betty had to be out of the house and long gone before her husband discovered that she was going to testify against him.

Pecoraro had rented a moving van and brought some young agents along to pack up any furniture Betty might want to take with her into her new life. She didn't want to take much. She took her clothes, her furs, her jewelry, and Michael's stuff—his furniture and toys. She took what cooking utensils she would need from the kitchen, plus her bed, her dresser, and a sofa, but she left some expensive-looking rugs and other furniture behind. Anything that was Tocco's, or a gift from his family, she left. She took only what she needed. By the time they had packed up everything she wanted, the house was still half full. As Betty worked with the agents, sorting through her possessions and helping to pack them up, she seemed to have no regrets about leaving the house.

Once the van was loaded, Bob Pecoraro and Wayne Zydron drove it away. In case anybody had seen them at the house, they switched vans down the road and loaded the stuff into another vehicle for the second part of the journey. Betty and Michael rode in a rented minivan with Jack Bonino and George Houston. The beloved yellow Eldorado was left behind to be sold.

It was late afternoon when Betty, Michael, and their escorts arrived at their destination. The idea of starting over was becoming more of a reality, but as they looked over their new apartment, the place had the slightly unreal feeling of a vacation spot. Michael was due to start at a new school. Betty had to get her bearings and think about what she would do next with her life, but the trial was looming, and it was hard to think of anything beyond that. And they still had their friends, the FBI agents, to link them to their old life.

After the move, whenever they had to meet with U.S. attorneys or FBI agents for interviews, Betty and Michael would be flown to another city and put up in a hotel. They were long, exhausting days, but Betty looked forward to them. It was a relief to be among familiar faces again, and to be doing something. She had become particularly close to Pecoraro—or Bobby, as she called him, over the months—and besides, Michael loved him.

People who leave the life of organized crime and start working with law enforcement seem to go through the same sort of emotional transference that patients of analysts experience. Having abandoned their loved ones and their past lives, most cooperating witnesses gratefully embrace their new friends in law enforcement. Men declare they want to join the FBI. Women fall in love with their contact agents— some because it's another dominant male presence in their lives, and some because the process makes them extremely isolated. The contact agent is often literally the only person they can talk to, or trust. Betty Tocco was no different. Her emotional dependence on Bob Pecoraro became intense.

In fact, Pecoraro had become the subject of a good deal of gossip among his fellow agents. They had noticed the rapport between him and his attractive lady informant and couldn't resist teasing him. But Pecoraro, who was acutely aware of the vulnerable position Betty was in, and who took the integrity of his work very seriously, did not find the suggestive office banter in the least bit amusing. He had become close to Betty, and yes, she was an attractive, funny, warm person. But he was determined that their work together not be compromised.

"When she was in witness protection," he recalls, "we'd meet in a neutral location like Kansas City. Never me alone but me with a prosecutor, or with an IRS agent, or an FBI agent. The interviews could take hours, and I would tell those guys, 'Don't leave me alone with her. When we're finished, I want to make sure Betty goes to her room first.' And they'd say, 'Well, why?' and I'd say, 'I just don't want any talk, and I want you guys to know it as much as you can, and I don't want to be in a room alone with her. The poor lady, we've taken everything away from her, she's got nothing except me—I picked her name, I'm like her link to her other life.'

"One time we finished and it took her about two hours to finally leave, and then the other guys left and I went to my room. Then there was a knock at the door, and it was Betty.

"She said, 'I just . . .'" Pecoraro paused for a long time as he recalled the incident, choking back tears. "'I just want to come in and talk to you alone.' I said no. Like a jerk. I said, 'Betty, you're a very good-looking woman, I don't have any . . . if this wasn't the situation . . . you know . . . But I have to leave here, and I'm going to have to look your husband in the face someday, and I'm going to have to look other FBI agents in the face, and a judge . . . There could never be anything between us.'"

But if Bob Pecoraro thought he had headed off malicious gossip by resolving not to have a relationship with Betty Tocco, he was wrong. Worse was to come as the trial approached. At the discovery hearing, when the government revealed its list of witnesses, Tocco first learned of his wife's cooperation with the FBI, and the identity of her contact agents. He slammed his fist on the table and shouted: "That motherfucker Pecoraro, he's divorced, he's got three kids, and now he's fucking my wife."

Pecoraro was not in court to hear the outburst, but he heard footsteps clattering down the stairs shortly afterward, as fellow agents sprinted down to tell him what had happened. To make matters worse, because of these accusations, the chief prosecutor, Larry Rosenthal, refused to let Pecoraro take the stand. After all his work in constructing a monumental case against one of Chicago's most notorious mobsters, after physically hunting him down and bringing him to justice, he was going to have to sit out the trial. Jack Bonino would testify in his place. The prosecution did not want the evidence to be muddied by allegations of an affair between the FBI agent and the witness.

Pecoraro was outraged. "I said, I'm not afraid for them to ask me one question. Goddammit, they can't ask me any questions I'm ashamed of."

Even so, Rosenthal would not take any chances that the jury might not believe him. To Pecoraro's immense chagrin, he was shelved for the whole trial. He had to read about it in the next day's papers, tut-tutting about details omitted or events incompletely described. It was a very trying time.

For Betty Tocco, it was even worse. Besides the dread of confronting her husband face-to-face, she was tormented by the thought that her past as a prostitute would be exposed in court. She didn't know how she would bear the public humiliation. By the time she took the stand, remembers Assistant U.S. Attorney Dean Polales, this woman who had been so attractive was drawn and thin. She looked awful.

Rosenthal's decision not to let Pecoraro testify was harsh, but it was wise. Albert Tocco had retained one of the most prominent defense attorneys in Chicago, Patrick Tuite, who was prepared to stop at nothing to attack Betty's credibility—and he would have relished an opportunity to besmirch Pecoraro's reputation. On one occasion, when Tuite and Pecoraro came face-to-face in an elevator, the attorney said, in a voice laden with sarcasm, "Well, well, if it isn't the knight in shining armor."

Much later, at a presentencing hearing, Pecoraro did briefly take the stand. When he had finished, and was walking out of the courtroom, Tocco snapped his fingers, summoning him over to the defense table. He leaned toward the agent and said, in a menacing tone, "You taking care of my kid?"

Pecoraro was taken aback but, conscious that the jury had seen and probably heard the exchange, replied brusquely, "Your kid's fine. Anything else?"

The trial of Albert Tocco and Clarence Crockett, the notorious mobsters from Chicago Heights, was a sensation. If it was unusual for a mobster of Albert Tocco's status to be brought to trial in the Chicago area, it was unprecedented for a Mafia wife to testify against her husband. Several witnesses, including the madam of a brothel, testified that they had been forced to pay street tax to Tocco. Some of Tocco's former collectors who had turned state's evidence described his role in four murders. On November 27, 1989, the first day of Betty's deposition, the normally crowded court was packed. Courtroom artists were frantically at work, trying to capture the dramatic face-off between husband and wife. When one woman went to the bathroom, she returned to find her seat had been taken, and there was no room for her to stand. The resulting commotion brought proceedings to a noisy halt, while the judge tried to restore calm.

In a witness room, Betty prepared herself to take the stand. Wearing an understated olive green silk dress, with her hair swept back behind big gold earrings, she steeled herself to confront the wrath of her husband. Before she was brought in, the judge, understanding Tocco's extreme pain as well as his rage, had asked him if he would be able to control his emotions upon seeing his wife and hearing what she had to say. The defendant said he would try to keep calm.

But his self-control lasted only a few moments. Betty, seated in the witness box, was asked why she had waived her legal right to refuse to testify against her husband. She replied haltingly, "Due to the circumstances, I had come to the decision that I had decided I was going to testify."

"For my money, right, Beth? For my money?" roared Tocco.

"All right, just one moment," the judge interrupted. But it was no use. Again Tocco broke in.

"That's what she wants, Your Honor. Why don't they ask her straight out what she wants?"

Again the judge reprimanded the defendant and told him that if he was unable to restrain himself, he could leave the courtroom. Tocco subsided into his chair, while his attorney asked his wife to recount her reasons for testifying.

"Because it's one of the ways to be done with living the life I've been living," she replied, "under tension, anxiety and fear. Having to constantly explain to my children what's going on, what's happening, is it true, is it not true. I don't want my son growing up in the same atmosphere that my daughter did. I became concerned about my own personal welfare."

She described how she had recently become afraid that her husband would try to harm her. As she spoke, she tried to ignore her husband and his codefendant, who were making loud, off-putting comments. Tocco's attorney claimed that she was testifying not because she was frightened of her husband but because she had been promised immunity for her part in the death of Tony and Michael Spilotro. Tocco could stand it no longer. He rose to his feet and headed for the door, declaring: "Your Honor, I'm going to leave. She's nothing but a liar. She'll always be a liar."

A marshal scurried after him, and Albert Tocco was escorted from the courtroom, to sit out his wife's testimony in a holding cell. Anything was better than listening to her treachery.

Tocco was called in one more time, to be informed what the jury was going to be told about his absence from court. Again, his rage erupted as he accused the prosecutor of tutoring his wife to speak against him: "Why don't you tell them that you put all lies to her? Why don't you tell them that?"

Again, he stormed out of the courtroom.

Betty's first statement before the jury about her reasons for testifying gave a strong indication that she meant to put up a good show. "There's many reasons, starting with the fact that I—when the reality hits you that you are an Outfit guy's wife, it may turn some people on, but it doesn't turn me on."

Betty described her life with Tocco, starting with their first meeting when he had pretended to be a dentist, and recounting everything, right up to his flight to Greece. She explained the "fear, anxiety and frustration" she felt after he had gone. The defense attorneys' agenda was to prove that she was, as her husband had alleged, motivated entirely by money. They accused her of selling out her husband to the FBI so she could get her hands on his millions. They itemized the funds he had given her—$400,000 in certificates of deposit and $200,000 in gold, as well as $250,000 he had left in safekeeping with his friend Lorenzetti, to which she had access, and $40,000 in gold coins that turned up on the doorstep, which she claimed was to pay for her husband's legal defense. They itemized the luxury goods he had lavished on her—four fur coats, two glamorous cars, a condo in Florida, a gold cigarette case and lighter, heaps of gold jewelry. They characterized her as a spoiled Mafia princess, bleeding her husband dry and spending her days shopping. What a tragic lifestyle, they said. Poor Betty.

Although she took quite a battering, Betty held her own. When they accused her of helping the FBI to catch her husband just so she could get her hands on his money, she hit back: "You know that's an outright lie."

Denying that she was ever pressured to cooperate with the FBI, Betty defended her new friends, declaring: "It's a damn shame that people have the perception of them that they do."

By the afternoon recess, Betty was fighting to keep her composure. She was accompanied to the witness room, where Agent Pecoraro brought her coffee and tried to bolster her morale. Once or twice she broke down in tears. She not only had pugnacious attorneys to deal with, but also a hostile press. The next day's papers gave a sarcastic commentary on her moneyed lifestyle and phony poor-me attitude. They passed harsh moral judgment on a woman who wanted to send her murderous husband to jail. Some things, it seemed, were beyond the popular imagination, including the idea that the wife of a criminal could ever change sides, unless she was doing it for money.

On the second day of her testimony, Betty's relationship with Tocco came under the spotlight. He had opted to sit out the rest of his wife's testimony, so at least she didn't have to contend with his outbursts in court. She did, however, have to listen to a recording of one of their vicious arguments, and cringed as she heard herself broadcast to the world, cursing a blue streak.

After hearing herself portrayed as a ruthless gold digger, Betty heard her husband described as a perfect father—putting up a tree house for his boy, play wrestling with him before bed, shooting hoops, taking him to carnivals and on trips to Disneyland. Then came the killer punch.

"You knew what the perfect bait was to catch Albert, didn't you?"

The defense's relentless searchlight was now turned on Betty's heartless wish to deprive her husband of his son. The defense described Albert's phone calls to his son from prison every morning before Michael went to school, and every night when he got home, until his telephone privileges were abruptly canceled and all communication with his son was stopped. By cooperating with the FBI, they said, Betty was callously cutting off the boy from his father. This was an aspect of the case that enflamed public debate: furious letters to the press denounced her selfish cruelty in tearing apart father and son; indignant readers replied that a lifelong criminal forfeits his right to raise a child.

The issue came to a head the day after Betty finished giving evidence, when Tocco's lawyers insisted that they wanted the boy to testify. They believed Michael could prove that Tocco had told his son he would be coming home soon, and thus disprove he was a fugitive from justice. But Michael did not want to be questioned in front of all those people, and threw a screaming fit outside the courtroom, crying and shouting that he did not want to see his father. Finally the judge interviewed the boy in chambers, with his mother and father, four defense lawyers, and two prosecutors present.

It was a pitiful scene. Eight-year-old Michael had not seen his father for several weeks, but it was his father's lawyer, Patrick Tuite, who spoke to him. His mother sat behind him, occasionally prompting the grown-ups to treat the child with kindness, and trying to make them see that the boy had not been tutored to hate his father.

The attorney's first question concerned a loving note that Michael had supposedly written to his father. To the attorney's disappointment, Michael denied writing it.

"I don't have any of that color paper."

Undeterred, Tuite moved on. "When you said good-bye to your father in Greece, what did he tell you about when he would see you again? Did he say 'I'll see you soon,' or 'I'll be home soon'?"

"I don't know," replied the boy.

"When you left your father in Greece," Tuite continued, "were you and he friends?"

"A little."

"And when you came back here, did you visit him over at the jail?"

"Uh-huh."

"And were you friendly with him when you were over at the jail with him?"

"A little, a little not," replied the boy.

"Has something happened that you are not friendly with him, besides moving?"

As the attorney probed for a response that would indicate that the boy's mother had turned him against his father, Michael, who had mostly answered "uh-huh," stopped talking altogether. His father, who had been silent until now, suddenly spoke up: "I love you, Michael."

When Tuite asked Michael whether he wanted to continue to visit his father in prison, the boy's answer was noncommittal. Betty spoke for him: "He does want to see you."

Tocco continued trying to strike up a rapport with his son. "How you doin'?"

"He does want to see you," Betty said again.

Before they could say anything else, the judge broke in with a gentle reminder, "Wait, folks, we are on the record here." But the judge still tried to keep it chatty, admiring Michael's T-shirt.

"You're getting big, Mike," his father said.

Again Tocco's attorney tried to get Michael to say he had written a note to his father, and again the boy denied it. Eventually, Tuite abandoned the attempt, and as he thanked the boy, Tocco cut in again: "Don't be bashful, Mike. Stand up."

As the questioning ended, Betty asked if Michael could have a word with his father.

"Don't be bashful," repeated Tocco.

"Could he give him a hug?" asked Betty.

The judge turned to the marshal guarding the prisoner. "Any problem with Michael giving Mr. Tocco a hug?"

The marshal couldn't think of one.

"He's scared," said the boy's father.

"No, he's not," said his mother.

The court made room for Michael and his father to sit together for a moment, for a hug and a few words, before Michael and his mother left together, and Tocco was taken back to the cells. It was the last time he would see his son.

Summing up at the end of the monthlong trial, Tuite made a final assault on Betty Tocco's reputation, pouring scorn on the idea that she could be afraid of this man—even though the court had been treated to a display of his violent temper. He had even produced the previous Mrs. Tocco, blonde-haired Penny, who sat in the courtroom smiling, to demonstrate that it's perfectly possible to divorce Albert Tocco and live. It was a tasteless gambit. Nobody mentioned that, rather than divorce Albert Tocco, Penny had been supplanted in his affections and thrown away like an old shoe.

The jury took two days to find Albert Tocco guilty of thirty-four counts of racketeering, extortion, tax fraud, and obstruction of justice, the first conviction of a Chicago Heights mob boss in thirty years. Crockett was also found guilty on twenty-three similar counts. As the verdict was read, Tocco scowled angrily. There was an angry exchange with prosecutor Larry Rosenthal, who claimed Tocco had accosted him in a court hallway during the trial, and threatened him with the words: "I'm going to get you, and I'm going to get those fucking FBI agents."

Glaring at Rosenthal, Tocco said: "Your Honor, he is lying. Unless I am going crazy, all they have done is tell lies since the first agent took the stand."

Between the verdict, delivered on December 7, and his sentencing on May 15, Tocco was held in isolation. He nonetheless managed to speak to other inmates, and repeatedly voiced his threats against the prosecutor, the FBI agents, and against his wife.

At the sentencing, Tocco stood before the judge clenching his fists, and bellowed: "I'm no crime boss! I never gave no orders for no murders!" He offered to undergo a lie-detector test, turning to the press bench as he said the test could be overseen by the media.

"The sentence is not to punish you," the judge said coolly. "It is to rid you from society." So saying, he sentenced Tocco to two hundred years. The prisoner stood for a moment, then blew a kiss. Now aged sixty-one, he would not be eligible for parole for sixty-seven years. Society had kissed Albert Tocco good-bye.

Betty Tocco heard the news over the phone. She felt bad, but at the same time she was relieved—it meant that everything she had gone through had been worthwhile. Tocco would not be coming out, and he would not be coming after her. Michael could grow up an ordinary boy, a long way from the grasping hands of the mob.

Bob Pecoraro, meanwhile, had become involved in another investigation. While he was building his case against Albert Tocco, he had uncovered evidence of corruption in local government: a number of figures in the Chicago Heights administration had been doing business with Albert Tocco, some taking bribes and issuing contracts in exchange for kickbacks. Pecoraro had subpoenaed records of contracts for public works, and Betty had been able to supply details of how most of these public figures were on friendly terms with her husband. The government would eventually secure convictions against the mayor of Chicago Heights, the police commissioner, the finance commissioner, and thirty-seven other government figures.

Pecoraro had little contact with Betty after the trial, just enough to know that Michael had settled into school and that she was doing all right. One day he got a call from a local FBI agent saying she was in some kind of trouble. It seemed that fifteen years with a mobster had not taught Betty to be street smart. Once she was on her own, she had been taken in by a con man who had talked her out of $100,000. Since she was unlikely to find a decent job at her age with no experience, she needed this money to live on.

Alarmed, Pecoraro called to find out what had happened. "Did you get anything in writing, a receipt of some kind?" She hadn't.

"But he seemed so nice," she protested.

"That's why he's a con man, Betty!"

The episode brought home to Pecoraro how alone and defenseless Betty was, but there was nothing he could do for her now. The FBI had done its part, finding her a home and moving her stuff. Armed with a new name and a new social security number, she would have to find her own way.

Pecoraro worries that, in a way, Betty was used by the FBI—once she had served her purpose she was on her own, cut off from the parents she adored, the places she knew. Would she have been better off to keep her mouth shut and live on her husband's ill-gotten gains? Pecoraro, having nursed her through the process of betraying her husband and destroying her family, just had to walk away.

"There's nothing more I can do for her. Then, I was doing my job. It's not my job anymore. It's very sad. I don't even know . . . I don't know if she's having a hard time of it, or if it's easy, I don't know if her life has really deteriorated or gotten better, all I know is I'm partially responsible."

He pauses for a long time.

"To do the right thing, which was to testify against her husband, she ruined her life."

Acknowledgments

One of the delights of researching this book was the opportunity it gave me to travel all over the United States—although this meant I was dependent upon those with local knowledge, and to these people I am extremely grateful. Special thanks to Mike Robinson of AP in Chicago, a fount of information and anecdotes; Assistant U.S. Attorneys Ruth Nordenbrook and Dan Dorsky in Brooklyn, always generous with their time and invaluable insights; Special Agent Bob Pecoraro, who took a risk and trusted me to tell his story; Detective Ron Jennings from New Jersey, who looked out for me; Larry Egan, formerly with the IRS in New Jersey, who knows everybody; Al Guart of the *New York Post*; mob historian Allan May in Cleveland, who was full of good ideas; and Jerry Capeci, whose Gang Land Web site (www.ganglandnews.com) gave me a great introduction to the New York Mafia.

Thanks to many generous and helpful colleagues in the media: Carol Marin of CBS, Mark Brown at the *Chicago Sun-Times*; Mark Madler at *Cicero Life*; George Anastasia at the *Philadelphia Inquirer*; Patrick Cox of the BBC; Andrew Gumbel of the *Independent* in Los Angeles; Shelley Murphy, Ralph Ranalli, and Kevin Cullen of the *Boston Globe*; J.M. Lawrence at the *Boston Herald*; David Krajicek, formerly of the *New York Daily News*; Channel 5's Dave Boeri in Boston; John L. Smith and Ed Becker in Las Vegas.

John O'Brien, formerly of the *Chicago Tribune*, who passed away in October 2003, was a goldmine of information.

Thanks to Chris Blank in the Brooklyn U.S. Attorney's Office;

Donald E. Conrad in Phoenix, Arizona; Eric Johnson in Las Vegas; Matt Schneider, Mitch Mars, and Dean Polales in the U.S. Attorney's Office in Chicago.

For ideas, insights, and information, thanks to FBI agents past and present: George Hanna, Jay Kramer, Charlie Maurer, Joe O'Brien, Jack O'Rourke, and George Vinson; IRS agents Tom Moriarty and Bill Paulin; to Phil DiPasquale for my tour of Chicago Heights; and to Deputy Chief of New York State Organized Crime Task Force Joe Rauchet.

I'd like to thank the friends who helped me along the way: Sharon Krum, David Usborne, Paula Froelich, Camilla Nicholls, Lola Bubbosh, Peggy Bayer, Rosanne Massa, Jackie Colucci, and Nadine and Dave Boyle.

Thanks to my mother, Jane Longrigg, and sisters, Francesca and Laura, who gave unfailing support, and my parents-in-law, Helen and Bruce Buchanan, who made the whole thing possible.

I'd also like to thank my editor, Chris Knutsen, my publisher, Jonathan Burnham, my lawyer, Devereux Chatillon, and my agent, Derek Johns.

Thanks to my husband, Adrian Buchanan, a brilliant manager, editor, and father.

Sources

Chapters 1–4

Author interviews with: Lana Zancocchio; Jeffrey Rabin; Assistant U.S. Attorney Ruth Nordenbrook; Deputy Chief of New York State Organized Crime Task Force Joseph Rauchet; Larry Egan, formerly with the IRS; Detective Ron Jennings, formerly of Wall Police Department, New Jersey.

Legal documents:

USA v. Bonanno family, CV87 2974.

USA v. Anthony Graziano, 90CR 334: Objections to presentence report filed by Jeffrey Hoffman for the Defendant.

USA v. John Zancocchio and Anthony Graziano, 90CR 333, New York Eastern District: Fatico hearing before Judge Nickerson.

USA v. Jennifer Graziano, 00CR 137, NYED March 3, 2000: Criminal cause for pleading before Magistrate Steven M Gold.

USA v. John Zancocchio and Lana Zancocchio, 01CR 692, New York Eastern District: Indictment; Memorandum in Opposition to Motion for Downward Departure, plus supplement, filed by Ruth Nordenbrook for the government; Sentence before Judge Jack B Weinstein.

USA v. Peter Cosoleto, a.k.a. "Petey Boxcars," et al, 02CR 0307: Indictment.

USA v. Anthony A Graziano, a.k.a. "TG" a.k.a. "The Little Guy," et al, 02CR 60049 Indictment; Pre-trial detention hearing, West Palm Beach, Florida, May 2, 2002.

Other sources:

Jerry Capeci's Gang Land Web site (www.ganglandnews.com).

Multiple articles in the *New York Post, New York Daily News, St. Petersburg Times.*

McPhee, Michele. *Mob Over Miami*. Onyx: New York, 2002.

Stutman, Robert M. and Richard Esposito. *Dead on Delivery: Inside the Drug Wars*. Warner Books: New York, 1992.

Chapters 5–6

Author interview with David Krajicek; Victoria Gotti's columns in the *New York Post*; articles in the *Post*, the *Daily News, Entertainment Weekly, People* magazine; Victoria Gotti interview on *Larry King Live*.

Bonanno, Joe. *Man of Honor*. Unwin: London, 1984.

Bonanno, Rosalie. *Mafia Marriage*. Avon: New York, 1990.

Gotti, Victoria. *The Senator's Daughter*. Forge: New York, 1997.

———. *Superstar*. Crown: New York, 2000.

Chapter 7

Author interview with Antoinette Giancana, February 13, 2003.

Giancana, Antoinette and Thomas C. Renner. *Mafia Princess*. Corgi: New York, 1985.

John Kass, "Mafia Princess sings a different tune," *Chicago Tribune*, August 2, 2001.

"Mafia Princess," *Playboy* magazine, February 1987.

Chapters 8–10

Author interviews with: Hal Rothman, chair history department, University of Nevada, Las Vegas; historian and author Ed Becker; journalist Lisa DePaulo; author Julie Smith; and journalist Stephen M. Silverman.

Berman, Susan. *Easy Street*. Dial Press: New York, 1981.

———. *Lady Las Vegas*. A&E Books: New York, 1996.

DePaulo, Lisa. "Who Killed the Gangster's Daughter?" *New York* magazine, March 12, 2001.

Hughes, Babette. *Lost and Found*. Permanent Press: New York, 2000.

Reid, Ed. *The Green Felt Jungle*. Trident Press: New York, 1963.

Rothman, Hal. *Neon Metropolis*. Routledge: New York, 2002.

Scott, Cathy. *Murder of a Mafia Daughter*. Barricade: New Jersey, 2002.

Smith, John. "With Mafia daughter's death, chronicling of Las Vegas history takes a hit," *Las Vegas Review-Journal*, January 7, 2001.

Also: Multiple articles on Susan Berman's murder published in the *Los Angeles Times* and the London *Observer*.

Chapter 11

Carpenter, Teresa. *Mob Girl*. Simon & Schuster: London and New York, 1992.

Carpozi, George Jr. *Bugsy: The Godfather of Las Vegas*. Everest: London, 1981.

Edmonds, Andy. *Bugsy's Baby: The Secret Life of Mob Queen Virginia Hill*. Birch Lane: New York, 1993.

Eisenbery, Dennis. *Meyer Lansky, Mogul of the Mob*. Corgi: London, 1981.

Jennings, Dean. *We Only Kill Each Other: The Story of Bugsy Siegel*. Penguin: New York, 1992.

Lacey, Robert. *Little Man*. Arrow: New York, 1991.

Chapters 12–15

Author interviews with: Special Agents Tom Moriarty (ret.) and William Paulin of the Chicago IRS; Thomas Bourgeois of the Chicago FBI; Tom Wronsky, formerly with the Chicago FBI; David Niebur and Phillip Bue, formerly with the Cicero Police Department; Richard Lindberg, Ray Hanania, Dawn Weleba, attorney David Boyle.

Legal documents:

USA v. Frank Maltese, 90CR 87-19, opinion by US District Court Judge Ann Claire Williams, 1993, confirming sentence.

USA v. Michael Spano Sr. et al, 01CR 348, transcript of trial.

————. Government's response to defendants' pretrial motion to strike the organized crime allegation from the indictment.

————. Government's motion for upward departure.

————. Government's consolidated response to defendants' sentencing memoranda.

————. Sentencing before Judge John F. Grady.

Brown, Mark. "Mob widow looked unbowed." *Chicago Sun-Times*, June 17, 2001.

Illinois Police and Sheriff News Web site (IPSN): www.ipsn.org.

Marin, Carol. "Married to the Mob." *60 Minutes II*, CBS, April 5, 2000.

Secter, Bob and Gary Marx. "La Presidenta." *Chicago Tribune*, July 5, 1998.

Also: Daily coverage of the trial of Michael Spano Sr., et al, *Chicago Tribune* and *Chicago Sun-Times*. May 28 to August 23, 2002.

Chapter 16
Author interview with Brenda Colletti, 1996.

Legal documents:
USA v. John Stanfa et al, CR94 127, November 1995.

Also: articles in the *Philadelphia Inquirer* by George Anastasia.

Chapter 17
Author interviews with Jackie Colucci and Roseanne Massa, July 23, August 19, September 6, 2002.

Legal documents:
USA v. Ernest Varacalli, et al, 2001 CRS 18283: indictment.

Also: Jerry Capeci's Gang Land Web site (www.ganglandnews.com); July 18, 2002, September 20, 2001, December 6, 1994.
"Police Pinch Mob Squeeze," *New York Daily News,* January 11, 2003.

Chapter 18
Bonanno, Rosalie. *Mafia Marriage*. Avon: New York, 1990.
Edmonds, Andy. *Bugsy's Baby: The Secret Life of Mob Queen Virginia Hill*. Birch Lane: New York, 1993.
Maas, Peter. *Underboss: Sammy the Bull Gravano's Story of Life in the Mafia*. HarperCollins: New York, 1997.
McPhee, Michele. *Mob Over Miami*. New York: Onyx, 2002.

Legal documents:
USA v. S Gravano et al, CR 2000-3511: Government's motion in limine to introduce evidence of other crimes and Guilty plea; presentencing memorandum on behalf of Salvatore Gravano by his attorney Lynn Stewart. *USA v. S Gravano et al,* CR 2000-3511: Karen Gravano presentence investigation; Debra Gravano: presentence investigation.
Phoenix Police Department Daily Call Report dated 01/14/00.

Chapters 19–21
Author interviews with: John and Carolyn Branco; FBI agent Charles Maurer (ret.); Assistant U.S. Attorney Eric Johnson; attorney John Momot.

Legal documents:

USA v. Stephen Cino and Robert Panaro, CR S 97 082, Las Vegas, Nevada: testimony of John Branco, April 1999; testimony of Charles Maurer.

German, Jeff. Series of articles on Operation Thin Crust. *Las Vegas Sun,* June 28–July 2, 2002.

Smith, John L. "Woman sees friend's killing as true loss in Blitzstein case," *Las Vegas Review-Journal,* June 29, 1997.

Chapters 22–24

Author interviews with: Assistant U.S. Attorney Daniel Dorsky and attorney Jerome Karp.

Legal documents:

USA v. Andrew Russo and Dennis Hickey, CR 98 817; testimony of Dorothy Fiorenza, January 12–14, 1999.

Jerry Capeci's Gang Land Web site (www.ganglandnews.com).

Chapters 25–30

Author interviews with: FBI Special Agent (ret.) Bob Pecoraro; Special Agent (ret.) Tom Moriarty, Chicago IRS; John O'Brien, former reporter, *Chicago Tribune,* Assistant U.S. Attorney Dean Polales; IRS Agent (ret.) Philip DiPasquale.

Legal documents:

USA v. Albert Tocco and Clarence Crockett, 88 CR 841: Transcript of trial, pre-trial hearings and pre-sentencing.

Trusteeship hearings of the Laborers' International Union of North America (LIUNA) 97-30T, testimony of Bob Pecoraro, July 18, 1997.

Pileggi, Nicholas. *Casino: Love and Honor in Las Vegas.* New York: Simon & Schuster, 1995.

Biography of Albert Caesar Tocco, IPSN Web site (*www.ipsn.org*).

Also: Multiple press accounts of the trial of Albert Tocco and subsequent investigations of the administration of Chicago Heights published in the *Chicago Tribune, Chicago Sun-Times,* the *Homewood-Flossmoor Star,* and the *Southtown Economist.*

Selected Bibliography

Anastasia, George. *The Goodfella Tapes*. New York: Avon, 1998.

Berman, Susan. *Easy Street*. New York: Dial Press, 1981.

Bonanno, Joe. *Man of Honor*. London: Unwin, 1984.

Bonanno, Rosalie. *Mafia Marriage*. New York: Avon, 1990.

Capeci, Jerry and Gene Mustain. *Mob Star*. New York: Dell, 1998.

Carpenter, Teresa. *Mob Girl*. London and New York: Simon & Schuster, 1992.

Durante, Georgia. *The Company She Keeps*. Nashville: Celebrity Books, 1998.

Giancana, Antoinette. *Mafia Princess*. New York: Corgi, 1985.

Ianni, Francis A. *Family Business: Kinship and Social Control in Organized Crime*. New York: Russel Sage Foundation, 1972.

Laurino, Maria. *Were You Always an Italian? Ancestors and Other Icons of Italian America*. New York: Norton, 2000.

Longrigg, Clare. *Mafia Women*. London: Chatto de Windus, 1997.

Maas, Peter. *Underboss: Sammy the Bull Gravano's Story of Life in the Mafia*. New York: HarperCollins, 1997.

Maas, Peter. *The Valachi Papers*. New York: Bantam, 1968.

McPhee, Michele. *Mob Over Miami*. New York: Onyx, 2002.

O'Brien, Joseph F. and Andris Kurins. *Boss of Bosses: The FBI and Paul Castellano*. New York: Island, 1991.

Pileggi, Nicholas. *Casino: Love and Honor in Las Vegas*. New York: Simon & Schuster, 1995.

———. *Wise Guy: Life in a Mafia Family*. New York: Simon & Schuster, 1985.

Pistone, Joseph D. *Donnie Brasco*. London: Hodder & Stoughton, 1987.

Puzo, Mario. *The Godfather*. London: Mandarin, 1969.

Ranalli, Ralph. *Deadly Alliance: The FBI's Secret Partnership with the Mob.* New York: HarperCollins, 2001.

Siebert, Renate. *Secrets of Life and Death: Women and the Mafia.* London: Verso, 1996.

Sifakis, Carl. *The Mafia Encyclopedia.* New York: Checkmark Books, 1999.

Sterling, Claire. *Crime Without Frontiers.* London: Little, Brown, 1994.

————. *The Mafia: The Long Reach of the International Sicilian Mafia.* London: Hamish Hamilton, 1990.

Stutman, Robert M. and Richard Esposito. *Dead on Delivery: Inside the Drug Wars.* New York: Warner Books, 1992.

Talese, Gay. *Honor Thy Father.* New York: Ballantine, 1992.